LITTLE BIGHORN & ISANDLWANA
Kindred Fights
Kindred Follies

Published in 2007 by Phantascope
phantascope@email.com

This book is copyright. Apart from any fair dealing for the purpose of private study, research, criticism, or review, as permitted by the Copyright Act, no part may be reproduced by any process without written permission. Enquiries should be made to the publisher.

Copyright © 2007 Paul Williams
All rights reserved.
ISBN: 1-4196-6579-0
ISBN-13: 978-1419665790

Visit www.booksurge.com to order additional copies.

PAUL WILLIAMS

LITTLE BIGHORN & ISANDLWANA
Kindred Fights
Kindred Follies

2007

LITTLE BIGHORN & ISANDLWANA
Kindred Fights
Kindred Follies

CONTENTS

Prologue xi

1 Their Land is Ours 1
2 Deception and Deceit 35
3 The Impossible Ultimatum 49
4 The Three-Column Plan 67
5 The Three-Column Advance 97
6 The Divided Command 147
7 The Last Man, The Last Bullet 189
8 Besieged 243
9 Finding the Dead, and the Living 271
10 So Who is to Blame? 299
11 The Fading Comet 319
12 Aftermath 343

Appendix A 353
Appendix B 367

Bibliography 381

Index 385

Maps

Sioux Country, 1865—1877 94
Zulu Field of Operations, 1879 95
Battle of the Little Bighorn, June 25 1876 186
Battle of Isandlwana, January 22 1879 187
The Defence of Rorke's Drift 242

Illustrations

LT. Colonel George A. Custer 33
LT. Colonel Anthony W. Durnford 34
Sitting Bull 47
Cetshwayo kaMpande 48
Captain Frederick W. Benteen 241

Paul Williams graduated from the Swinburne School of Film and Television, after working as a painter and graphic artist. He has since worked in the television industry as writer, producer and director, having the following books published along the way:

History— *Matthew Brady & Ned Kelly; Kindred Spirits, Kindred Lives*

Novel— *The Shenandoah Affair*

Children's—*A Kid's Guide to Cubby Houses*
The Adventures of Black Ned
Grandfather's Dream Machine (Illustrator)

PROLOGUE

The triumphant warriors slashed, battered and hacked the prostrate figures sprawled amidst the dry, summer grass. Uniforms were stripped off, captured rifles and ammunition hastily gathered, the blood smeared barrels glinting in the late afternoon sun. The bodies of fallen soldiers and horses were scattered and intertwined, their flamboyant colonel lying dead amidst a knot of fallen men. Fingers of ridicule would be pointed at this man, and many would say the blame rested with him. But was it the impossible ultimatum thrust upon the natives by an administration bent on territorial conquest that was at fault? Government and general public alike would be shocked and awed, and all the world would wonder how 'stone age' men could inflict such a blow. Poems would be written celebrating the regiment's heroic stand, and patriotic paintings of soldiers defending their colors to the last would be admired by the crowd.

But mistakes had been made. Three columns of troops had invaded in an unjust and unprovoked war, misjudging the fighting capacity of the so-called savages who, it was thought, would not stand against a modern army. Bringing the fleeing natives to battle would be the problem. Then the overconfident invaders had weakened their strength by dividing their force, thus allowing the savage annihilation to take place.

But more soldiers not too far distant were at that moment being surrounded by the triumphant warriors. The victors made their way across country bent on finishing what the day's bloody fighting had begun.

This disaster occurred twice. The first time was at the Little Bighorn River, Montana, on June 25th 1876, and the second at Isandlwana, Zululand, on January 22nd 1879. The British Army fighting the Zulus had taken no heed of the mistakes made by the army of the United States fighting the Sioux Indians, and a bloody repeat of history had been the result.

1
THEIR LAND IS OURS

Ulysses S. Grant was something of an enigma. Who would have believed that the bearded farmer eking out a living by selling firewood on the streets of St. Louis in 1855 would, within the next decade, become the nation's most celebrated soldier since George Washington, and, like Washington, later become president of the United States?

Grant's luck changed when the Civil War erupted in 1861. Being an ex-military officer, he rejoined the Federal Army, met with success and eventually promotion to lieutenant general. Four years after the first shots were fired, he accepted the surrender of the Confederate forces under Robert E. Lee. Apart from a few minor engagements and one errant, rebel commerce raider sinking Yankee shipping on the high seas, the War Between the States was over.

But the year 1875 found President Grant entangled in a quandary of considerable proportions. The previous year a military expedition under the command of Lieutenant Colonel, brevet Major General George Armstrong Custer had been sent into the Black Hills of Dakota, part of the Sioux and Cheyenne Indian reservation. The expedition had been ostensibly for military reasons, but prospectors taken along had declared 'gold at the grass roots,' and the inevitable rush of fortune seekers had begun.

Now there was a demand by many whites that the Black Hills be taken from their rightful owners. But such a seizure would be in violation of United States treaty obligations. The Sioux, or Dakotas, had been the pre-eminent tribe of the northwestern plains opposing white encroachment on traditional hunting grounds. Now they watched with sullen venom as their sacred Black Hills were desecrated by white miners with no regard for native rights.

'Go west young man,' had been Horace Greeley's advice ten years before when the Civil War's gruesome battlefields had fallen silent. Helping the immigrant push was the construction of three railroads, the Union Pacific towards California, its eastern division across Kansas to Denver, Colorado, and the Northern Pacific out to the Dakota Territories. Here plans were being made for the iron horse to steam out further onto the northwest plains following the Yellowstone River through Montana.

Combined with ever-increasing wagon roads, the white man's intrusion dissected the huge buffalo herds and left them open to the prey of many whites who shot them not only for food and hides, but for sport and other activities, as Custer recalled:

> I know of no better drill for perfecting men in the use of firearms on horseback, and thoroughly accustoming them to the saddle, than buffalo-hunting over a moderately rough country. No amount of riding under the best of drill-masters will give that confidence and security in the saddle which will result from a few spirited charges into a buffalo herd.

The buffalo was the basis for the red man's way of life. The meat supplied food and the horns provided glue and a variety of tools and other implements. 'Buffalo chips,' the dried droppings, supplied fuel for fires on the plains where wood was sparse, and the hide furnished shelter and clothing.

Pretty Shield, a Crow women, recalled:

Ahh, my heart fell down when I began to see dead buffalo scattered all over our beautiful country, killed and skinned, and left to rot by white men…Even the flowers could not put down the bad smell. Our hearts were like stones. And yet nobody believed, even then, that the white man could kill *all* the buffalo.

Whites did not only decimate the buffalo, but also introduced diseases to which the carriers had developed at least a partial immunity. Measles, smallpox and venereal disease made big inroads into the Indian populations who considered this to be 'bad medicine' deliberately thrust upon them by aliens bent on stealing their lands.

June of the year 1866 saw the arrival of a government commission at Fort Laramie, Wyoming, to barter with the Sioux chiefs for permission to open a new immigrant wagon road through their hunting grounds. John M. Bozeman had blazed a new trail providing a more direct route from the upper Platte River to the Montana goldfields, discovered in 1860. Negotiations between the chiefs and the commissioners were still in progress when a military force under the command of Colonel Henry B. Carrington tramped into the post with orders to construct three army posts along the Bozeman Trail. He had command of 700 soldiers of the 27th infantry, more than half raw recruits. They carried outmoded muzzle-loaders, and the colonel had requisitioned 100,000 rounds of ammunition, but was despatched with 1000 rounds only. With the troops were 260 non-combatants, including officer's wives, children and colored servants. Carrington himself had no experience in Indian warfare, and had not seen action during the Civil War, but his command was expected to provide military protection for travellers whether the Indians liked it or not. General

Sherman had instructed him to avoid war with the Sioux 'if possible.'

Chief Red Cloud pointed at the eagles on Carrington's shoulder straps, shouting that he was the 'white eagle' who had come to build a road through the Sioux hunting grounds. He stormed from the sham of a conference vowing to make the Bozeman Trail run with blood.

The forts Carrington constructed found themselves in a siege-like state, venturing beyond the walls inviting attack. In the first six months over 54 soldiers and civilians were killed, over 40 wounded and over 700 horses, cattle and mules driven off.

But worse was to come.

Captain William Fetterman and a force of eighty men were despatched from Fort Phil Kearney to relieve a wood-cutting party under attack. Fetterman, disobeying his orders, was lured from the road by Sioux decoys. His command was cut off and wiped out to a man, a prelude to the Little Bighorn 10 years later. One of the Sioux was a young warrior named Crazy Horse, who no doubt took note of the over-confidence of the bluecoats when approaching his fellow tribesman. A blizzard struck, stalling Sioux plans to attack and destroy Fort Phil Kearney itself. A heroic ride by the scout Portuguese Phillips through ice and snow brought a column to relieve the beleaguered garrison.

The nation was shocked and the blameless Colonel Carrington replaced. 'Of course,' wrote General William 'War is Hell' Sherman, 'this massacre should be treated as an act of war and should be punished with vindictive earnestness, until at least ten Indians are killed for each white life lost.'

Congress, however, did not see it Sherman's way and instead recommended that President Andrew Johnson set up a commission to investigate the matter. The Sanborn Commission duly reported what every one already knew; the cause of the current conflict was the military occupation of the Bozeman Trail across unceded Indian hunting grounds. It went on to recommend that aggressive warfare against the wronged Sioux should cease, and negotiations should commence to induce the tribe to accept a special reservation.

At the same time further south, a bungled military campaign under the charge of General Winfield S. Hancock against the southern Cheyenne in Kansas resulted in the burning of one deserted village and a subsequent escalation of hostilities on the part of the aggrieved tribe. A party of mounted soldiers under Lieutenant Kidder carrying dispatches was surrounded and wiped out, their bodies discovered a few days later, as George Custer recalled 'Lying in irregular order, and within a very limited circle, were the mangled bodies of poor Kidder and his party, yet so brutally hacked and disfigured as to be beyond recognition save as human beings.'

Wanting harmony at all costs, a Peace Commission was appointed by President Johnson to negotiate treaties with the plains tribes, addressing their just grievances, civilising them, and ensuring safety for the whites, both in settlements and along the rail and wagon routes. The 'Indian Peace Policy' was applauded by some sections of the white community and decried by others, including many senior military officers, who felt crushing the tribes with armed force was the only way to solve the Indian question once and for all.

President Johnson appointed four supporters and four opponents of the Peace Policy to the Commission. One of those opposed was Colonel W. S. Harney, who had gained a reputation as an Indian Fighter by ravaging a Sioux camp in 1855. Whites had been shocked and disgusted when Fetterman's men had been found mutilated, but would have chosen to know nothing of Harney's 'civilised' men having mutilated the dead and hacked the pubic hair from fallen squaws, an outrage repeated by Colonel Chivington's men when they attacked peaceful Cheyennes at Sand Creek in 1864. At least on the second occasion, the government acknowledged the crime and paid compensation to the tribe involved; cold comfort to the dead.

The Peace Commission decided the best course of action was to confine the tribes of the southern plains to a large reservation south of Kansas, and the northern tribes to another north of Nebraska, areas unsettled by whites and not in the path of any planned railroads. The government would undertake to transform their charges into civilized farmers, and peace would reign supreme. The opponents of this scheme, including General Sherman, felt that the tribesmen would not give up their traditional way of life until they had been crushed with bayonet and rifle.

Some military officers must have been galled when orders were received to lower the stars and stripes, Fetterman's death unavenged, and abandon the forts along the Bozeman Trail. No sooner had the troops marched out than the Sioux swarmed in, and clouds of smoke billowed skywards as the walls, barracks and blockhouses were consumed by flames. Chief Red Cloud had won his war.

A treaty had been negotiated with the Sioux but, with legal representation denied them, it is inconceivable that the 159 signatories fully understood what they had signed. What the right hand gave, the left hand took away. The Indians were guaranteed a large reservation including all of South Dakota for their exclusive use, they were to be instructed in the use of the ox and plough, and would be provided with schools, teachers and clothing for 30 years. One pound each of meat and flour per day would be supplied for four years as they gave up the nomadic buffalo chase and became farmers.

These conditions were unacceptable to the proud warriors of the plains, so it was permitted that they could hunt outside the reservation in what was termed 'unceded Indian territory' upon which 'no white person should be permitted to settle, or to pass through the same without the consent of the Indians first had and obtained.'

But yet another clause nullified these conditions, stating that the Indians 'will not in future object to the construction of railroads, wagon-roads, mail stations, or other works of utility or necessity, which may be ordered or permitted by the laws of the United States.' This included not only the unceded lands but the reservation as well.

The treaty 'confined' the Indian to the reservation while allowing him to hunt on unceded non-reservation lands that were, in fact, ceded whenever the whites wished. But it was also specified that these unceded lands would eventually be relinquished by the Indian, the treaty not specifying a time frame, or who would decide when that time came. Four months after the treaty's proclamation, General Sherman issued a general order 'All Indians, when on their proper reservations, are under the exclusive control and jurisdiction of their agents...Outside the well-defined limits of their reservations they are under the original and exclusive jurisdiction of the military authority, and as a rule will be considered hostile.'

So much for peaceful buffalo hunts without fear of molestation by whites.

In April of 1869, shortly after Ulysses S. Grant entered the White House, Congress authorized the appointment of a new Board of Indian Commissioners to oversee the operations of the Bureau of Indian Affairs. Its role was to ensure justice to the Indians when evaluating policies, both current and new, and see to the appointment of honest agents, and inspect the quality of provisions and stores supplied to the reservations. This move was well intentioned, but implementation would prove to be easier on paper than in reality.

And while one branch of government made an honest attempt to represent the Indians' rights, others took them away. During 1873 the government supported the construction of the Northern Pacific Railroad by supplying escort troops to surveyors mapping the route along the Yellowstone River. Sioux under the leadership of Sitting Bull took exception to the planned dissection of their unceded hunting grounds and harassed the troops and surveyors as they worked. The chief well realised the railroad would bring settlers, soldiers and hunters who would destroy the buffalo herds and the Indians' free-roaming way of life. Board Commissioners travelled west to Fort Peck to seek Sitting Bull's consent to the intrusion of the iron horse across the prairies. The chief did not show up at a proposed meeting, and sent a message that he would talk to a truthful white man if they could find one.

Sitting Bull had replaced Red Cloud as the bane of the whites. The old chief had tired of war and chose to stay on the reservation. Sitting Bull was an Unkpapa, one of the seven sub-tribes of the Teton Sioux Nation, the others being the Oglalas, Two Kettles, Sans Arcs, Brules, Miniconjous and Sihasapas. He was an extraordinary man, emerging as an influential and shrewd politician after being a famed warrior in his youth. He was the pre-eminent Sioux chief and medicine man of his day. Newspaper reporter John Finerty saw Sitting Bull in 1879, in Canada:

> An Indian mounted on a cream-colored pony, and holding in his hand an eagle's wing which did duty as a

fan, spurred in back of the chiefs and stared stolidly, for a minute or so, at me. His hair, parted in the ordinary Sioux fashion, was without a plume. His broad face, with a prominent hooked nose and wide jaws, was destitute of paint. His fierce, half-bloodshot eyes gleamed from under brows which displayed large perceptive organs, and, as he sat there on his horse, regarding me with a look which seemed blended of curiosity and insolence, I did not need to be told that he was Sitting Bull...After a little, the noted savage dismounted and led his horse partly into the shade. I noticed that he was an inch or two over medium height, broadly built, rather bow-legged I thought, and he limped slightly as though from an old wound. He sat upon the ground, and was soon engirdled by a crowd of young warriors with whom he was especial favorite as representing the unquenchable hostility of the aboriginal savage to the hated palefaces.

During 1873 General David S. Stanley escorted the railway surveyors with military units including Custer and 10 companies of 7th Cavalry. Custer, like his superiors Sheridan and Sherman, heartily backed the extension of railways over traditional Indian hunting grounds:

> The experience of the past, particularly that of recent years, has shown too that no one measure so quickly and effectually frees a country from the horrors and devastation of Indian wars and Indian depredations generally as the building and successful operation of a railroad through the region overrun...So earnest is my belief in the civilizing and peace-giving influence of railroads through an Indian country...would for ever after have preserved peace with the vast number of tribes...

But Custer fails to mention that the building of wagon and railroads over Indian country caused the 'depredations' in the first place. When the railway surveyors and troops appeared, the Indians, not surprisingly, felt it was they who were being 'overrun.' Both Stanley and Custer may well have approved the railroad's transgression, but otherwise they did not blend, two officers less alike being hard to imagine. Stanley was a stolid, short man, overfond of alcoholic refreshment, as opposed to the milk-drinking Custer; tall, slim, vibrant, and a lover of theatrical display. He had graduated from West Point just in time to make the First Battle of Bull Run where his coolness under stress had been noted. Slouchy and unkempt early in the war, upon being promoted from captain to brigadier general he donned a startling uniform of black velveteen lavishly emblazoned with gold swirls on the sleeves, and grew his yellow locks long. He was, at 23, the youngest general in the Union Army, 'the Boy General' and became the darling cavalier of the north, like a pop star of a later era, his fame eclipsing other generals of equal merit.

And he liked it.

Officers and men serving under Custer varied considerably in their opinion. Some said he was the idol of his men, others the very opposite. The 7th Cavalry's last survivor, Jacob Horner, said he was not liked because he was too hard on both men and horses, and often changed his mind. He said, however, that Custer would not order a man to do anything that he was not prepared to do himself. Other evidence suggests some did not like Custer until they followed him into battle where his flamboyant dash and bravery provided 'a partial compensation for the ordeal of serving under him.' But General Stanley, in 1873, did not like him. 'I have seen enough of him to convince me that he is a cold-blooded, untruthful and unprincipled man,'

Stanley wrote to his wife, 'He is universally despised by all the officers of his regiment excepting his relatives and one or two sycophants.' Perhaps because of his drinking habits, Stanley's venomous feelings towards Custer took a somewhat illogical focus on the mobile stove used to cook his meals by his black servant, Aunt Mary. Six times Stanley ordered Custer to get rid of it. Custer would agree and the black metal monster would seem to vanish. A little further down the track, however, the offending luxury would reappear, having been squirreled away in the wagon of some 'sycophant.'

But there were more important conflicts than disputes over stoves. The Sioux were not happy with the intrusion, and during August, the 7th fought two lively skirmishes with them. Custer wrote in his official report:

> Everything was in readiness for a general advance, the charge was ordered, and the squadrons took the gallop to the tune of 'Garryowen,' the band being placed immediately in rear of the skirmish line. The Indians had evidently come out prepared to do their best, and with no misgivings as to their success, as the mounds and high bluffs beyond the river were covered with groups of old men, squaws and children, who had collected there to witness our destruction. In this instance the proverbial power of music to soothe the savage breast utterly failed, for no sooner did the band strike up the cheery notes of 'Garryowen' and the squadrons advance to the charge, than the Indians exhibited unmistakable signs of commotion, and their resistance became more feeble, until finally satisfied of the earnestness of our attack they turned their ponies' heads and began a disorderly flight.

Perhaps Custer should have taken his band to the Little Bighorn?

Then construction of the railroad stopped. But it was the power of the dollar and not the Sioux that was the cause, an economic crash causing the tracks to halt at Bismarck, North Dakota. The 7th took quarters at the recently established Fort Abraham Lincoln just across the Missouri River from the township.

A few months after Custer's clash with the Sioux, on the other side of the world, another minor action took place in the Drakensberg Mountains of South Africa, a continent rapidly being dominated by the wealth and might of the British Empire. Major Anthony William Durnford of the Royal Engineers was ordered to prevent the escape of rebel Hlubi natives under Chief Langalibalele from the British colony of Natal into neighboring Basutoland. On November 2nd 1873 he set out with a small mounted force of 55 Natal Carbineers and 30 native Basutos. He was to link up with 500 black troops under the command of Captain Allison at Bushman's River Pass amid the rocky crags atop the Drakensbergs, then command the operation to halt the Hlubis' flight.

The Natal Carbineers were the oldest volunteer horse unit in the colony, first raised in 1855. They were part-time soldiers, typical of many such units throughout the Empire at a time when militarism was fashionable. The government supplied the Carbineers' wages, arms and ammunition, but they elected their officers and supplied their own uniforms and horses. They came from established white colonial families, drilled four times per year, and were expert with both horse and gun, but had rarely been put to the test under fire.

It was rough going as Durnford, mounted on his grey Basuto pony, Chieftain, led his men up the craggy climb towards Bushman's River Pass. Trooper Henry Backnall recalled:

Everyone was too tired to give more than a passing glance at the stupendous masses of projecting rock above us like a rugged wall, half a mile high. We would scramble up 20 or 30 yards then sit down, scramble another 20, and sit down again, leading our horses, which made it much more tiring than it would have been without them, for in keeping out of their way we would slip down at almost every step.

Durnford's mount lost its footing and he fell, cracking two ribs, gashing his head and dislocating one shoulder. He was helped to remount his uninjured horse and soldiered on. Captain Barter, a white-bearded farmer in his fifties, commanded the Carbineers. He was exhausted by the rugged climb and recalled one vista:

The scene before us was savage in the extreme. Down the bare side of the mountain hung ribands of water, showing the spot to be the very birthplace and nursery of rivers; above, huge crantzes frowned while the masses of unburnt dry grass, hanging like a vast curtain, gave a sombre and malignant aspect to the scene

But at least he and Durnford made it to the top, their force now reduced to 36 Carbineers and 15 Basutos, most not managing the climb and some Basutos out on scouting patrol. To add to their problems, Captain Allison's force of 500 had been unable to locate its proposed route in the rugged terrain, thus Durnford's main body of troops never arrived.

Early on November 4th Durnford reached the pass. But he was too late. Most of the tribesmen had already crossed into Basutoland, and it was the cattle guard that appeared before his thin line of Basutos and Carbineers. He negotiated with their headman giving assurances of the government's peaceful intentions, but young warriors appeared from along the pass, armed, grim and menacing. Durnford had been ordered not to open hostilities by firing first, thus he had to watch in helpless frustration as the Hlubi, having seen the sparseness of his force, scrambled through rocks to outflank him. Durnford later reported 'had a shot been fired, I could have swept the natives down the pass.' Captain Barter urged Durnford to withdraw his exhausted men to a more secure position, saying some thought they would be killed if they stayed. Durnford gathered his men before him. 'Will nobody stand by me, then?' Only five agreed. Durnford, seeing his position untenable, gave the order to fall back. They turned their horses' heads and started to withdraw in good order, but then a single shot rang out, fired by an Hlubi warrior. A crashing volley from the other natives followed. 'Ride out of this,' someone cried, and the Carbineers spurred their mounts into a headlong, galloping retreat, all discipline lost. Three Carbineers and one Basuto were shot and killed during the scramble, but Durnford, in the rear, performed with cool courage. His Basuto interpreter had his horse stabbed from under him, and Durnford attempted to pull him up onto his mount. But the interpreter fell killed with a bullet through his head. Durnford was surrounded by warriors who thrust at him with assegais, slashing his jacket, and one grasped his bridle. One hostile thrust cut into his side and sliced a nerve in his left elbow, but he fought back, shooting down two assailants with his revolver. A bullet grazed Durnford's cheek as his frightened horse bolted through the cordon, another warrior knocked tumbling to one side. Durnford, his wounded left arm limp, attempted to rally the fleeing Carbineers but had no success. He turned to face the Hlubi alone, and started back, but one of his loyal Basutos grabbed Chieftain's bridle and turned him around. 'I could not let him fling away his life by riding back alone amongst 300 fighting men who had tasted blood.'

Durnford and his downcast command returned to civilisation, their mission a failure. Debate, accusation and recrimination would follow.

On the North American plains, meanwhile, the problem of the hostile Sioux and Cheyenne remained, those white believers in Manifest Destiny scratching their heads as they wondered what to do next. These savages, they thought, could not hold up the inevitable spread of civilization. General Sheridan, now commanding the Military Division of the Missouri, wished to establish a military fort on the reservation, 'so that, holding an interior point in the heart of Indian country, we could threaten the villages and stock of the Indians, if they made raids on our settlements.' Such a fort would be a violation of the treaty, yet sanctioned by it, depending upon which clause is read. Where better to establish such an intrusive and antagonising post than the Black Hills of Dakota, sacred to the Sioux and Cheyenne, and who better to command an expedition of exploration into this little known region than the redoubtable George A. Custer?

On June 8th 1874 Custer received orders from his department commander, General Alfred H. Terry, to organize a reconnaissance of the Black Hills, and on July 2nd twelve companies of cavalry and infantry accompanied by Arikara, or Ree, Indian scouts, sworn enemies of the Sioux and Cheyenne, marched from Fort Abraham Lincoln.

They entered the reservation and moved into the Black Hills, so called by the Sioux because the timbered slopes appeared deep blue or black from the surrounding prairies. The hills extend 120 miles from north to south with a width of between 40 and 60 miles. It was one of the few hunting grounds untouched by the white invader, game such as deer, antelope, elk and bear in abundance. Custer led his expedition into the sacred hills where work commenced, exploring the streams, knolls and valleys, the soldiers hunting the Indians' game. The simmering natives did not attack, but kept their distance. 'The Thieves' Road,' they dubbed the trail of Custer's advance. On one occasion the hidden Indians were treated to a theatrical display when Custer had his sixteen-piece band dismount, struggle with their instruments up a rocky slope, and start playing.

It was not, however, the work of the band, surveyors or topographers that had the most effect, but the discoveries of two prospectors brought along for more than just a ride. The news, 'gold in the grassroots,' was quickly splashed across the newspapers. A stampede of gold-hungry miners followed. The first intruders established a stockade in the aptly named Custer Gulch, but the army was ordered in to drive them out in an attempt to abide by the treaty, no clause allowing such an overt violation. But as they left, hundreds of other fortune seekers poured in from all sides, the government failing to mobilise enough troops to stem the flow.

Thus President Grant found himself with an impossible dilemma. The only solution to the problem, it seemed, was to take the Black Hills from the rightful owners one way or another. Legal means would be tried first but as by the treaty of 1868 three-fourths of the adult male Sioux would have to give their consent for the hills to be ceded to the United States, it seemed doubtful that this would ever happen. But by that same treaty, food was to be supplied to the Indians for four years, a period now expired. The government had continued to supply the provisions realising how dependant the agency

Indians had become. Perhaps the threat of starvation could be used to coerce the Indians into a sale of their sacred hills?

A delegation of chiefs was coming to Washington during May of 1875 to discuss another matter, the relinquishment of hunting rights along the Republican River in return for $25,000. This was also a chance to overawe these stone-age men with the sights and sounds of modern civilization, convincing them armed resistance to the white tide was hopeless. Also on the agenda, unknown to the chiefs, was the cessation of the Black Hills and the vast unceded hunting grounds. When this was proposed the chiefs refused to even discuss the matter. President Grant then spoke personally, reminding the chiefs that the food supplies were gratuities that could be terminated at any time. The white man, he informed them, outnumbered the Indian by 200 to one. Nothing could stop the miners swarming into the hills, so the only sensible course of action was their cessation to the United States. Any hostilities on the part of the tribes, he said, would lead to the rations being withheld. The chiefs were also shocked to hear a proposal that they consider relinquishing their current homeland entirely, and move far south to Indian Territory. (Later the state of Oklahoma)

The disgruntled chiefs returned to their western homelands, and told their fellow tribesmen of the wonders of white civilisation and cities in the east. Sitting Bull rejected their stories as figments of the imagination induced by the powerful white man's medicine, to which they had been subjected and seduced.

A commission was despatched from Washington in an attempt to buy the Black Hills. The reservation Indians agreed at prices ranging from twenty million dollars to fifty million, but not the six million on offer. The non-reservation Sioux, however, clinging to the old life, refused to sell at any price, warning the whites to get out. The commission returned to Washington, nothing accomplished.

On June 25th, exactly one year before the Battle of the Little Bighorn, Bishop W. H. Hare wrote in the New York *Tribune* 'We should not be surprised if, insisting now on buying with money what the Indian does not wish to sell, we drive him to frenzy, our covetousness end in massacre, and we pay for the Indians' land less in money than in blood.'

Another expedition, meanwhile, had journeyed to the Black Hills to confirm or deny Custer's original report of abundant gold. Professor Walter P. Jenny with scientists and prospectors left Fort Laramie on May 25th escorted by eight companies of troops under the command of Colonel R. I. Dodge. They dug and panned for gold samples for several months alongside hundreds of other invaders, without molestation by the Sioux, and returned with glowing reports.

The day following Jenny's departure for the Black Hills the steamboat *Josephine* left Fort Buford for a reconnaissance up the Yellowstone River into the unceded Sioux territory. On board with a military detachment were Colonel James Forsyth and Lieutenant Frederick Grant, the president's son. General Sheridan had written, 'it may be necessary, at some time in the immediate future, to occupy by a military force the country in and about the mouth of the Tongue River and the Big Horn. You will therefore make special examination of these points with this in view.'

They returned on June 10th after completing a pioneering trip up the Yellowstone, only turning back when the river became too shallow near present Billings, Montana. There had been no hostile encounters with Indians and this encouraged a large party of traders and hunters to establish Fort Pease at the mouth of the Big Horn River, an unwelcome intrusion.

Further south, the invasion of the Black Hills continued and General George Crook, an Indian fighter of some renown, was assigned the task of attempting to keep the intruders out. On July 29th 1875 he issued a proclamation ordering them to vacate the Black Hills by August 15th, and called for a meeting of miners so that they could register their claims to 'secure to each when the country shall have been opened, the benefit of his discovery and the labor he has already expended.' Thus it was a forgone conclusion that the Indians were going to lose their land in the not too distant future. 169 gold diggers assembled at Custer Creek on the appointed day and registered their claims, drew lots for future town-sites and elected a committee to stay and protect their interests till June 1st 1876. Crook agreed to intercede with General Sheridan regarding the committee staying on, in violation of the proclamation, and very few of those who did leave stayed out for long.

As fresh strikes were reported hundreds more miners slipped through the thin military cordon and more disillusioned Indians slipped away from the reservation to join the free-ranging tribes under chiefs like Sitting Bull and Crazy Horse. General Sheridan once remarked, 'It is absurd to talk of keeping faith with Indians,' which may help explain the army not keeping the prospectors out. But despite the provocation the warriors held the peace. On November 1st the Indian Commissioner reported that 'during the year passing in review there has been less conflict with the Indians than for many previous years… and complaint of marauding has been much less than usual.' And on January 1st 1876 the Board of Indian Commissioners reported 'during the past year there have been no organized acts of hostility by any tribe or band of Indians. This is more noteworthy from the fact that two years ago all the bands of Sioux threatened to wage war upon any individuals or parties who might visit the Black Hills.' General Sheridan's *Record of Engagement with Hostile Indians* listed, for the year 1875, one minor episode involving the Sioux, and this was in a remote part of Montana, far from the Black Hills of Dakota.

The quiet before the storm.

Ulysses S. Grant found himself caught between the extremes of those whites demanding the tribes relinquish their hold on the Black Hills, and the irrefutable terms of the 1868 treaty, which guaranteed the Black Hills as part of the Sioux reservation. The Indian Board and whites with a sense of justice sided with the Indians, but as Grant gave assurances that the Peace Policy was alive and well, war with the Sioux must have been very much on his military mind. The army's campaign would, naturally, be directed against the 'hostiles' at large on the open range, the unceded hunting grounds where, by the terms of the treaty, they had a perfect right to be. They had been peaceful so far, but for how long? In 1862 the Santee Sioux further east in Minnesota had erupted from their reservation without warning, 644 settlers being killed before the army quashed the uprising. Andrew Myrick, a Minnesota trader, had remarked about the Indians, 'If they're hungry, let them eat grass.' Myrick's body was discovered with his mouth stuffed with grass. The Santee Sioux agent, James McLaughlin, wrote afterwards decrying the loss of innocent life, and if the Indians had been more discriminate in taking their reprisals, 'the red man would long ago have made an attack on the national Capital.'

No doubt Grant felt secure from Indian attack in the White House. But a shock and awe campaign on the prairies would nullify any chance of the Dakota Sioux making a preemptive strike, and could well intimidate the three-fourths of the agency Indians into finally ceding the Black Hills to the

United States. And once fighting broke out, the treaty would be in tatters in any case, the hills annexed as spoils of war. Such a campaign would end once and for all the conflict on the northern plains between white man and red. The Indians would be settled on the reservations to become Christian farmers, and the Northern Pacific Railroad would move west without further hindrance, opening vast tracts to civilisation. Such a course of action would certainly please his old wartime lieutenants, Generals Sherman and Sheridan, who had been in favor of war all along. Yes, a final bloody contest with the red man of the plains was the best way out.

***

Sir Bartle Frere arrived aboard that modern marvel of the Victorian era, the steam ship, to become governor of the Cape, South Africa, in April of 1877. A prominent British administrator of his auspicious background would not normally have considered such an ordinary posting, but he came with big plans afloat, the confederation of the various South African colonies under British rule. Therefore, like President Grant a few years before, he had a problem on his hands; how best to annexe native lands. During this period of British colonial expansion, confederation was becoming an increasingly desired policy, having previously born fruit in the Leeward Islands, India, and more recently, Canada. The home government wished to minimise the costs of colonial administration, not only making them self-supporting, but generating profitable trade with Britain.

At that time, in addition to the Cape, the southern portion of South Africa was divided into various colonies including Natal, controlled by the British, the Transvaal, recently annexed by the British, but colonized by Boers of Dutch descent, and

Zululand, on the eastern border, still governed by the natives themselves. It was considered 'the most politically sophisticated, administratively integrated and militarily powerful' black state south of the Sahara. Little wonder the word Zulu meant 'of heaven.' It was ruled by their king, Cetshwayo kaMpande, whose uncle had been the great Zulu warrior Shaka who, with ferocious determination, had carved out the Zulu empire with territorial conquests of his own during the early 19th century.

The colonial secretary in London, Lord Carnarvon, had given Frere the challenging task of confederating these colonies. Carnarvon had been planning, 'taking Cetshwayo and his Zulus under our protection.' in the summer of 1876. No doubt the recent stories in English newspapers of the disaster at Little Bighorn, the American government's attempt to take the Sioux under their 'protection,' sounded no warning bells. Yankee colonials might well make a mess of things, but not the British, the world's dominant colonial power, well used to crushing natives when the need arose.

If Frere were to succeed in this formidable task he had been promised the post of South Africa's first governor-general. In addition to governing the Cape, meanwhile, he was high commissioner of Native Affairs in South Africa, giving him an influential voice in the other British colonies. As an added inducement, his salary of 7000 pounds per year would rise to 10,000 following confederation.

Such a union would enable the British Empire to exploit the vast trading and mineral resources of South Africa. Diamond fields had been discovered in the almost uninhabited Griqualand West, and the British had acquired these by simply moving the border. Boers of the Orange Free State were silenced with the payment of 90,000 pounds, and the annexation of the Transvaal had resulted in new gold fields coming under British control.

Prior to his appointment to the Cape, Frere had spoken of the relatively small trade carried on with Africa, considering the huge resources on hand. He suggested 'welding together the loose elements of a great South African Empire,' and made reference to African labor as a 'mine of wealth to the employer.'

There was a strong push within South Africa for the British to annexe Zululand, and tales of Cetshwayo's cruel mistreatment of his own subjects were fed to the new governor. In August of 1876 he had executed young girls who had refused his marriage arrangements with the Zulu regiment of 37-40 year olds. In response to an inquiry instigated by the acting British Secretary for Native Affairs, John W. Shepstone, Cetshwayo, considering this an intrusion into his domestic affairs, replied 'Did I ever tell Mr Shepstone I would not kill? Did he tell the white people I made such an arrangement? Because if he did he has deceived them. I do kill...It is the custom of our nation and I shall not depart from it.' This gave the high moral ground to those wishing to see Zululand under British control. But possibly these same people would be dismayed to hear of British troops bayoneting hundreds of Zulu wounded or torturing captives when war finally came.

With the help of Natal newspapers, British, German and Norwegian missionaries set about white-anting Cetshwayo's throne, especially after they were expelled from Zululand in April of 1878. The missionaries wished to convert the 'savages' and the colonists in Natal and elsewhere wanted what they saw as a military threat quashed. Cetshwayo did pose a threat to Boers who settled on Zulu lands, but his association with the British had always been one of friendship, and no British traveller or settler had been harmed, the Zulu nation having been at peace for 23 years.

Frere was informed that Cetshwayo kept a standing army of 40,000 warriors ready to invade Natal at short notice. The renowned writer Anthony Trollope journeyed through South Africa in 1877. 'I have no fears myself that Natal will be overrun by hostile Zulus,' he wrote perceptively, 'but much fear that Zululand should be overrun by hostile Britons.'

In September of 1877 Frere wrote to John Shepstone's brother, Sir Theophilus Shepstone, the British administrator in the Transvaal:

> To maintain a standing army of 40,000 unmarried young men, would task the resources of a country as rich & populous & industrious as Belgium, & if Cetywayo can manage it, without a constant succession of conquests, he is fit to be War Minister to any great military power in Europe.

Shepstone, despite favouring Zululand's occupation by the British, felt obliged to enlighten Frere by pointing out that the army did not only consist of unmarried young men, and they provided their own food.

It was also a fact that the Zulu army was not 'standing', but spent most of the year in their home villages. Their supposed military service consisted mainly of working for the king, growing crops, tending herds etc. It was this labor, in lieu of paying taxes as in the British colonies, that allowed the Zulu government and social system to function.

Shepstone, who spoke fluent Zulu, had attended Cetshwayo's coronation in 1873 and was impressed with the new monarch:

> Cetshwayo is a man of considerable ability, much force of character, and has a dignified manner; in all conversation

with him he was remarkably frank and straightforward, and he ranks in every respect far above every Native Chief I have ever had to do with. I do not think that his disposition is very warlike, even if it is, his obesity will impose prudence; but he is naturally proud of the military traditions of his family, especially the policy and deeds of his uncle and predecessor, Chaka, to which he made frequent reference.

The British supported Cetshwayo's ascendance to the throne on certain conditions, to which he gave verbal consent. Shepstone read out the Coronation Laws following a 17 gun salute; an end to indiscriminate bloodshed in Zululand, no one to be executed without trial or appeal, no lives to be taken without the king's permission, minor crimes to be punished by fines rather than death. 'His sagacity enables him,' wrote Shepstone, 'to see clearly the bearing of the new circumstances by which he is surrounded, and the necessity for so adjusting his policy as to suit them.'

But Cetshwayo did not rule as an absolute monarch, his plans sometimes thwarted by the chiefs of his council of state. Following the coronation they continued to execute whom they pleased without reference to the king, which they considered their hereditary right. Shepstone wished to bring western values to Zululand, but he also knew that breaches would give the British an excuse for future intervention, which he felt would eventually come. As time passed he became an advocate of war with Cetshwayo, but would have thought twice, no doubt, had he known one of his own sons would be a victim. George Shepstone was an officer of the Royal Natal Carbineers and his brother Theophilus (Offy) commanded them. George would fall in the bloody carnage of Isandlwana alongside many of his men.

Not all in the London's corridors of power, however, were in favor of Zululand becoming another British responsibility. Many in Parliament were concerned at the rising financial cost of imperial expansion, and the possible diplomatic ramifications with other European powers. In June of 1877 Lord Carnarvon wrote that the annexation of Zululand, 'must and ought to come eventually, but not just now.'

While Governor Frere contemplated the grand scheme for the confederation of South Africa, Theophilus Shepstone tackled a local problem inherited by the British when they annexed the Transvaal; a long running dispute between the Boers and Zulus regarding exactly where the border lay between the two countries.

Previously the British had chosen to see the Zulu viewpoint as a way of denying the Boers access to the sea, but the waters had now become muddied by these same Boers becoming British subjects. Shepstone travelled across the Disputed Territory, most of the Transvaal's eastern border with Zululand, then continued on for a conference with Cetshwayo's prime minister, Chief Mnyamana. They met on a large flat-topped hill near Blood River within Zululand on October 18th 1877. The negotiations did not go smoothly. Chief Mnyamana stated that the rightful boundary should be the Buffalo River as far as the Drakensberg Mountains, and then north following that river to the headwaters of the Vaal. This was unacceptable to Shepstone who suggested Blood River and the Lynspruit as an alternative, with an unoccupied strip on the Zulu side for administration by a British agent who would, in about five years time, award it to either the Zulus or the Boers. But Mnyamana was not happy. He wanted Boer infiltration of Zulu territory formally investigated before any agreement could be reached.

The Zulu demands would later be softened by Cetshwayo, but by then Shepstone had actually increased the Transvaal's demands by claiming land supposedly ceded by the Treaty of Waaihoek in 1861. This included territory currently occupied by the Zulus on their side of Blood River, and Shepstone informed Lord Carnarvon that the Boer case was 'incontrovertible.' But Shepstone was well aware of growing Boer dissatisfaction with his administration of the Transvaal, and he had a clear conflict of interest in his assessment of the border dispute. Tensions grew and many Boer homesteads lay abandoned, the occupants having fled for fear of Zulu attack.

The lieutenant governor of Natal, Sir Henry Bulwer, now entered the dispute. He was not convinced of Cetshwayo's supposed war-like intent, and in December of 1877 wrote to him offering to appoint, with the home government's consent, an independent arbitrator. Cetshwayo readily agreed, but requested, in the meantime, that a committee of Natal Commissioners carry out a preliminary investigation. Bulwer agreed and set the wheels in motion.

Shepstone, however, remained convinced that war was the only solution, and a dissatisfied Bulwer wrote to him in January of 1878:

> You make no reference to the possibility of this being settled by peaceful means in any one way or another, but are giving reasons for the destruction of the Zulu power, and for the Zulu Nation ceasing to exist as an independent Nation...We are looking to different objects—I to the termination of this dispute by a peaceful settlement, you to its termination by the overthrow of the Zulu kingdom.

Sir Bartle Frere, watching these proceedings from Cape Town, supported Shepstone's pro-war policy, but somewhat cynically came out in favor of Bulwer's attempt to settle by arbitration, allowing time for an increase in British forces and preparation. The attempt at arbitration would also give the British a respectable veneer to the outside world before the inevitable crushing of the Zulus by firepower came.

The Natal government selected three men to sit on the Boundary Commission; Attorney-General M. H. Gallway, acting Secretary for Native Affairs John Shepstone and Colonial Engineer Lieutenant Colonel Anthony Durnford. In 1873, when a major, Durnford had led the expedition to Bushman's River Pass attempting to stop rebel tribesmen escaping into Basutoland, resulting in the deaths of five of his command including three white Natal Carbineers. Durnford would play a controversial and prominent role in the military disaster at Isandlwana that was to come.

On March 12th 1878 the commission began work at Rorke's Drift on the Buffalo River, the border between Natal and Zululand. Most assumed a decision favorable to the Boers would eventuate, to be followed by hostilities with the Zulu nation. This, however, undervalued the impartiality of the commissioners, and did not take into account changing attitudes in London. Lord Carnarvon, the chief driver of South African confederation, had resigned his post as colonial secretary shortly before the committee began work, being at odds with the British government over its attitude towards a war then being waged between Russia and Turkey. His successor, Sir Michael Hicks Beach, had different priorities and was not especially interested in the African question.

Sir Bartle Frere was shattered by Carnarvon's resignation. He could see the grand plan for confederation, his governor-generalship and his pay rise slipping away. He considered a military campaign against the Zulus as being necessary to bring about confederation, and his fears were confirmed with these words from Hicks Beach in March of 1878:

> I presume that the presence of a considerable force in Natal, with some (not too large) augmentation of that in the Transvaal would not be without its useful effect on Cetywayo: though I think Shepstone would have to be discouraged from taking the opportunity to make war. The negotiations, through Bulwer, with Cetywayo should be pushed on, and the dwellers in the disputed territory be protected from aggression meanwhile; but our power should not make us relax our best efforts to obtain a peaceful solution.

The new colonial secretary also cast doubt on the fairness of the existing treaties with the Boers and suggested giving that part of the Disputed Territory settled by Boers to the Transvaal, and the remainder to the Zulus.

Bartle Frere would, naturally, prefer the whole-hearted support of the home government, but in his long career as a colonial administrator he had been known to act unilaterally and escape reproach because his actions had resulted in success. This, no doubt, would have considerable influence over his future intrigues. And, of course, there was the example set by Lord Lytton, the Viceroy in Afghanistan, who had successfully contrived to start a war, despite the home government's disapproval, in 1878.

Frere regarded black Africans as uncivilised and their chiefs and institutions not worthy of preservation. Once their 'reign of barbarism' was ended, trade and civilization could prosper. A war with the Zulus would see his goals come to fruition, but now he was being frustrated by those very Britons he felt should be supporting him; the likes of Bulwer and Hicks Beach.

The next blow to Frere's colonial ambitions came when the Boundary Commission handed down its report in July. It found that the Zulu cessions of land both in 1854 and 1861 were defective and that the Zulu king did not have the power to cede land without the consent of the council of chiefs, representing the Zulu people. Lieutenant Colonel Anthony Durnford wrote to his father 'I think our views will be maintained—at least I hope so. You see we have gone in for fair play.' The Transvaal, however, was to receive the territory to the west of Blood River because it had, in fact, exercised control there without interference from the Zulus. The Boers with land east of Blood River would find no comfort in this award, and Bartle Frere was appalled at these findings. This would not help bring on the desired war, but he could not ignore the decision. Frere, in his capacity of high commissioner for Native Affairs in South Africa, decided to allow the Boers to stay on their farms in the disputed territory under a guarantee of British protection, while granting Cetshwayo nominal sovereignty over the land. One colonial official said this was 'giving the shells to the Zulus and the oysters to the boars.' Frere knew this would please no one in the long term, and continued his intrigues to bring on armed conflict, the only way, he felt, to settle the matter once and for all.

Lieutenant General Sir Frederic Thesiger was a tall, robust and handsome teetotaller of fifty. He was not only keen on amateur dramatics and a talented clarinettist, but also an experienced military campaigner, having seen action in both the Crimean War and the Indian Mutiny. He was a skilled rider, had proven himself calm under fire, and won the devotion of those who served alongside him with his gentlemanly, modest demeanour.

Lieutenant General Sir Arthur Cunynghame was recalled from South Africa in early 1878. Thesiger, who became Lord Chelmsford on the death of his father later the same year, was given command, but more through connections than being the best man for the job. Although competent and efficient, he tended to be indecisive and obsessed by petty detail, having little flair and vision for the big picture.

But early signs indicated that the new commander in South Africa would have no trouble handling Cetshwayo's Zulus when the time came. Chelmsford speedily quashed a native rebellion on the eastern Cape frontier, which lulled the general and those around him into a false sense of security regarding his capabilities. Bartle Frere wrote to Colonial Secretary Hicks Beach:

> He has broken up every strong hold in which the Kaffirs have attempted to rally. He has cut off their supplies of food and ammunition, & some very important chiefs have been captured, & others killed. In no previous war have the Kaffirs been so signally, speedily & completely defeated & the disturbance brought within the limits the police can manage.

Following his easy victory, Chelmsford stayed as Frere's guest at Government House in Cape Town. This gave the governor an ideal opportunity to mould the general's thoughts regarding South African confederation. War with the Zulus, he said, was inevitable, claiming Cetshwayo's regiments were a constant military threat.

For reasons of defence, Frere informed Hicks Beach and Bulwer, Chelmsford was to move his forces into Natal. The general was ready for action, and wrote to Sir Theophilus Shepstone:

> If we are to have a fight with the Zulus, I am anxious that our arrangements can be as complete as it is possible to make them. Half measures do not answer with natives, they must be thoroughly crushed to make them believe in our superiority, and if I am called upon to conduct operations against them, I shall strive to be in a position to show them how hopelessly inferior they are to us in fighting power, altho' numerically stronger.

Frere and Chelmsford began their plans for the invasion of Zululand, another link in the Empire upon which the sun never set.

Lieutenant Colonel George A. Custer
(Little Bighorn Battlefield National Monument)

Lieutenant Colonel Anthony W. Durnford
(Institute of Royal Engineers Library, Chatham)

2
DECEPTION AND DECEIT

If war must come with the red man of the northern plains, now was as good a time as any for President Ulysses S. Grant. The army had been drastically slashed following the Civil War as the surviving farm hands, shopkeepers, lawyers and accountants returned home. Those troops remaining had become thinly spread carrying out reconstruction duty in the shattered rebel states, and along trouble spots on the western frontier. But as the nation's wounds healed, and conflict with the tribes on the southern plains declined, a military thrust to settle the menacing Sioux and Cheyenne was more than feasible. They, like the Zulu, represented a constant military threat to a nation determined upon expansion.

The only trouble was, the so-called hostiles were refusing to cooperate. By being so tolerant of the white invasion of their sacred Black Hills, there was no reason to call for a military strike. Grant could, no doubt, imagine the screams of rage from those members of the public who believed in fair play, and those newspapers and politicians hostile to his administration, if the army simply marched in. Yet there seemed to be no other way out. Subterfuge would have to be used, a campaign planned in secret, the hostile free-roamers not on the reservations quickly crushed, the job accomplished by the time the wails of protest were heard. Army commander General Sherman would be a staunch supporter of such a plan, having pushed this course of action for years, and General Philip Sheridan, known as 'Little Phil,' whose department would be the scene of the action, would back Grant to the hilt.

Some people in positions of power within the government might make life difficult, however. Both the secretary of the interior, Columbus Delano, and the commissioner of Indian Affairs, E. P. Smith, would not look with favor at such a militant scheme. But then Delano became involved in one of many scandals to rock Grant's administration. Professor Othniel C. Marsh had met Chief Red Cloud during an expedition hunting fossil bones of extinct dinosaurs, and heard first-hand his many grievances regarding the administration of Indian Affairs. There is no doubt that many of the Indian agents were corrupt, extracting receipts from gullible tribesmen for clothing and food far in access of that actually supplied. The balance would be sold off to whites, the profits pocketed by the agents. And both clothing and food supplied to the tribes were often sub-standard, while the government was paying first-class prices. Newspapers hostile to Grant were only too glad to spread the news, and Columbus Delano was forced to resign on October 1st 1875. But the newspapers had unwittingly done Grant a favor. With Delano gone, he was able to substitute a replacement far more amenable to his plans for war against the Indians in the person of Zachariah Chandler of Michigan, an ex-senator of considerable power in Republican politics. Not only the public were surprised by this, but Grant's cabinet also, who did not receive the customary consultation. Chandler had made no secret of his view that Indian Affairs should be taken away from the Department of the Interior and returned to the Army, which had this responsibility prior to 1848. One week before Chandler accepted his appointment Grant requested a conference with key military personnel at the White House regarding a solution to the Black Hills problem. On November 1st the New York *Herald* reported:

> Several pastors in this city of different denominations, who were apprehensive that the Government was about to abandon its peace policy towards the Indians, called upon the President today to express their conviction that such a course would greatly disappoint Christian people...The President replied with great promptness and precision that he did not regard the peace policy as a failure, and that it would not only not be abandoned while he occupied that place, but that it was his hope that during his administration it would become so firmly established as to be the necessary policy of his successors.

The very next day Generals Phil Sheridan and George Crook arrived for their conference with Grant at the White House. That night Zachariah Chandler arrived in Washington to assume his new duties as Secretary of the Interior. On November 3rd newspapers reported:

> Secretary Chandler, accompanied by Assistant Secretary Cowen, called at the Executive Mansion today and had a long talk with the President, mainly in regard to Indian affairs. Secretary of War Belknap and Generals Sheridan and Crook participated in the conference and gave expression to their well-known opinions concerning the Indian question, besides furnishing much information respecting the practical administration of the peace policy within the limits of their past and present commands.

Grant now had about him only those who would cooperate with his plans for war. Conspicuous by his absence from this conference regarding Indian affairs was E. P. Smith, the Indian

Commissioner, known for his pro-peace stance towards the Sioux. Grant and his cohorts mulled over the Sioux problem, and it was decided that miners were no longer to be excluded from the Black Hills, although the public order for their exclusion would remain intact. The Sioux, under pressure from the influx, may well decide to cede the land, or hostilities may erupt. Should the Sioux attack, it would justify Grant withholding rations from those Indians still on the reservations, increasing pressure on them to cede the Black Hills, and white deaths would cause an outcry for military retribution.

A military campaign against those 'hostiles' who refused to come into the reservation was also discussed. This was to be kept secret until justification could be found in hostile action by the Sioux. Or if they did not cooperate, the Indian bureau was to fabricate outrages by the Indians that would justify a punitive expedition. Winter was the best time to strike, when the Sioux would be far less mobile, snowed into their villages along icy streams. A repeat of Custer's attack on the Cheyenne village at the Washita was now required.

News regarding the miners not being excluded from the Black Hills was made public, but some perceptive newspaper reporters felt there was far more to the White House conference than was being divulged. William T. Curtis of the *Chicago Inter-Ocean* had accompanied Custer's Black Hills expedition and was now chief of his newspaper's Washington bureau. On November 7th he wrote a despatch regarding rumours that 'the military are to have more to do with Indian matters in the future than they have had in the past,' and the following day, 'The roving tribes and those who are known as wild Indians will probably be given over entirely to the military until they are subdued enough to remain on their reservations and adopt civilized modes of life.'

The next day, November 9th, saw the signing of a report by Erwin C. Watkins regarding the Sioux Indians. Watkins was one of three Indian inspectors who made annual tours of the Indian reservations. He was an ex-army officer who had served with Crook and Sheridan during the Civil War and had, conveniently, just returned from a tour of the Indian agencies in the Dakotas and Montana. His report makes no mention of the breaches by whites of the treaty of 1868 including the invasion of the Black Hills, but accuses Sioux under chiefs like Sitting Bull of being disrespectful of white authority, and being lofty, boastful, scornful, savage, untameable, uncivilized. The Indians, Watkins reported, claimed sovereignty over their country, as well as murdering innocent settlers, emigrants and hunters, and attacking submissive tribes who have made peace with the whites.

It is hard to believe that a mere Indian inspector was the genuine author of what was to be the nation's recommended military strategy, as Watkins had no qualifications for that role. What was supposedly written by him smacks of the hand of senior military minds:

> In my judgement, one thousand men under the command of an experienced officer, sent into their country in the winter, when the Indians are nearly always in camp, and at which season of the year they are the most helpless, would be amply sufficient for their capture or punishment…
> The true policy in my judgement, is to send troops against them in the winter, the sooner the better, and *whip* them into subjection. They richly merit the punishment for their incessant warfare on friendly tribes, their continuous thieving, and their numerous murders of white settlers and their families, or white men found unarmed.

The Government owes it, too, to these friendly tribes, in fulfilment of treaty stipulations. It owes it to the agents and employees, whom it has sent to labor among the Indians at remote and almost inaccessible places, beyond reach in time to save. It owes it to the frontier settlers who have, with their families, braved the dangers and hardships incident to frontier life. It owes it to civilization and the common cause of humanity.

The Sioux had, in fact, been surprisingly well behaved since the invasion of the Black Hills, though many cynical Indians left the reservation to join the untamed Sioux living by hunting on the open range.

Thus these allegations were invented for fear that they *might* come true, and, like Cetshwayo's Zulu army, it was a force that could possibly unleash destruction on the white population. The report provided an excuse for a pre-emptive strike, but even those responsible realised that only the gullible would believe such a concoction, thus it was withheld from official publication. Reporter William Curtis of the *Chicago Inter-Ocean*, however, had the report leaked to him and quoted from it, but in the form of a face to face interview with Watkins.

Indian Commissioner E. P. Smith, one of those in the peace camp, sat on the report for three weeks before forwarding it, on November 27th, to Secretary Chandler who in turn forwarded it to William Belknap endorsed 'for the consideration and action of the Hon. Secretary of War.'

***

Sir Henry Bulwer, the Governor of Natal, did not share Bartle Frere's enthusiasm for a war with the Zulu nation. He was far from convinced there was any hostile intent on Cetshwayo's part, as Frere would have the world believe.

When army commander Lord Chelmsford arrived in Natal during August of 1878, friction erupted as Bulwer felt the arrival of British troops in force would make the Zulus feel threatened and create needless tensions. Chelmsford complained to Frere, requesting his presence, saying that Bulwer would not permit him to take 'the most ordinary measures of precaution for fear lest they should be misconstrued by Cetewayo and the Zulus.' Any alarm on Cetshwayo's part would, of course, not be misconstrued, but be an accurate reading of the British design. Bulwer's fears were realised when he received from Chelmsford, on August 28th, a memo titled 'Invasion of Zululand; or, Defence of the Natal and Transvaal Colony from Invasion by the Zulus.' The document only detailed an invasion of Zulu territory by five separate columns of troops; nothing to do with defence. Chelmsford's plan called for eight battalions of troops, but as there were only six available in Natal and the Transvaal, he requested two more to be shipped from England along with two companies of Royal Engineers and additional staff officers. Chelmsford stated that an invasion of Natal by the Zulus was more 'imminent' than it had been for years. He also planned the use of battalions of Natal Africans, one out of every ten men armed with a rifle, the others with traditional native weapons, the assegai and shield. European officers and NCOs would lead them

Bartle Frere arrived in Durban, Natal, on September 23rd, in response to a request from both Chelmsford and Bulwer. The general wanted his support to help overcome Bulwer's opposition to the military build-up, and Bulwer did not want the responsibility of announcing the Boundary Commission's recommendations, unfavorable to the Boers, without him present. A week later Frere wrote to Colonial Secretary Hicks Beach in London 'The people here are slumbering on a volcano,

& I much fear you will not be able to send out the reinforcements we have asked, in time to prevent an explosion...The Zulus are now quite out of hand, & the maintenance of peace depends on their forbearance.'

This would have been as much a surprise to the Zulus if they read it as, three years earlier, the Watkins report would have been to the Sioux who were supposedly murdering white settlers along the frontier.

On October 14th Frere wrote to Hicks Beach saying that he was waiting to hear from Cetshwayo regarding an 'explanation regarding violations of the frontier already reported.' The first occurred when two wives of Zulu Chief Sihayo absconded into Natal with their lovers. A large war party was despatched and crossed into Natal. The wives were captured, dragged back over the border and executed. Natal settlers were outraged at this invasion of their soil and Bulwer demanded that the antagonists be sent to Natal for trial. Cetshwayo refused, knowing that Natal police had often transgressed into Zululand to arrest criminals, and instead offered 50 pounds in compensation.

The second cause for complaint occurred when Zulu tribesmen took a surveyor and his companion in charge. They were inspecting a drift on the Thukela River to see what work was required to allow wagons to cross. The Zulus, keeping a close watch on the border, questioned them for some time before their release. The surveyor was unperturbed by the event, but his companion reported the incident to the Natal authorities. Frere wasted no time in reporting to Hicks Beach that the surveyor had been 'seized and assaulted by an armed party of Zulus which crossed to our side of the river.' They had actually been apprehended mid-stream, but Frere was not about to let the truth spoil a good story, which might mislead the government regarding Zulu intentions. Bulwer placed the cause of the problem with the colonial engineer's department for sending the surveyor's mission at a time when British troops were gathering in Natal, heightening border tensions.

Another border incident occurred when Chief Mbilini kaMswati raided a group of Swazi refugees on the Ntombe River. The disputed Boer settlement of Luneberg was nearby and the magistrate blamed Cetshwayo for ordering the raid, describing it as 'a feeler of great significance.' A few weeks later, however, he further reported that Cetshwayo had, in fact, ordered the arrest of Mbilini for the transgression. Bartle Frere was not interested in the second piece of news, however, and described Cetshwayo as initiating acts to keep up the terror he had inspired 'and to try how far he might go.' Bulwer, on the other hand, received the following from Cetshwayo:

> I hear of troops arriving in Natal, that they are coming to attack the Zulus and to seize me; in what have I done wrong that I should be seized like an 'Umtakata' (wrongdoer), the English are my fathers, I do not wish to quarrel with them, but to live as I have always done, at peace with them.

The British prime minister, Benjamin Disraeli, was preoccupied with a tense situation in Europe and did not relish the prospect of a South African war soaking up vital resources. It was possible that Britain might be at war with Russia in the not too distant future, and Disraeli angrily described the colonies as 'millstones round our neck.' Distant from the actual events, he blamed Sir Theophilus Shepstone for the looming conflict in South Africa. 'He has managed to quarrel with English, Dutch and Zulus; and now is obliged to be recalled, but not before he has bought on, I fear, a new war.'

Even the real architect of the coming war, Sir Bartle Frere, was unhappy with Shepstone's somewhat overbearing approach to his duties, as were the Boer subjects in his jurisdiction. Despite Shepstone's pro-war stance, Frere requested his recall and was pleased to see acting Transvaal administrator Colonel Lanyon take over as his replacement.

As Frere made preparations for war, the time lapse in receiving communications from Britain worked to his advantage. The telegraph cable from London stopped at St Vincent in the Cape Verde Islands, and messages had then to be carried by ship to Cape Town, thus it took at least sixteen days for a telegram to reach its destination. Written material such as despatches and personal letters took from three weeks to a month. Frere would benefit stating that he could not wait such long periods for the home office to endorse his decisions, and, in any case, it had been made clear by the government that the Zulus would have to be brought to heel sooner or later. But not yet, having also clarified an earnest desire to avoid war. There was, however, this call for reinforcements from both Chelmsford and Frere which would have to be dealt with. On October 17 Hicks Beach, after discussing the South African problem with Cabinet members, informed the prime minister:

> We decided to send out the 'special services' officers asked for...but no more troops at any rate for the present. And I have sent by to-night's mail a despatch to Frere to this effect, throwing as much cold water as possible upon his evident expectation of a Zulu war, and telling him that the imperial forces now in South Africa...should suffice for all other necessities. I much fear, however, that before this can reach him, we may hear of the beginning of a

fight with the Zulus; and then the troops will probably have to go.

On November 1st Hicks Beach received Frere's 'slumbering on a volcano' letter and Cabinet considered the situation once more. But their answer remained the same, and the colonial secretary wrote to Frere informing him of more urgent matters in Eastern Europe and India, saying that a Zulu war was out of the question. He urged Frere to settle any dispute with the Zulus by peaceable means. 'The only serious recent act on the part of the Zulus…as giving ground for complaint on our part, is the taking and killing the two refugee Zulu women…This can surely be settled without a war.'

But there were those within the corridors of power who felt Chelmsford and Frere should have more military support. What if war broke out and a British defeat was the result? They had heard of the size and strength of the Zulu army. The government would be assailed by all and sundry for not having heeded the call for troops. It was decided to send out two more battalions after all, but Hicks Beach wrote to Frere saying that the Cabinet 'wished me to impress upon you most strongly the necessity of avoiding aggression, and using all proper means to keep out of war.' But the troops were coming, much to Frere's delight. He probably thought that if there was to be no war, why send more troops? Frere could read between the lines, and was convinced that if the British struck first a short, successful conflict would add more territory to the Empire, and Chelmsford's victory laurels would also be his. Lord Salisbury, who had previously served with Frere on the India Council, described him as 'quarrelsome and mutinous' and had noted his 'impetuosity of disposition' and added 'Impatience of control is a common defect in men of able and fearless character.'

Chelmsford's success in the brief border war using the breech-loading rifles now supplied to British redcoats convinced Frere a successful campaign was a forgone conclusion. Chelmsford agreed, 'the first experience of the power of the Martini-Henrys,' the general wrote, 'will be such a surprise to the Zulus that they will not be formidable after the first effort.'

The results of such misplaced confidence would stun not only Chelmsford, but also Great Britain and the rest of the world.

Sitting Bull
(Little Bighorn Battlefield National Monument)

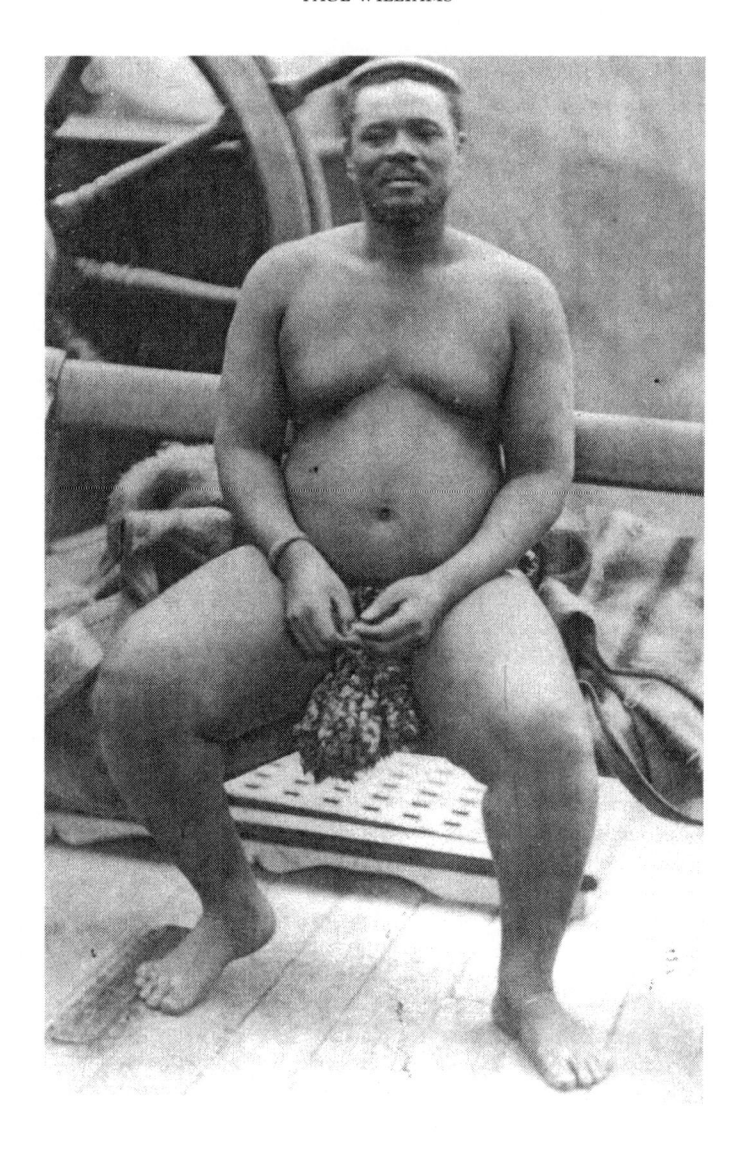

Cetshwayo kaMpande
(National Army Museum)

3
THE IMPOSSIBLE ULTIMATUM

The Watkins Report, recommending military action against the Sioux and Cheyenne, landed on the desk of Secretary Chandler in Washington D.C. on November 27th 1875. One week later he sent a communication to Secretary for War William Belknap, which included:

> I have the honor to inform you that this day I have directed the Commissioner of Indian Affairs to notify said Indians that they must remove to a reservation before the 31st of January next; that if they neglect or refuse so to move, they will be reported to the War Department as hostile Indians and that a military force will be sent to compel them to obey the orders of the Indian Office.
> You will be notified of the compliance or non-compliance of the Indians with this order; and if said Indians shall neglect or refuse to comply with said order, I have the honor to request that the proper military officer be directed to compel their removal to and residence within the bounds of their reservation.

Three days later Indian Commissioner E. P. Smith sent copies of the January 31st ultimatum to Devil's Lake, Cheyenne River, Spotted Tail, Red Cloud, Fort Peck, Crow Creek and Standing Rock Agencies, with instructions to communicate the contents to the winter-bound villages not within the reservation. There was never any chance the Indians could have complied even if they wished to. The despatch did not arrive at remote Fort Peck agency till January 21st, but the agents sent runners across the frozen plains to locate the Indian bands and deliver the impossible ultimatum.

The Watkins Report landed on General Phil Sheridan's desk on December 14th. Without waiting for the deadline to expire, he sent copies to his departmental commanders Generals Terry and Crook requesting their opinion on a winter campaign. Crook replied on December 22nd that he was ready to move 'whenever in the opinion of the War Department such action becomes necessary.'

Terry replied that because of the need for secrecy, he had not been able to make any preparations or find out exactly where Sitting Bull's camp lay, although it was believed to be on the Little Missouri River. He continued:

> If this information is correct, it will be possible, in ordinary winter weather, to reach their camp by a rapid march from Fort A. Lincoln. For such an operation there are available five well-mounted companies of cavalry at Lincoln and two at Fort Rice, a force which I think would be sufficient. Such an operation must, of course, be conducted with secrecy and rapidity, for it would not be possible to follow the Indians for any considerable distance, should they receive notice of the approach of troops and seek safety in the dispersion and flight. It would be very impractical to carry food and forage for more than a very few days.

The ultimatum wiped out the government's treaty obligations with the stroke of a pen, and none of the supposedly hostile Sioux took it seriously. Nor were they meant to. Little Phil Sheridan was to write on February 4th 'The matter of notifying the Indians to come in is perhaps well to put on paper, but it will in all probability be regarded as a good joke by the Indians.' Even if they had wished to comply, few could have travelled the distances required through snow and ice with squaws and papooses on ponies weakened by sparse grazing in winter. When runners returned to their respective agencies, the replies were as cool as the frigid weather. Sitting Bull is reputed to have sent the message 'You won't need to bring any guides. You can find me easily. I won't run away.'

As it was, the reservations this severe winter were having enough trouble feeding the Indians there. The agency rations were slow to arrive and then news spread across the plains of the Platte River Sioux being moved eastwards to the detested Missouri in order to minimize freight charges.

On Christmas Eve, 1875, General Terry sent word to headquarters 'Capt. Poland telegraphs that, although there is no game in the vicinity, the Indians at Standing Rock are selling all their hides for ammunition…'

On January 18th, the new Indian Commissioner, J. Q. Smith, placed a ban on the sale of arms and ammunition. Despite this, many braves would await the coming troops armed with late model Winchester and Henry repeaters, their cartridge belts full, with abundant ammunition in reserve.

On January 3rd 1876, Sheridan advised General Sherman that both departments under his command were ready for 'decisive' movements against the hostiles. He requested 'should such operations be determined upon that directions to that effect be communicated to me as speedily as possible, so that the enemy may be taken at the greatest possible disadvantage.'

The January 31st deadline arrived and, to no one's surprise, the 'hostiles' had not appeared on the frigid landscape and surrendered themselves to the penury of reservation life. A few days later Secretary Chandler forwarded a recommendation to Secretary of War Belknap 'the said Indians are hereby turned over to the War Department for such action as you deem proper under the circumstances.'

So much for President Grant's assurance to the Christian deputation on November 1st that the Peace Policy would 'not be abandoned' while he was president of the United States.

On February 8th Generals Crook and Terry received confidential wires from Phil Sheridan 'the War Department has ordered operations against hostile Indians.'

Terry reported to Sheridan:

Letters from Fort Stevenson show conclusively that Sitting Bull has left the Little Missouri for the Yellowstone, probably as high up as Powder River. I report this not for the purpose of making objection to any orders I may receive, but to put the Lieutenant General in the possession of all the information which I have.

Sheridan replied:

I have no specific instructions to give you about Indian hostilities. If Sitting Bull is not on the Little Missouri, as heretofore supposed to be, and cannot be reached by a quick march, as you formerly contemplated, I am afraid that little can be done by you at the present time. I am not well enough acquainted with the character of the winters and early spring in your latitude to give any instructions, and you will have to use your judgement as to what you may be able to accomplish at the present time or early spring.

On February 18th a merchant named Paul McCormack staggered into Fort Ellis, Montana, and reported that hostile Sioux surrounded Fort Pease, the trading post on the Yellowstone River. A few whites had been killed and more wounded, but friendly Crow Indians had ambushed and killed eight Sioux after driving off their ponies. Major James Brisbin commanded, who, like the other senior officers, had a distinguished Civil War record, having joined the Union army as a private, then risen through the ranks to brigadier general of volunteers. But he was as much a farmer at heart as a soldier, being known as Grasshopper Jim, expounding at length on the possibilities of butter, cheese, sheep and cattle ranching in Montana. 'The time will come,' he wrote, 'when we will have both shepherds and shepherdesses on the plains when the patriarch, as of old, with his sons, daughters, and sons' wives and daughters will follow the herds, crook in hand. Any large family can become rich by following the herds.' If, presumably, the grass they ate was not devastated by the grasshopper plagues that periodically wiped out all vegetation for miles around. 'They came in swarms,' recalled Libby Custer, 'and when we looked up at the sun, we seemed to be gazing through clouded air...Having finished everything, they soared away, carrying on their departing wings our dreams of radishes and young beets!'

Grasshopper Jim listened to McCormack's story, then wired General Terry with the news. Terry realised that this was an opportunity for troops in his department to strike a winter blow, and ordered Brisbin to march to the relief of Fort Pease. On February 22nd the major set out at the head of four companies of the 2nd Cavalry, a party of civilian volunteers and 54 Crow Indian scouts who joined them en route. Crossing the ice-bound Yellowstone several times, the stockade was reached on March 4th to find 19 traders and trappers there safe, but six had been killed, eight wounded, and 21 had left for the safety of white settlements. Brisbin's scouts searched the area, finding no sign of the hostiles, but the remaining men were evacuated along with supplies, including a sizable quantity of whiskey, the consumption of which helped keep the cold at bay as the column marched through snow back to Fort Ellis.

George Custer returned with his wife from a five-month leave back east and began planning, with Terry, the spring offensive. Only nine of the twelve companies of the 7th U. S. Cavalry were on duty in Terry's department, and he requested transfer of the remaining three from the Department of the Gulf, along with a detachment of the 20th Infantry with Gatling guns. Terry theorised that a force of only 550 men attacking the hostiles, if located in one large camp, would be at 'great risk of defeat.' His prophetic words would bear fruit when Custer attacked the huge village on the Little Bighorn with 566 enlisted men and 31 officers.

Terry's initial request for the extra three companies was rejected by the War Department, but Custer knocked on the right doors during a trip to Washington, and the additional troops arrived at Fort Abraham Lincoln on May 1st 1876. Custer also enlisted additional Indian scouts for a period of six months who were provided with arms, uniforms, army rations and a private's pay of $13 per month. On March 15th the following slightly distorted story appeared in the Bismarck *Tribune*:

> General Custer's command will consist of eight companies of the 7th Cavalry, six companies of infantry, and detachments from several other companies and a battery of Gatling guns. It will cross the Little Missouri and then be governed by circumstances, probably establishing a base of supplies at the mouth of the Big Horn, or at

Glendive Creek. The expedition will be out all summer, probably.

General George Crook, at Fort Fetterman in Wyoming, meanwhile, had been making his own quiet preparations with the intention of striking winter villages in the vicinity of the Big Horn, Rosebud, Powder and Tongue Rivers. Crook was a seasoned veteran of the Civil War and had defeated the Apaches in the south. Crazy Horse, said to have been one of those responsible for the Fetterman disaster in 1866, was believed to be in Powder River area, and the army had a score to settle with him. Little did the army realise the Fetterman fight had only been a prelude of worse things to come.

On March 1st Crook rode out at the head of a combined force of infantry and cavalry, a little under 700 men. Although the senior officer, he was, theoretically, only an observer, having turned over direct command to General Joseph J. Reynolds, a campaigner of repute from Civil War days. The sun shone brightly on the drifts of snow deposited by a blizzard just the night before. 'The worse it gets the better,' Crook told his men, 'always hunt Indians in bad weather.' The column of foot-slogging infantry, mounted cavalry, heavily laden pack mules, cumbersome wagons and beef cattle plodded northwards, the fur-clad scouts, Indian, mixed blood and white, fanning out ahead.

Only two nights later, with the troops under canvas, shots were heard followed by the pounding of hundreds of hooves as the Indians supplemented their winter diet at Uncle Sam's expense. The beef herd thundered off into the darkness amidst the whoops of Sioux raiders, the cattle never to be seen again. One herder was killed and the troops' rations cut to compensate for the lost beef, hardly an auspicious beginning to the new campaign.

On the night of March 5th a party of six scouts rode quietly out of camp on unshod ponies, thus leaving an 'Indian' trail. Crook had ordered them to seek out the hostiles' villages. No sooner had they disappeared into the night than sentries saw dark shapes approaching the camp. The soldiers started shooting, but the flash of return gunfire erupted from the darkness as the Indians darted about, constantly changing position. A ball sliced through the cheek of Corporal Slavey.

'Lights were snuffed out in a twinkling, camp fires were kicked to smithereens, men were in their ranks, and rifle pits were sunk in an incredibly short time,' wrote Robert Strahorn of Denver's *Rocky Mountain News*. The skirmish continued, but after about half an hour the attackers melted into the night. The junior officers had been astonished at Crook's lack of concern as bullets whistled about him. As he reclined on buffalo robes he explained it was only a small party hoping to repeat their previous success by stampeding the mules and horses.

The scouts had come back at the gallop when firing first broke out, but with the hostiles on the alert, their mission was postponed.

The column creaked and plodded through the snow the following day, their progress obviously followed as smoke signals wafted into the clear blue sky warning the Sioux ahead. As Crook watched, the next big step in a communications revolution after the electric telegraph was taking place back east, Alexander Graham Bell taking out a patent on the first telephone. The days of smoke signals, despatch riders, semaphore, heliographs, signal lights and flags were numbered in a rapidly changing world. Four years later, after many Sioux had fled to Canada, the United States government tried to tempt them back. A delegation met Colonel Nelson Miles who demonstrated both the jumping spark of the telegraph terminal and the telephone.

Half the delegation was shown to a separate building, then spoke to each other through the new invention, 'huge drops of perspiration coursed down their bronze faces,' Miles recalled, 'and with trembling hands they lay the instrument down.' The Indians who tried this could see the white mans' medicine was strong, and became proponents of peace. Sitting Bull, at a later time, also tried the phone. 'Hello. Hello! You bet, you bet,' he said, using the little English he knew, and then was startled when the voice on the line replied in fluent Sioux. He had assumed such a machine could only use English.

But that was a few years away yet as the troops watched smoke signals herald their advance. What hope had the column of striking an unsuspecting village when the Indians closely followed their march? But Crook was an old campaigner with a few tricks up his sleeve. On the night of March 7th he led, in secret, the ten companies of cavalry out under the frigid winter moonlight with fifteen day's rations. The intention was to strike whatever hostiles the scouts could locate. Next morning the infantry made a very visible display of escorting the wagons back to camp at the ruins of old Fort Reno, one of the posts constructed to protect the Bozeman Trail, to distract the enemy from the strike force's march.

The cavalry column probed northwards through freezing temperatures but deserted campsites were all the scouts discovered. They crossed into Montana Territory, and when about 160 miles north of Fort Fetterman, on March 16th, scout Frank Grouard surprised two Sioux warriors out on the hunt. They wheeled their ponies about and dashed off, but left a trail in the snow back to their village. The scouts followed the trail southeast along Indian Creek, and Grouard knew the likely village sight on the Powder River.

Crook split his force, sending General Reynolds forward with six companies totalling 375 men on a night march with orders to hit the village at dawn. They carried nothing but one day's rations and ammunition. Crook, with the remaining four companies and pack train, would continue north to the mouth of Lodgepole Creek on Powder River and rendezvous with Reynolds after his force had struck the village.

As Reynolds led his men out they felt buoyant and eager despite heavy, black clouds overhead. Then snow flurries descended and Reynolds feared the trail would be lost, but Grouard astonished the soldiers with his tracking abilities, sometimes following the trail squinting by match light on hands and knees. The son of a Mormon missionary and a Polynesian wife, he knew the country like the back of his hand having lived amongst the Sioux including the bands of Sitting Bull and Crazy Horse. While the soldiers shivered in a ravine without food or coffee, the scouts went ahead and discovered a fresh trail leading down to a village on the banks of the Powder, just as Grouard had predicted. As the pale light of dawn shimmered on the frosty horizon, the troops made their way down snow-covered slopes into the river valley. A village of about one hundred Sioux and Cheyenne lodges slumbered on the near bank at the base of bluffs covered with snow encrusted trees and brush. A pony herd grazed nearby on the grassy flat.

Grouard was questioned by Reynolds, who then devised his plan of attack. Captain Noyes' battalion would strike from upstream, cutting off the pony herd, while Captain Egan's company would charge directly into the village firing their pistols from horseback, to be backed up by reserves under Captain Mills. Captain Moore's battalion was to dismount and occupy the bluffs overlooking the village where they could open fire on Indians fleeing before the charge.

The sun was well up by the time the three battalions moved in for the kill along diverse paths. They were still some distance from the village and had to cover rough, icy terrain, but Egan's troops assembled for their initial assault without alerting the Sioux. The village was just beginning to wake as Indian boys began moving ponies towards the river. Captain Bourke advanced at the head of one battalion to find himself confronted by a Sioux youth, about fifteen. He levelled his revolver and the boy 'wrapped his blanket about him and stood like a statue of bronze, waiting for the fatal bullet.' Bourke did not shoot, not wanting to alert the enemy. Realising the peril, the boy suddenly sounded a war whoop but in the next instant Bourke heard the first shots fired.

Egan had ordered the charge, the cavalry horses bolting forward, and he led his 47 men at the gallop, yelling as they fired. The surprise was complete, Indians bolting from their tepees and darting between the trampling hooves. Firing from moving horses, the troopers caused panic and confusion, but actually hitting a running Indian was not so easy. The warriors snatched up weapons and herded their women and children into the cover of surrounding scrub. They quickly regrouped and scrambled up the surrounding bluffs. But where was Captain Moore's battalion; the men who were supposed to be on those same bluffs firing down on the Sioux? He and his men had failed to arrive on time.

The Indians started returning a heavy fire on the troops in the village as Captain Noyes' men drove much of their pony herd away. With bullets ripping through tepees and thudding into the ground around them, Egan's men dismounted, holstered their pistols and opened a return fire with carbines at about 200 braves now encircling them on the snowy heights. Mills' reserve battalion belatedly rode in and joined Egan's men in the defence, then Moore's battalion also arrived in the village, having lost their way to the heights through rugged terrain. The attackers now found themselves fighting a defensive battle within the hostiles' village, the roles reversed. While their fire seemed to be having little effect on the Indians darting about the bluffs, four soldiers were killed and others wounded as the enemy bullets hit home. Reynolds ordered the tepees and their contents destroyed before moving out. The furious Indians on the hills could do nothing to save their homes as flames shot up and smoke billowed into the winter sky. Tepees loaded with ammunition exploded sending lodge poles and burning debris flying into the sky. Reynolds ordered his men to retire and they began their withdrawal, the Indian herd of 700 ponies being driven along in the rear.

The soldiers realised this was a bleak victory. Not only were they in retreat, but they had failed to bring out their dead for a decent burial. And rumour had it that one of the wounded had been left behind to die by torture at the redskins' hands. At dawn the discontent of the exhausted and cold soldiers turned to anger when the Indians swooped, recapturing most of their unguarded ponies, disappearing with them across the frozen hills.

Reynolds reunited with General Crook who was initially delighted to hear the hostile village had been attacked and burned. But then as the full story emerged his high spirits turned to wrath. After the weary command straggled back into Fort Fetterman on March 26, Crook was quick to prefer court-martial charges against the two officers he held to account; General Reynolds for generally bungling the attack and withdrawal, and Captain Moore who had failed to occupy the heights as ordered.

The Sioux had got off lightly as far as casualties were concerned, but they had seen their homes and possessions destroyed by the rapacious white man in a war that was not of their making. They had been forced to flee to take shelter with kindred tribesmen, the crushing of their race what the whites wanted. Now was the time for the various Sioux and Cheyenne bands to unite in one huge village for defence; the time for a last-ditch fight for survival was at hand.

***

On December 11th 1878, three years after the ultimatum to the free-ranging Sioux had been drafted, another ultimatum concocted by Sir Bartle Frere was read to a deputation of three senior Zulu indunas and 11 chiefs. With their retainers, they sat under an awning spread beneath the 'Ultimatum Tree' at the Lower Thukela Drift near the threatening earthworks of the recently completed Fort Pearson.

Despite holding their composure, the listeners were shocked at the translation of what amounted to a dismantling of the social structure of the Zulu state. Unlike the brief demand thrust upon the Sioux, Frere's ultimatum was a long-winded and inconcise 5,000 words, which demanded the surrender of the Zulus responsible for the raid into Natal and those responsible for abducting the refugee women. There was a fine of 500 cattle for these offences, and a further 100 for the incident with the surveyor, the animals to be delivered within 20 days. Cetshwayo was also to respond within thirty days to a variety of demands which included the current Zulu army be disbanded and the warriors return to their homes. The ultimatum claimed that the army was not for self-defence, but used for the 'oppression of the people.' The current military system was to be abolished and replaced with one sanctioned by the British, a British resident in Zululand was to enforce the regulations, and no one was to be expelled from Zululand without his permission. All Christian missionaries and converts who had fled Zululand since 1877 were to be allowed to return. Cetshwayo was accused of misruling his people and there were a variety of other conditions which interfered with the existing Zulu laws, all of which posed no threat to white settlers in bordering territories. To add injury to insult, John Shepstone, brother of Sir Theophilus, read out the terms. He had once parleyed with a wanted Zulu, Chief Matyana, at a meeting where arms were not to be carried. Matyana barely escaped with his life after being shot and wounded by John Shepstone. The Zulus, not surprisingly, were suspicious of this man, despite him having been on the Boundary Commission which found in their favor. It was impossible for Cetshwayo to comply with these demands, which Bartle Frere well knew. Those conditions, which abolished the army, would render the king virtually powerless and it would be impossible for him to keep his throne. But Cetshwayo was, of course, no more expected to comply than the Sioux had been expected to surrender at the reservations in 1876. In both cases the imposers of the impossible terms knew that they must lead to war, the ultimate aim being the taking of their lands.

Governor Bulwer of Natal, who had discouraged the build-up of troops, endorsed the ultimatum, but later said that he was 'very sore at having been induced by Frere to sign,' and 'That's the worst thing I ever did in my life…The Zulus have always been our friends.'

The astonished Zulu delegates replied that they could not understand why such an ancient and necessary tradition such as their army should be disbanded. They were informed that it posed a threat to the citizens of Natal, while the British posed no threat to them. One chief pointed at the British soldiers present and asked what they were for. 'For defence,' he was told. The Zulus said that a mere thirty days was not long enough for discussion on such an ultimatum, and requested more time. This was refused, and the disgruntled Zulus left the meeting, crossing the river back into Zululand.

Colonial Secretary Hicks Beach, on the same day, was penning a letter to Bartle Frere. He had seen a copy of a puzzling letter Frere had written to Theophilus Shepstone. 'It seems to contain proposals I don't understand,' he wrote to Frere, 'Your letter to Shepstone speaks of "final proposals" and an "ultimatum". I really do not know what you contemplate in this direction, nor do I at present see the necessity for such an ultimatum...As you will see from my despatch, we entirely deprecate the idea of entering on a Zulu war in order to settle the Zulu question.' Due to the tyranny of distance, this letter did not reach Frere till after hostilities had begun. Frere had avoided informing Hicks Beach in a letter of December 8th writing that Cetshwayo was about to be informed of the Boundary Commission's award and 'further communications' on 'our relations, past & future.' This, of course, was an oblique reference to the ultimatum.

On Christmas day Hicks Beach finally learned from an official despatch of Frere's machinations. Incensed, he wrote back:

> When I first came to the Colonial Office I told you might rely on my support; and so you may. But (bearing in mind all I have written to you against the Zulu war, at the instance, remember, of the Cabinet) I think you will see how awkward a position you may have placed me in by making demands of this nature without my knowledge

or sanction...Cetywayo may very possibly prefer fighting to accepting them, and then, if the Cabinet should not be satisfied that you were right in making them, it will be too late to draw back, and we shall find ourselves involved in this war against our will.

John Dunn, an influential Zululand settler who acted as Cetshwayo's advisor on European matters, sent word to Frere that the king was prepared to hand over those Zulus who had transgressed into Natal, and was gathering cattle for delivery as required by the ultimatum. Recent heavy rains, however, made travel over boggy ground difficult, and he needed more time for discussion regarding the other demands with his council. But Frere showed no mercy. 'The word of the government as already given cannot now be altered unless the prisoners and cattle are given up within the time specified.' Troops would be ordered across the border into Zululand, Cetshwayo was informed, if the conditions were not met, then halt at convenient posts to await the expiry of the thirty-day deadline. They would, however, not take any 'hostile action' without provocation.

John Dunn sent further word that Cetshwayo was still collecting the cattle, but had no hope of delivering them on time. But on December 30th he wrote that the king had 'quite changed his tone' and was 'determined to fight, as he says that, for what he hears of the Forces that are to be sent against him, he can easily eat them up one after the other.' Seeing the country on the verge of war, Dunn fled across the river from Zululand into Natal with 2,000 retainers and 3,000 cattle. The Zulu king had treated Dunn well, rewarding him with a large chiefdom in southern Zululand. His flight was, not surprisingly, seen as a betrayal, and the Zulus retaliated by burning his kraals (native villages). Dunn would ride with the British troops and aid Chelmsford's campaign by supplying valuable intelligence regarding the Zulu forces ranged against him.

Cetshwayo realised that if Frere would not even grant more time to deliver cattle, there was no chance that he would ever rescind the more stringent demands. But he could not possibly agree to dismantle the traditional, entrenched military system which gave the monarchy its authority, thus war was inevitable.

The time was coming for the Zulus' annual First Fruits Ceremony when, under a full moon, the king and his warriors underwent purification ceremonies. These were to strengthen and cleanse the Zulus of evil, and unify the people. But this year he ordered that the Zulu regiments assemble without the usual decorations and ornaments. They were to come 'with only their arms and ammunition prepared for immediate and active service.'

As the Sioux had not appeared by January 31st 1876, the twenty-day deadline of December 31st 1878 came and went without the appearance of any cattle or those Zulus responsible for the incursions into Natal. On January 1st 1879 Chelmsford warned Frere that the Zulus might be tempted to attack first, raiding into Natal, if there was any delay in the advance of his troops. Three days later Frere gave Chelmsford the responsibility of 'further enforcement' of the demands stated in the ultimatum. Back home in winter-bound London, the colonial secretary could only guess at what was happening, not knowing that Sir Bartle's war was about to erupt on the Zulu people.

4
THE THREE-COLUMN PLAN

General Crook's winter campaign had resulted in the burning of one Indian village, but then ignominious retreat. A spring offensive was planned which called for the advance of three columns of troops towards the Little Missouri River, North Dakota, where the hostiles, according to reports, were most likely to be found. General Crook would move northwards once again from Fort Fetterman, Colonel Gibbon would move eastwards along the Yellowstone River from Fort Ellis, and General Custer would move west from Fort Abraham Lincoln.

But politics were to intervene.

Secretary of War William Belknap has been described as a 'pouchy-cheeked, beetle-browed, curly-headed man with a tremendous flowing beard and the air of an unctuous politician.' He had, in 1870, 'privatised' the position of army sutler into a post trader, to be appointed by himself, and subject only to supervision by his office. The position of sutler had previously been appointed and supervised by a board of local army officers. A wave of protest erupted as the new arrangement encouraged corrupt appointments and the monopoly position the trader held allowed unfair exploitation of soldiers in isolated garrisons. In 1873 Belknap issued orders forbidding army officers from public comment on military matters except through the auspices of his office.

The Indian agencies, often with a military post close by, also had their own agency traders licensed by a different department, the Office of Indian Affairs.

During the autumn of 1874 all trading licenses, Indian and army, in the upper Missouri region were revoked without warning or any apparent cause. Orvil Grant, the president's brother, then appeared travelling from trader to trader to barter over the price for the licence's renewal. Those who coughed up continued in business while those who did not had to sell to the highest bidder. The Bismarck *Tribune,* following Orvil's progress, dubbed him the 'The Christian Capitalist.'

In 1875 the New York *Herald* sent reporter Ralph Meeker on an undercover operation to discover the facts. Collaborating with him were residents of Bismarck, including the newspaper editor, the post-mistress, and George A. Custer, commandant at Fort Abraham Lincoln, who seemed displeased by the apparent corruption and wished to see it stamped out. The *Herald* commenced exposing the trading scandals in a series of articles starting in July, and when William Belknap visited Fort Abraham Lincoln during September, he was coolly received by Custer who believed he was in league with Orvil Grant. Mrs Custer, however, a lady of grace and charm, more than made up for husband's reticence. But Belknap was less than charmed when he visited Bismarck to find insulting handbills, in the form of a circus promotion, stuck up on walls making fun of his alleged involvement with graft.

This, along with his cool reception of Belknap, would count against Custer in Washington's corridors of power. He would be accused of instigating the demand for an inquiry into Belknap's activities, but George A. Armes, a former captain of the 2nd cavalry, and associate of Custer's, was responsible. Armes had been drummed out of the army by Belknap in March of

1870 and, out for revenge, wrote in the New York *Herald* on February 9th 1876 revelations regarding Belknap's activities with evidence to back him up. The following day the newspaper carried an editorial calling for Belknap's impeachment. It also accused President Grant's brother, Orvil, of being implicated, and suggested that Grant ask his brother how much he 'made in the Sioux country starving the squaws and children.'

Heister Clymer, the Chairman of the House Committee on Military Expenditures, had carried out an investigation into Belknap, and advised him to tender his resignation without delay to avoid impeachment. Armes wrote, 'Belknap went to President Grant this morning before nine o'clock and tendered his resignation as Secretary of War. Great excitement prevails this evening all over the city, and I have been congratulated by hundreds of people during the afternoon who give me credit for exposing him.'

On March 15th 1876, shortly after Belknap's resignation, Custer received a subpoena at Fort Abraham Lincoln to appear in Washington. He arrived in the capital on March 28th and testified before the Clymer committee the following day. During the follow week he twice attempted to make courtesy calls on the president, but was left waiting and ignored. He testified again on April 4th, no doubt frustrated by being absent from his post when the imminent Sioux campaign was being prepared. Custer's testimony was just as damaging to the president's brother Orvil as it was to Belknap, but he had, in fact, no hard evidence to back up his claims, his testimony only being based on hearsay. Far more damaging to William Belknap and Orvil Grant was the testimony of the post traders of Fort Abraham Lincoln and other garrisons. But Custer was now in the enemy camp as far as Grant and his cohorts were concerned, a marked man. Some within the Clymer committee claimed Custer was the author of an article which appeared in the New York *Herald,* on March 31st, republished from the Bismarck *Tribune*:

> Last summer when your correspondent first visited this country...and engaged in ferreting out and making public through the columns of the *Herald* the corruption and fraudulent management of the Indian Department, as regulated by the Delano-Orvil Grant ring, the working of the latter was described as that of an anaconda, whose head was in Washington and whose tail was on the upper Missouri.

The article included a copy of the circus handbills pasted up in Bismarck attacking Belknap during his visit. The post trader at Fort Abraham Lincoln, Robert C. Seip, testified that he suspected Custer to be the article's author, having cashed bank drafts for the general against the New York *Herald.* Reporter Ralph Meeker, however, testified that the money came to him, Custer acting as the go-between while he was working under cover in Bismarck. He too was curious regarding the author's identity, he said, but his editor would not allow him to make such a disclosure even if he knew.

Custer felt vindicated by Meeker's testimony, but this newspaper story appeared on April 18th:

> Ex-secretary Belknap and his friends are collecting material to make out a case against Gen. Custer with a view to having him tried by court martial before Gen. Terry at St. Paul...it is charged that Custer swore falsely and it is on this ground that an attempt is to be made to court martial him.

It was of little surprise that President Grant took a savage view towards those who alleged corruption in his administration, especially when they concerned his own family. Custer was about to command a major military expedition, and to leave him in command would appear to validate Grant's confidence in both him and his testimony. The attempt to have charges laid was going nowhere, but Grant could have his revenge by removing Custer from command of the expedition, the worst humiliation an officer could suffer short of losing a battle. On April 28th Grant gave the vital order, and it sped through channels to General Terry, who was directed to 'send someone other than Custer in charge of the expedition from Fort Lincoln.' Terry suggested one of his three infantry colonels be the replacement, but Sheridan was not happy, 'the command will be better satisfied,' he wired, 'in having the department commander in charge.' Terry telegraphed back, 'I will go myself.'

Custer, shattered by his removal, saw General Sherman the following day. The army's top officer felt Custer should at least be able to accompany the expedition in command of the 7th, and advised he see the president personally, explain his actions, and request the return of his regiment. Early on Monday, May 1st, Custer appeared in the presidential waiting room and presented his card only to see others being shown into Grant's office while he was left to cool his heels once more. After hours of waiting in humiliation, General Rufus Ingalls, acting quartermaster general, took pity and offered to approach the president on Custer's behalf. But Ingalls returned with the sorrowful message of Grant's refusal. Frustrated, Custer dashed off the following note to Grant:

> Today for the third time I have sought an interview with the President—not to solicit a favor, except to be granted a brief hearing—but to remove from his mind certain unjust impressions concerning myself, which I have reason to believe are entertained against me. I desire this opportunity simply as a matter of justice, and I regret that the President has declined to give me an opportunity to submit to him a brief statement, which justice to him, as well as to me, demanded.

A despondent Custer left the White House and proceeded to the War Department where the inspector-general and adjutant-general gave him leave to return to Fort Abraham Lincoln. Unable to see Sherman, who was in New York, he boarded the 7 o'clock train and steamed westwards. The following day Sheridan heard from Sherman:

> I am advised at this moment that General Custer started last night for St. Paul and Fort A. Lincoln. He was not justified in leaving without seeing the President or myself. Please intercept him at Chicago or St. Paul, and order him to halt and await further orders. Meanwhile, let the expedition from Fort Lincoln proceed without him.

When Custer alighted at the Chicago railway station he was astonished to find himself held in detention by the military. He shot off three wires to General Sherman explaining his actions, reminding him that he had agreed that Custer should retain command of his regiment, if not the expedition, and asking that he be detained at Fort Abraham Lincoln with his wife rather than Chicago. After consulting Grant, Sherman agreed to the last request.

Custer, in a state of agitation, proceeded by train towards his post but stopped at Terry's headquarters at St. Paul. According to Terry's brother-in-law, Colonel Robert Hughes, Custer, with tears in his eyes, actually fell to his knees and implored the general for help. Terry was anxious that the redoubtable Custer should retain his command and helped compose a letter to Grant, dated May 6th:

> I respectfully but most earnestly request that while not allowed to go in command of the expedition, I may be permitted to serve with my regiment in the field. I appeal to you as a soldier to spare me the humiliation of seeing my regiment march to meet the enemy and I to not share its dangers.

Terry sent this letter through channels with his personal request that Custer be allowed to serve, and Sheridan added his own endorsement.

The same day the New York *Herald* attacked Grant for Custer's arrest in Chicago and observed that 'no formal charges are preferred against Custer, and he is disgraced simply because he did not "crook the pregnant hinges of the knee" to this modern Caesar,' and Grant was an 'irresponsible despot…with an absolute power to decapitate anybody offending his Highness or his favorites.' The Chicago *Times* joined the chorus detailing the entire affair, 'the facts in the case present the President of the U. S. in one of the most humiliating and disreputable of the many humiliating and disreputable plights he has ever been put in this winter.'

On May 8th Terry received word from Sherman that the president 'sent me word that if you want General Custer along he withdraws his objections. Advise Custer to be prudent, not to take any newspaper men, who always make mischief, and to abstain from personalities in future.' It was far more likely that the 'mischief' made by the newspapermen was the cause of Grant relenting, rather than Custer's plea.

While Custer was being ground through the Washington political mill, General Terry met with delay after delay moving from Fort Abraham Lincoln. This worked to Custer's advantage, giving him time to join the troops before their departure. But Terry could take solace in the fact that Crook's column from Fort Fetterman was suffering similar problems and would not set out until after his own.

An improvement in weather conditions towards the end of April allowed steam trains to get through to Terry from the east carrying vital supplies. Brevet colonel, Major Marcus A. Reno was in command of the 7th while Custer was absent, and made little secret of his hope that he would never return. He wired Terry 'From Custer's telegrams and the papers it seems he will not soon be back. In the meantime the expedition here is making large expenses and Sitting Bull waiting on the Little Missouri. Why not give me a chance, as I feel I will do credit to the army?' Having his offer rejected, he went over Terry's head to Little Phil. 'Expedition ready when transportation from Abercrombie and cavalry companies from Rice arrive. Why not give me a chance, sending instructions what to do with Sitting Bull if I catch him. He is waiting for us on the Little Missouri.' Reno must have been desperate to think Sheridan would ride roughshod over Terry's wishes. To do so would have broken the chain of command and caused considerable friction between Terry and Sheridan on one hand, and Terry and Reno on the other. Sheridan's response was appropriate, 'General Terry has entire charge of the expedition. I do not feel like interfering with him in his plans.' Reno had seen much action during the Civil War and had received four promotions for *gallant and meritorious services,* the last being to brevet colonel in the regular army and brevet brigadier general of volunteers shortly before Lee's surrender at Appomattox Court House. Despite this, he would later be branded by some as 'the one coward of the regiment.'

Amongst the scouts recruited was 'Lonesome' Charley Reynolds, something of an enigma, being a quiet, educated gent who had earned the reputation of being the best guide and hunter in the Dakotas. Another asset was one of Custer's favorite scouts, Corporal Bloody Knife, the son of a Ree and a Sioux. He had served with Custer for several years including the Black Hills expedition. Both he and Custer would pay a heavy price for their incursion into the Black Hills. But nepotism was not the exclusive domain of President Grant, Custer's younger brother Boston having been taken on as a guide. He had only been employed as forage master at Fort Lincoln and would be lucky to track a grizzly across fresh snow. Other relatives who would share Custer's fate were his civilian nephew Autie Reed, brother-in-law James Calhoun, commander of Company L, and brother Tom, commander of Company C. Tom was a Civil War hero too, having twice been awarded the Congressional Medal of Honor. On the Black Hills expedition he had awoken one morning after oversleeping to find the grass outside his tent ablaze at the hands of the practical joker brother George. No one knew what the erratic Custer would do next.

The Indian scouts employed were mainly Arikaras, commonly called Rees. This tribe was often called Corn Indians due to living in relatively stable villages while they supplemented hunted game by growing pumpkins, corn, squash and other vegetables. The Sioux regarded such employment with the utmost contempt, but a few friendly Sioux rode as scouts for the expedition alongside the Corn Indians, traditional enemies.

Isaiah Dorman, an African-American married for years to a Sioux, was employed as Sioux interpreter and Frederick Gerard was employed to translate for the Rees. He was the best translator in the Dakotas, but friction erupted between himself and Reno resulting in his sacking on May 6th. Custer promptly reinstated him on his return, another cause for tension in a factionalised command

The late start did have its advantages, the ice on the frozen Missouri breaking up allowing steamboats to carry both supplies and infantry support to a depot upstream. The riverboat *Josephine* belched smoke into the clean, spring air as she steamed off from Bismarck on May 9th. Four days later she tied up at Fort Buford and took on board Major Moore's infantry battalion of 127 men, 3 scouts, and Dr. George E. Lord. The *Josephine* continued upstream entering the Yellowstone on May 14th, and four days later reached a stockade built a few years before opposite the mouth of Glendive Creek, when the 7th was protecting surveyors for the Northern Pacific Railroad. The gangplanks were lowered and the troops tramped ashore with supplies for the coming campaign.

On the evening of May 10th Terry and Custer arrived at Bismarck by rail where, at Fort Abraham Lincoln, the expedition's preparations were nearly complete. No doubt Major Reno, responsible for the organisation, felt miffed at Custer being the beneficiary of his sweat and toil.

Terry, having assumed formal command, wrote to Sheridan on May 15th:

> Information from several independent sources seems to establish the fact that the Sioux are collected in camps on the Little Missouri and between that and the Powder

River. I have already ordered Colonel Gibbon to move eastwards and suggest that it would be very desirable for General Crook's column to move up as soon as possible. It is represented that they have 1,500 lodges, are confident, and intend to make a stand. Should they do so, and should the three columns be able to act simultaneously, I should expect great success.

Terry may well have said he expected great success, but did he? He must have known what Custer well knew, as recounted in *My Life on the Plains*:

> the experience of both officers and men went to prove that in attempting to fight Indians in the summer season we were yielding to them the advantage of climate and supplies; we were meeting them on ground of their own selection, and at a time when every natural circumstance controlling the result of a campaign was wholly in their favor; and as a just consequence the troops, in nearly all these contests with the red men, had come off second best.

Second best indeed.

As the spring thaw allowed navigation up the Missouri and easier troop movements, it also encouraged restless young Sioux and Cheyenne braves to forsake the reservations and head out into the unceded hunting grounds where they were warmly received by Sitting Bull and Crazy Horse. The Sioux at the Spotted Tail and Red Cloud agencies had been especially discontent that long winter, being closest to the Black Hills invasion, and feared rumours that they were to be removed to the Missouri River. But of more importance was the lack of food. The Great White Father in Washington had been slow to live up to his promises, as usual.

Following Reynolds's attack on the Powder River village, the restraint exhibited by many Indians had ceased. Governor Thayer of Wyoming urged General Crook to protect travellers on the trail between the town of Cheyenne and the Black Hills. On May 7th Captain James Egan of the 2nd Cavalry was detailed to patrol the road with one company of infantry and a troop of cavalry, and on May 17th his men galloped to the rescue of a wagon train surrounded by Sioux. Despite this, the few soldiers could not police the entire trail, and traffic came to a standstill under a reign of attacks during May. But these took place within the reservation, not even on unceded lands. The Indians were the only ones who, by treaty, had any right to be there.

Governor Thayer travelled in person to the White House with his plea for protection, and a curious policy emerged whereby travellers entering the Black Hills could not be afforded protection—unless they were conveying supplies to those already there—and travellers leaving the Black Hills were entitled to protection. Were army officer arriving with troops at the scene of an Indian attack expected to ascertain whether the braves had the right to be scalping the victims or not?

The hazy morning of May 17th finally saw the impressive vista of Terry's column ready to march. Assembled on the plain outside Fort Abraham Lincoln were twelve companies of the 7th U. S. Cavalry, along with three and a half companies of infantry from the 6th and 17th regiments, 4 surgeons, 1 vet and a battery of four Gatling guns, each drawn by four horses, tended by Lieutenants Low and Kinsie with 32 men of the 20th Infantry; a total of 879 men. In addition, there were 39 Indian scouts commanded by Lieutenant Charles Varnum, 7th Cavalry,

3 scouts employed by the Quartermaster's department, or 2 if Boston Custer is discounted; Bloody Knife and 'Lonesome' Charley being the other two. There were 2 interpreters, a wagon train, a pack train and a beef herd. Despite orders to the contrary, Mark Kellogg from the Bismarck *Tribune* was mounted and ready to go.

The 7th Cavalry's band struck up a stirring rendition of Garry Owen, and then played The Girl I Left Behind Me in deference to the weeping women, some holding babes in their arms, who waved farewell to their men as the column marched past. It was to become a day to be remembered by many with more sadness than they thought possible at the time. Custer's wife Libby wrote:

> As the sun broke through the mist a mirage appeared, which took up about half the line of cavalry, and thenceforth for a little distance it marched, equally plain to the sight on the earth and in the sky...and already there seemed to be a premonition in the supernatural translation as their forms were reflected from the opaque mist of the early dawn.

Mrs Custer rode out alongside her husband, who looked back in admiration at the two-mile column stretched behind him. Sights like that were uncommon since the Civil War. She stayed the first night in camp at Heart River, thirteen miles from the fort. The campsite was well sighted with plentiful grass, wood and water. One drawback was the number of rattlesnakes also finding the area to their liking, numbers being killed as the soldiers set up camp. As the regiment marched the following morning Libby rode out alongside Custer. When it was time to return, she threw her arms around his neck, holding him tight. With tears in his eyes, Custer told her she was a soldier's wife, and must return to the fort. Turning her pony's head, she reluctantly rode back with the army paymaster who had distributed the troops' wages the night before. The Ree scouts would welcome this thoughtful consideration, as the soldiers would have cash to buy game they brought in while on the trail. Terry had not allowed the troops to be paid before marching to avoid the expedition being weakened by desertion, debauchery and drunkenness care of the seedy side of Bismarck's back streets.

The same day the troops moved from Fort Abraham Lincoln, a letter from one Joseph G. Bemis appeared in the Fairbault *Republican*:

> The miners are bringing in their bottles and buckskin pouches well filled with the yellow, and from the expression of their faces one would think they had been brought up on laughing gas. Improved claims are selling for two and three thousand dollars apiece, and everything is lovely except the accursed Indians. They seem to be trying to get a corner on horse-flesh, and so far, they are ahead.
> On Friday the 14th inst., they attacked a party at Buffalo Gap…and at the same place, a man by the name of Woods, from this place, on his way to Spotted Tail Agency, lost his life, horse, saddle and scalp. On the same day a party of five persons were killed in Red Canyon, fifty miles south of here, on the Cheyenne road, and two others severely wounded. Among the killed were a Mr. Metz and wife, and Mrs. Mosby, (colored); did not get the names of the others. The women were ravished, then filled with arrows and bullets, and their brains beaten out.

Eight days later General Crook's column marched from Fort Fetterman and headed north, following his trail of the previous winter. Colonel Gibbon's column was already in the field, heading east along the Yellowstone. John Gibbon was a quiet, old school officer, dependable, and without Custer's flair. He walked with a limp due to an old Civil War wound, and was known to the Crows as 'No-Hip-Bone' or 'The One who Limps.'

General Sherman's long awaited campaign to finally crush the Sioux and Cheyenne was under way. History would have dealt more kindly with American attitudes of the day had these columns converged on the Black Hills and ejected the trespassing miners, the cause of the strife.

***

On December 23rd 1878 Sir Bartle Frere wrote to Colonial Secretary Hicks Beach in London, 'I hope that Chelmsford's plans for moving in three converging columns on the Royal Kraal will go far to paralyse opposition, & to ensure success with as little opposition as possible.'

Three columns had superseded the original five-column plan, a shortage of transport vehicles causing the change. Chelmsford had been hard at work since his arrival in Natal during August of 1878, and Border Agent F. B. Fynney prepared at his request a detailed appraisal of Cetshwayo's military capabilities. The Zulu army was divided into age-graded regiments with warriors as young as fourteen, Fynney reported. The highly disciplined regiments were composed of companies of 60 men each, and each corps contained two or more regiments which were divided into two wings. Married and unmarried men formed different regiments. He estimated the size of Cetshwayo's army at 15 unmarried and 18 married regiments, but as men over 60 composed 7 of these, there were 26 regiments for effective use in battle, a mere 40,400 men!

They had no need of wagon trains as did the Europeans, 3 or 4 days provisions of millet or maize along with blankets being carried by boys who also drove a herd of cattle to supply meat.

Chelmsford wrote to Secretary of State for War Colonel Stanley, in London:

> In conducting operations against an enemy like the kaffir or Zulu, the first blow struck should be a heavy one, and I am satisfied that no greater mistake can be made than to attempt to conquer him with insufficient means. He has the advantage of being able to march in one day at least three times as far as the British soldier, and has no commissariat train to hamper him.

The young Zulu warriors were eager for combat, wanting to 'wash their spears' in the blood of battle. The Zulu tactic was to surround and annihilate the enemy using the 'horns of the buffalo;' a central column would charge head-on into the enemy while two enveloping wings, the horns, would fan out around the flanks and crush their foe from each side. But this did not worry Lord Chelmsford. He was quite confident that the killing power of his artillery and the Martini-Henry breech-loader would shatter any mass Zulu assault. He wished to encourage the Zulus to attack by dividing his relatively small force, confident that each column could defeat the enemy.

The backbone of each column was to be regular British infantry supported by artillery, mounted infantry and European colonial volunteers. A large number of native African auxiliaries would also be employed, but Sir Henry Bulwer discouraged this course of action fearing the eventual consequences of supplying them with arms and believing that enlisting Natal's natives would aggravate the Zulus. Bulwer was pressured by both Chelmsford and Frere, however, and in late November approved the raising of three regiments of native infantry, five mounted troops and 300 pioneers from Natal's black population.

Lieutenant Colonel Anthony Durnford was given the job of mustering and training the black auxiliaries. Durnford had created for himself a visual image not unlike that of George Armstrong Custer who wore a fringed buckskin jacket, red scarf, and hunting knife in a fringed scabbard. At the Little Bighorn he wore a broad-brimmed hat pinned up on the side. While Custer was called 'Long Hair' by the Indians, Durnford was known for his superb, extremely long, dangling moustache and 'stage brigand' outfit, as he described it himself:

> Boots, spurs, dark cord breeches, serge patrol jacket, broad belt over the shoulder and one round the waist—to the former a revolver and to the latter a hunting knife and ammunition pouch. A wide-awake soft felt hat with wide brim, one side turned up and a crimson turban wound around the hat.

Although an engineer, it seems Durnford was a cavalier at heart. He was a superb horseman, six-foot tall, slim, handsome and witty, but with a quick temper under stress. He was happiest in the saddle, crossing challenging terrain and bivouacking in tents, and personally trained the native horsemen for the coming campaign. But a Durnford family man had been an officer of the Royal Engineers since 1759, so the mould was cast. It is fascinating that both Custer and Durnford created a similar image, as both would die in virtually the same circumstances, and then be accused of disobeying orders, thus causing the annihilation of their commands. Whether or not Custer and Durnford were responsible for the tragedies in which they played pivotal roles has been debated ever since, but they were not similar men in all respects. While Custer graduated from the bottom of his class of 34 at West Point, Durnford had been a brilliant student graduating with first-class passes in French, fortification and mathematics from the Royal Military Academy, Woolwich, in 1848. Custer had knocked up a huge score of demerits for a variety of offences, but Durnford was commended for his 'intelligence, abilities, zeal and high principles.' But, as fate would have it, it was Custer who had the brilliant military career, thanks to the intervention of the Civil War on his shaky graduation from West Point.

Durnford, born in Ireland in 1830, was the son of a British army officer, Edward Durnford, who would rise to the rank of Major General of Royal Engineers. Following graduation, Anthony Durnford was posted to Scotland, then Ceylon where he was appointed civil engineer. In 1854 he married Frances Tranchell, the daughter of a retired colonel of the Ceylon Rifles. On the outbreak of war with Russia in the Crimea, he applied for transfer to the field of action but, delayed by bureaucracy and illness, did not arrive till after the battle smoke had cleared. He was not present in India at the time of the Mutiny of 1857, and in 1860 separated from his wife. Two of their three children had died in infancy, apparently causing great distress and straining their relationship. Durnford arrived in South Africa in 1872 as a captain, but was soon promoted to major, and posted to Natal. Present at Cetshwayo's coronation in September of 1873, he was impressed by the ceremony, 'They sang a war song, a song without words,' he recalled, 'wonderfully impressive as the waves of sound rose, fell and died away, then rose again in a mournful strain, yet warlike in the extreme.'

Shortly after the coronation, Chief Langalibalele's Hlubi tribe of Natal refused to register guns given them in payment for work done in the Kimberley diamond mines. When summoned by Lieutenant Governor Pine to Pietermaritzburg, the chief declined the invitation and prepared his tribe to take flight over the Drakensberg Mountains into neighboring Basutoland. Durnford was ordered to prevent their escape, and the skirmish at Bushman's River Pass occurred, resulting in the deaths of five of his men including three white Natal Carbineers.

The defeated force returned to safety, so ending Durnford's baptism of fire, but the heat was not over yet.

George Armstrong Custer's first fight after the Civil War had been at the Washita River in Indian Territory when the 7th attacked the Cheyenne camp of Black Kettle. The village was taken and destroyed, but Indians from a neighboring village cut off and killed Major Joel Elliot and 14 troopers. Threatened by the Indian reinforcements, Custer withdrew his regiment without news of the missing detachment. Some felt Custer had deserted these men and although the destruction of the village was hailed as a victory, the fate of the dead soldiers was a lingering wound which aggravated rifts within the 7th Cavalry until the Little Bighorn wiped the slate clean.

In a similar way, the fight at Bushman's River Pass became a wound which plagued Durnford, despite the courage he had displayed. One of the three Carbineers killed was a young man of some prominence, Robert Erskin, son of the colonial secretary of Natal. He had been one of those five who had offered to stay by Durnford's side, and the colonial establishment was not happy with the outcome. Durnford's leadership was considered by many to have been the cause of the debacle. The *Natal Witness* wrote, 'pride in his profession as a soldier was buried in the graves of the three Carbineers.' Durnford refuted the allegations saying that he was 'blameless' for the deaths, and in his written report criticised the order from the Lieutenant Governor not allowing his command to fire first. But he also stated that when the first few shots were fired panic ensued and 'the Carbineers fled, followed by the Basutos.' These words caused outrage amongst the surviving Carbineers, and the families of those killed.

A Court of Inquiry was called for. After weighing up the testimony, all were exonerated and Durnford was praised for his devotion to duty and courage displayed. The Carbineers had fled due to 'extenuating circumstances' it was decided. After all, the sons of Natal's leading families could not possibly be doubted. But Durnford's accusations were on the record for posterity, and the wound would not heel.

Durnford held a congenial attitude towards black Africans, which caused some anguish when this clashed with his role as a soldier. 'The death of those three boys lies heavy on my heart and I shall never be content till I have avenged them' he wrote to his friend Bishop John Colenso, but 'on a fair field, remember, for I am not an assassin, and would never countenance the slaughter of hunted creatures who know not which way to turn...'

Did the slaughter of Major Elliot and his men weigh heavily on Custer's heart? The episode would dog Custer till the day he died at the Little Bighorn, and in the same way the deaths of the Carbineers would dog Durnford till the day he died at Isandlwana—and beyond. Following Isandlwana the colonial press would refer to Bushman's River Pass as 'Durnford's first disaster.'

Many in Natal's colonial establishment had another axe to grind; Durnford's friendship with the somewhat radical and unorthodox Bishop Colenso, a man who created waves. Since his arrival in 1853 Colenso had battled bureaucratic incompetence and been an outspoken advocate for black African rights. The natives called him *Sobantu*, the Father of His People. He also fought his own superiors within the church, leading to a rival Anglican Archbishop of Maritzburg being appointed in 1869. Durnford, however, liked Colenso and supported many of his views, but another inducement to visit the Bishopstowe Mission was the attractive Frances Ellen Colenso, the second of the bishop's five children. She and her two sisters taught at the mission school and, despite being 18 years Durnford's junior, they became very close. Marriage was out of the question as Durnford had never divorced, socially unacceptable for a career officer at the time, but whether their relationship became intimate is not known. That an intense friendship developed there can be no doubt, obvious with her passionate defence of his name after Isandlwana.

Durnford left South Africa in May of 1876 but, after serving in Ireland, returned the following year. Being one of the few senior British officers stationed in Natal experienced in handling native troops, he was selected by Chelmsford to muster black auxiliaries for the coming war. The Natal Native Contingent, called the NNC, was to be no small gathering. It comprised 7,000 men in total, with white officers and non-commissioned officers in command. The companies were divided on a tribal basis, each with its own name and guidon, but only the whites and one native in ten were equipped with firearms; outmoded Enfield muzzle-loaders and Snider breech-loaders. The remainder carried traditional assegais and shields. This calmed Sir Henry Bulwer's fears about arming a black populace with guns which may one day be turned on their white masters. Durnford, concerned that the blacks would be mistaken for Zulus by their own side, wanted scarlet tunics for his men. He also felt uniforms would help intimidate the enemy. But Chelmsford decreed that a red bandanna would suffice, concerned that European clothing would hamper the natives' natural agility and their use as scouts. 'Friendly fire', however, would take its toll on black troops in the course of the war.

Most of the senior officers were experienced men of good calibre, but good junior officers and NCOs for the native infantry battalions were in short supply. The Natal Carbineers and the Natal Native Horse had attracted most white colonial volunteers, so NCOs had to be recruited from the remains, riff-raff whites who, as a rule, could not speak the native tongue.

The NNC was never intended by Chelmsford to be used as front line troops, able to withstand a Zulu onslaught. Their role was to be that of auxiliaries, protecting the flanks of the invading columns and assisting the supply train when required. Should they be subjected to Zulu attack, they were to form up on the flanks of the white battalions, with mounted troops protecting their rear. The attacking Zulu line would, it was supposed, be shattered by rapid-fire volleys from the British line, then the fleet-footed natives, ideal for use over broken terrain, would pursue the enemy, bringing them to ground.

The cream of the black infantry was the Natal Native Pioneers. Durnford, being the Commanding Royal Engineer, had seen the need for a special unit to erect earthworks, construct and repair roads and bridges. They were recruited from Zulu refugees and equipped with a uniform, rifles and, most importantly, picks and shovels.

The Natal Native Horse, trained by Durnford personally, were troops of a higher calibre than the infantry. They wore yellow cord uniforms and each was supplied with a Martini-Henry carbine. Established white colonial families supplied most of the officers, crack shots and expert horsemen experienced in handling natives in everyday life.

Durnford was firm but fair with his men. On one occasion the white officers under his command decided to give their horses a day off, and turned up on parade without them, in contravention of standing orders. Durnford was told that all the horses were on the sick list. 'Oh, very good,' he replied quietly. After the usual drill, he said, 'Now gentlemen, I think we will do a little skirmishing.' The officers' faces fell, with good reason. 'He kept us at it for two hours, skirmishing over some very rough ground,' recalled Captain Dymes, 'All the drill was done at the double. I can honestly say that, what with the pace, and the encumbrance of my arms and accoutrements—not to mention the rough ground, and the tumbles into antbear holes, etc—I felt thoroughly knocked up when the drill was over.' At the end of the trial, Durnford rode over to the sweating senior captain. 'I hope your horse will be fit for work tomorrow morning, Captain Hay.'

Captain Dymes recalled 'He was a slave to duty and expected everyone who served under his command to be the same, but he never gave an order involving hardship or fatigue to the column without himself sharing the fatigue and hardship.' He could have been describing "Iron butt' Custer, who, it will be recalled, was to have commanded the whole expedition from Fort Abraham Lincoln, but then had to settle for command of the 7th only. Durnford now went through a similar experience, being promised by Chelmsford command of the entire native force of 7,000 men, only to have him go back on his word. Associates of Durnford's later insisted this had happened, including Frances Colenso who wrote, 'At first the General promised him the control and command in chief of the *whole* of the native force—& I *know* that the whole matter was talked over between them & settled, *but not on paper.* Consequently Col. Crealock was able to over-persuade that weak General into altering everything, & giving only a third to him.' At that stage it was planned to send 5 columns into Zululand. Durnford was relegated to command of one of these. 'I shall have some 3000 men, infantry, cavalry and rocket battery,' he wrote to his parents on November 11th, 'so the command is at least a respectable one for a Lieutenant Colonel.' But Chelmsford's decision to reduce the number of columns to three left Durnford's force in a support role, a decision that was to have a crucial bearing on future events.

Frances Colenso placed the blame for Durnford's removal on Brevet Lieutenant Colonel John N. Crealock, Chelmsford's military secretary. Crealock, a veteran of the Indian Mutiny, had previously served with Chelmsford at Aldershot and applied to join his staff when he the general was appointed to his South African command. Described as 'a sort of military wasp' an 'arch-snob' and 'evil genius,' Chelmsford used Crealock as his head kicker, issuing most unpleasant orders, a role he quite suited. One officer stated that Chelmsford was 'governed by Crealock & kept in ignorance of all going on about him.' The Wasp, however, had an artistic side to his abrasive nature, and would paint informative watercolors of the Zulu War.

Eight battalions of white, redcoat regular British infantry formed the nucleus of Chelmsford's attack force. This included the two battalions sent out from Britain as reinforcements at Chelmsford's request, and these were his only troops unused to the African climate. The extent of the Empire taxed Britain's reserves of manpower and Colonel Wood would later complain to Queen Victoria, 'these poor young fellows had not the metal nor the health & strength to make them really good soldiers, & this was the reason why so many officers were killed.'

Each battalion was commanded by a colonel and consisted of eight companies of 100 men each. The senior officers had all purchased their commissions, but many were veterans of the Indian Mutiny, the Crimean War and other lesser conflicts in New Zealand, Ashanti, Abyssinia and China. The purchase system had been abolished in 1871, thus the junior officers were selected only on merit—theoretically. In class-ridden British society one's position in life counted for a great deal, and the officers were usually 'gentlemen' who still came from the upper echelons of London's drawing rooms and parlours.

In all, Chelmsford amassed 17,000 men, European and African, for the conquest of Zululand. This says something for Britain's extreme self-confidence in her ability to wage war against those considered inferior, the Zulus reputedly having an army of 40,000. But, of course, there was the white man's technology to help even the score. Chelmsford had at his disposal three batteries of light field artillery, each consisting of six, 7-pounder, rifled, muzzle loading guns mounted on light gun carriages, drawn by six horses, relatively easy to move across rough ground. He also had a 9-pounder rocket battery which could send a shrieking, sparking, missile gushing smoke to a range of 1,500 yards, better at terrifying the enemy than doing a great deal of actual damage. And, as with Terry's Dakota column, a battery of Gatling guns was brought along.

Supplying the three columns in enemy territory was a huge logistical hurdle for Chelmsford to overcome. Ammunition and rations had to be stored and crated, ready for use, then sent into the field in the wake of the troops. 2,500 wagons and other vehicles were required, along with over 27,000 oxen and 5,000 mules. The locals profited, charging outrageous prices for animals, conveyances and accoutrements of all kinds. Acquiring these campaign essentials would have been far easier and cheaper if Sir Henry Bulwer had allowed Chelmsford to simply requisition the animals and vehicles required, but permission was refused. Natal's governor was one of the few in a position of power to have qualms about the unjust war, and he was concerned about the effect on Natal's economy should too many vehicles be taken off the roads.

It was impossible to take the enemy by surprise with such a baggage train, the oxen only being capable of about two miles per hour, and that was without crossing gullies and streams.

Chelmsford's grand three-column strategy called for Colonel Pearson's No. 1 column, on the right, to cross at the Lower Drift on the Thukela River and march for Eshowe Mission, 15 miles due north. The No. 3 central column, under Colonel Glyn would Cross at Rorke's Drift on the Buffalo River and march due east, and Column No. 4, on the left, commanded by Colonel Wood would move southeast from Utrecht. These three columns would move in a pincer movement against Cetshwayo's capital of Ulundi, and crush it like a shell—so Chelmsford thought.

Colonel Durnford's No. 2 column would not march until the other troops were well within Zululand, then act in support of Pearson's No. 1 column on the left. Colonel Rowland's No. 5 column was to be held in reserve and take a defensive stance on the Phongolo River.

January seemed the right time to strike, the spring rains being late. This delayed the Zulus getting in their harvest, thus they would be poorly prepared to repel the British invasion. The border rivers were expected to be in flood, providing a barrier to a Zulu counter-invasion of Natal, and grass would be plentiful for grazing the horses and oxen.

As the troops assembled at their posts, an air of excitement, adventure and optimism pervaded the troops. Lieutenant Henry Curling wrote his mother:

> Our ultimatum has been sent to the Zulu king, but it asks so much that he cannot, even if he wishes, give in. The only thing the natives understand is force. They will promise anything but always break their promises, so the only thing to be done is to take all their cattle, burn all their huts and kill a few thousand of them; if they make a fight and get beaten, so much the better.

A sergeant of the Second Battalion, 24th Foot (2/24) was a little more discerning than his superior officer. 'I think we shall lose a good many,' he wrote, 'for they are too strong for us.' The perceptive sergeant was one of the many to lose his life at Isandlwana.

On January 6th 1879 British troops, their red coats and white helmets vibrant beneath the African sun, moved from Utrecht marching towards the Disputed Territory and, beyond that, Zululand. They had orders not to 'push on too far.' On January 11th soldiers of the central column splashed across the Buffalo River into Zululand at Rorke's Drift, and the following day the third column crossed the Thukela River at the Lower Drift. The troops smiled in expectation of the action to begin, and the wagons groaned and jingled as their drivers cursed the oxen on.

No doubt Sir Bartle Frere smiled when he received word of the advance. At last his war had begun.

Sioux Country 1865 - 1877

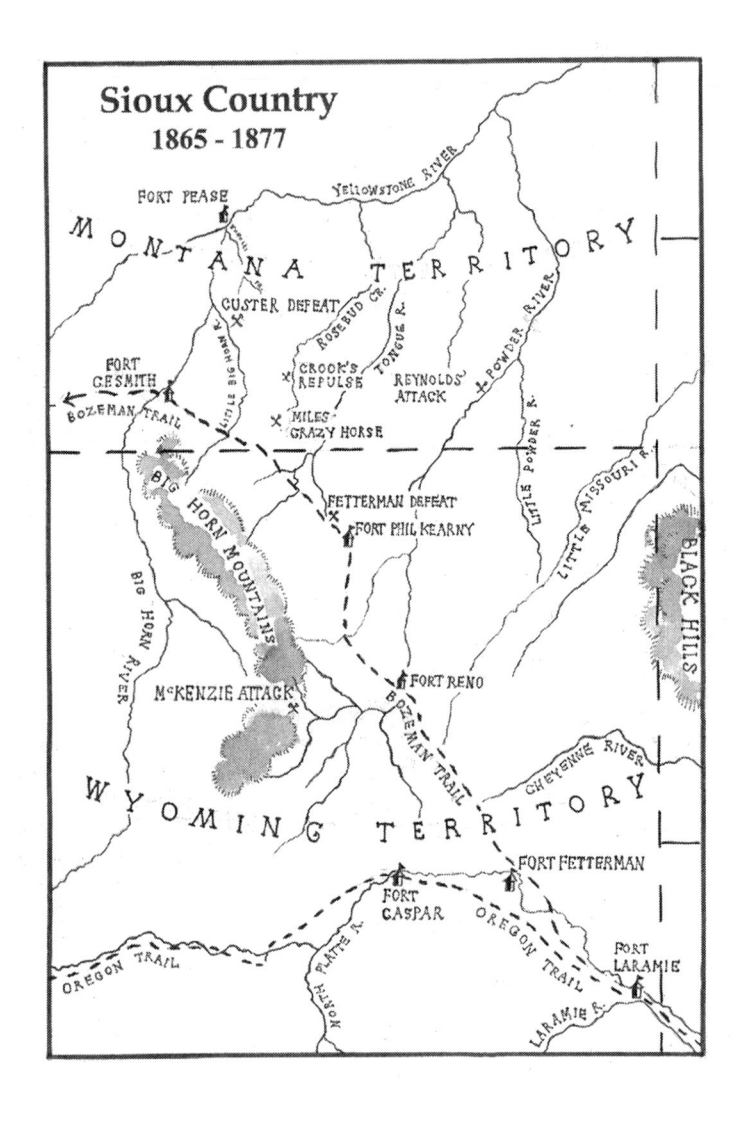

Zulu Field of Operations 1879

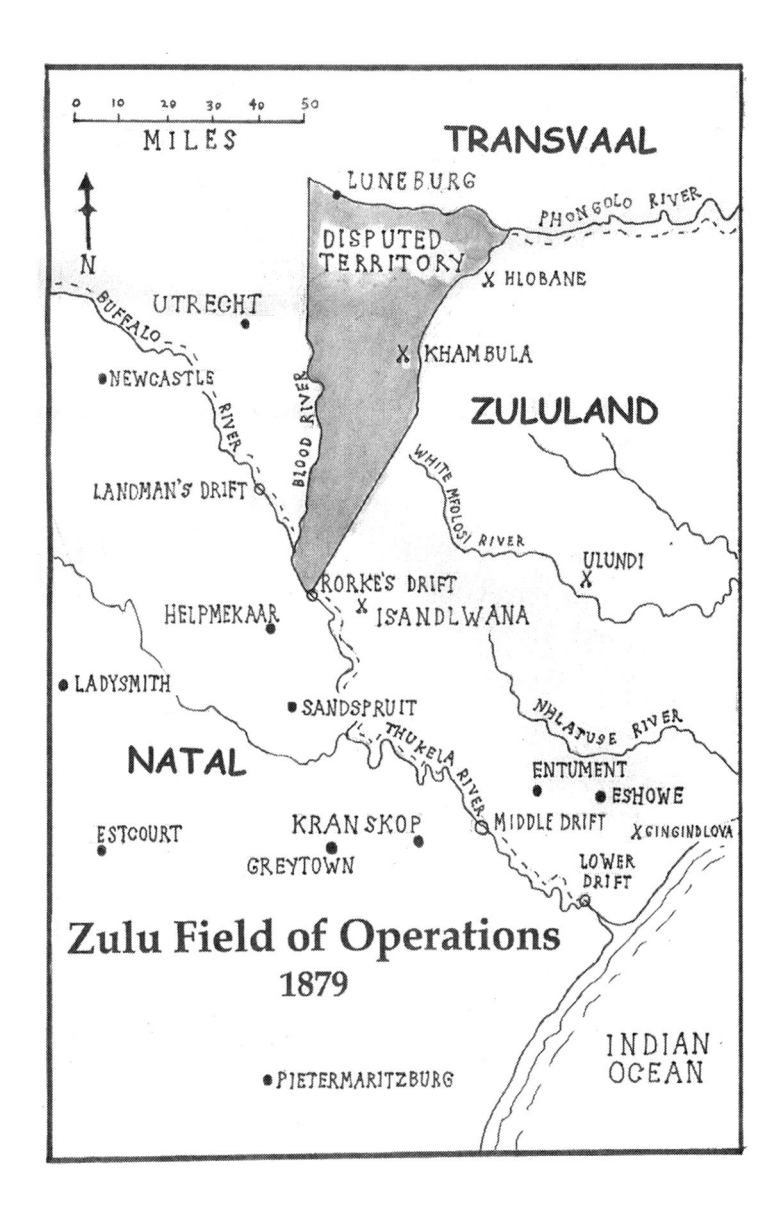

5
THE THREE-COLUMN ADVANCE

The first sunny day of General Terry's march was followed by four of pelting rain. The 48 year-old general probably cursed Grant for removing Custer from command of the expedition, rather being snug under shelter in his headquarters in St. Paul. Born in Hartford, Connecticut, Terry had been a lawyer in civilian life prior to the outbreak of the Civil War. He had raised a regiment of volunteers to fight for the Union and had been there from the start. Both he and Custer had seen action at the first big union defeat of the war; Bull Run in 1861. Terry served with distinction and for his capture of Fort Fisher, guarding the entrance to Wilmington Harbor, was promoted to brigadier general in the regular army. Captain John Bourke met Terry during the Sioux campaign of 1876 and contrasted the general's persona with that of his own commanding officer, the brusque and forthright General Crook:

> General Terry's manners are most charming and affable; he had the look of a scholar as well as a soldier; eyes, blue-grey and kindly; complexion bronzed by wind and sun to the color of an old sheepskin-covered bible. He won his way to our hearts by his unaffectedness and affability

But Bourke added 'I thought I detected slight traces of indecision and weakness.'

He could have been writing about Lord Chelmsford. And as it would transpire, Terry and his Lordship would have far more in common than a gentlemanly demeanour.

The Dakota column edged its way forward, the pioneer soldiers moving in advance, building timber crossings over flooded gullies and filling troughs with brush, rocks, soil and wood. Custer's orderly, John Burkman recalled, 'It don't sound much in the tellin' to say a wheel come off'n a wagon, or a wagon got stuck in the mud but for us that had to tug and sweat and cuss in the blazin' sun for maybe half a day, it meant a lot.' The cavalry rode and the infantry tramped out onto the plains, the routine always the same. Reveille was sounded at 4 o'clock, followed by breakfast, and the troops would be on the trail about an hour later. The distance travelled each day varied with the roughness of the terrain and availability of water, wood and grass, but camp was usually pitched in the late afternoon on a site of Custer's selection.

Only eight miles were covered on May 23rd, a campsite being selected because of good water, wood and forage for the horses. And that morning Custer, while chasing an elk in advance of the column, found a freshly abandoned Indian campfire. As the sun set that evening Sioux were spotted watching from a bluff about three miles away. They were apparently braves who had left the reservation to join their fellow tribesmen on the open plains, but a thorough scout of the area the following day revealed no further sign.

After days of marching they arrived at the headwaters of the Heart River, 135 miles from Fort Abraham Lincoln. Lonesome Charley Reynolds moved in advance tracking the route used by General Stanley's railway surveying expedition which Custer had accompanied during 1873. Reynolds led the troops to the head of Davis Creek, the only way known down to the Little Missouri.

As Custer rode towards his destiny at the Little Bighorn, another soldier impressed a large audience with his ability in the saddle. Anthony Durnford, despite considerable pain in his disabled left arm, attended a grand parade. One witness reported in the *Natal Witness*, noting his 'complete horsemanship' as he 'dexterously controlled an apparently restive animal.' The British Imperial garrison in Natal, South Africa, was holding a review for outgoing commander, Sir Arthur Cunynghame. The general paid tribute to Durnford, who was also about to leave his post as colonial engineer and return, for a time, to England. He had clashed with the new commander, Sir Garnet Wolseley, over his financial expenditures on public works. He had greatly improved the colonies infrastructure with slender resources, but Wolseley had noted 'It is high time that he ceased to be head of a spending department…Yet he is a fine fellow with many soldierlike qualities.' Durnford was also known to have a gambling problem. Perhaps money management was not a strength, but the new editor of the *Natal Witness* regretted his departure from the post, despite that paper having previously savaged Durnford for his role in the Bushman's River Pass affair:

> The Colonel was a brave, sensitive and high-principled man, and of a blameless life. He was a thorough-going soldier and had a quick eye to what was wanted, but possessed in a remarkable degree the power of encouraging and seeing to all the wants of his subordinates. He was moreover, one with whom one could not converse with ten minutes without learning something, and that is a very special merit in a place like this.

On May 27th 1876, three days after the parade, both Durnford and Cunynghame left South Africa aboard the steamer *Kafir*. Durnford was hoping English doctors could help his injured arm, and looked forward to a reunion with family and friends.

That same day, May 27th, General Terry wrote in his diary 'Custer in the advance with scouts and Weir's company looking for the trail...Bearing of hills supposed to be Sentinel Buttes shows us far south of Davis Creek. Our course plotted on the map agrees with bearing. Turned back at 1 o'clock, scout having reported that he had found Stanley's trail to the northward.' Lonesome Charley had lost the scent, but it was found again by Custer recalling the shape of Sentinel Buttes from the 1873 expedition.

The column moved through picturesque scenery, the banks of Davis Creek dotted with trees, but the pioneer troops in advance were forced to bridge the stream repeatedly as the clumsy wagons ground their way down to the banks of the Little Missouri. On May 29th tents were pitched amidst the cottonwoods alongside the flowing waters. It had taken 13 days for the troops to cover 166 hard-won miles.

The men had set up camp, but where were the hostile villages they had come to attack? The Ree scouts had been out searching, but had seen no sign of the Sioux and Cheyenne. A chagrined Terry had sent word to Colonel Gibbon's Montana column to close in on an enemy who were not to be seen.

Custer suggested he lead a scouting mission to the south, and Terry heartily agreed. Four companies of the 7th and 12 Ree scouts set out at dawn the following morning, the men in high spirits, following the twists and turns of the Little Missouri.

Custer wrote to his wife:

When we lunched all the officers got together and we had a jolly time. Only think, we found the Little Missouri so crooked and the badlands so impassable that in marching fifty miles today we forded the river thirty-four times. The bottom is quicksand. Many of the horses went down, frequently tumbling their riders into the water but all were in good spirits, and everyone laughed at everyone else's mishaps.

No signs of hostiles were found and Custer returned to report the disappointing news. On May 31st the Dakota column splashed to the west side of the Little Missouri where the Boy General stayed at the rear, 'to play wagon master' wrote Terry, directing the ponderous vehicles across the ford. The troops climbed up through the badlands, then Custer moved far ahead in company with younger brothers Tom and Boston. In a somewhat mischievous frame of mind, the two elder brothers separated from young Boston and moved back around behind him. They took their revolvers from their holsters and fired a barrage over his head. Convinced the whole Sioux nation was after him, Boston was riding hell for leather back towards the troops to sound the alarm when his two laughing brothers overtook him.

But General Terry was not so amused. Charley Reynolds was out bagging game, and the scouts had lost the scent once again. Terry wrote in his diary, 'a message was received from Lt. Col. Custer, who left the column early in the day without any authority whatever, that we were not on Stanley's trail… turned back and examined the ground. Found that to return would take too much time and marched on.' Custer received a verbal rebuke from Terry, which must have been a painful reminder of days gone by. He had been court-martialled in 1867 for offences including being absent without leave, having gone chasing across the plains to locate his wife. Custer had been suspended from duty and pay for 12 months, only to be recalled early for the Washita campaign. He responded to Terry's displeasure on May 31st 1876:

> At the time I proposed to accompany the advance battalion I was under the impression that it would probably be sufficiently far in advance of the main column to constitute a separate command, and that I could be of more service to you and to the expedition acting with the advance than elsewhere. Since such is not the case, I will, with your permission, remain with, and exercise command of, the main portion of my regiment.

The scouts relocated the correct trail, but an unseasonable blanket of snow fell on the morning of June 1st. The cold weather caused the animals to suffer from exposure and the lack of grazing, the snow being from one to two feet deep on flat ground, with drifts halfway to the top of some tents. The Rees were not happy with this turn of events, feeling such a misplaced storm to be a bad omen. The wagons would be severely slowed, so the troops stayed in camp for a few days while Lonesome Charley scouted the trail and the pioneers worked reshaping deep ruts and mounds, levelling the way ahead.

The sun shone, the snow melting away, on the morning of June 3rd and the troops, wagons and pack train climbed their way from the badlands onto the grassy, flat plains. As the column marched towards Beaver Creek three horsemen, two white and one Indian, appeared on the horizon; couriers bringing news from Gibbon's Montana column. The despatch, dated May 27th, had travelled from the mouth of the Rosebud down the Yellowstone by skiff, the steamer *Far West*, and then overland by rider:

> I have reached this point and have scouted the countryside on both sides of the Yellowstone. No camps have been seen, but war parties of from twenty to fifty have been seen to the south of the river and a few on the north side. One of these latter murdered three of our men whilst out hunting on the 23rd inst.
>
> As soon as my train arrives from Fort Ellis, which is expected about the first of June, I will resume the march down the Yellowstone with supplies which will last until about July 10th, and I can draw no more from there, the supplies being nearly exhausted. In the meantime I will keep scouting parties out up and down the river, and watch closely for any movement of Indians to the northward.
>
> A steamboat, if you have one at your disposal, will be of great assistance in passing troops across the river for effective cooperation if necessary. I have a few small boats which can be used, but they require, of course, a good deal of time…
>
> P. S. A camp some distance up the Rosebud was reported this morning by our scouts. If this proves true, I may not start down the Yellowstone so soon.

Gibbon's despatch is a curiosity, especially his claim 'no camps have been seen.' Gibbon's chief of scouts, Lieutenant James Bradley had, in fact, sighted a large village on May 16th on the Tongue River, then sighted it again at a new location on the Rosebud only eighteen miles from his column the day Gibbon wrote the despatch. But Gibbon did nothing. Bradley wrote in his diary, 'Everyone wondered why we were not ordered over to attack the village; but the General probably had good reasons.' Dr. Paulding recorded:

Don't know whether Gibbon's instructions or disposition will allow us to go for them...I suppose he will wait for Crook or Terry, hoping our untutored friends across the river will await their arrival. In the meantime Bradley can go over and take a look every day or so to see that they are still there. His party will be accommodated in a small grave 30x8x4 ft. some day.

Terry was probably frustrated by Gibbon's lack of detail regarding the 'camp some distance up the Rosebud.' The word 'camp' could mean just a few lodges rather than the main hostile village they were seeking, which was, in fact, what Bradley had seen. Gibbon had certainly understated the importance of the Indian signs in his surroundings, thus Terry sent instructions by rider to suspend his movements.

The following morning, June 4th, Terry's column began a 92-mile circuitous southern sweep towards the Powder River. Two days later Charley Reynolds, in advance, had trouble discerning the best route to the Powder, the various heads of O'Fallon's Creek causing confusion. Custer offered to take the van with an assurance that he would be able to locate an appropriate trail by 3 o'clock the following day. Terry let him off the leash, and the cocksure cavalier led a detachment out at dawn. Few believed he would succeed, but he fulfilled his promise only half an hour late, and sent a note back to Terry:

> We arrived here at 3.30. Considering the character of the country, the road is good, but will require some work. The valley of the Powder is over a mile in width, well timbered and well grassed. The river is about 100 yards wide and fordable. The scouts report the trail of four Indians made since the rain. No other signs. A few buffalo. If you can find camp grounds it would be best not to march here

tonight, as we will bivouac in preference to going back, as our horses have ridden hard. I believe we came by the only practicable route within several miles.

Terry, anxious to move ahead, not only gave the order to keep marching but dismounted and joined the pioneers with pick and shovel helping clear the way. The column reached Custer by the river at 7 p.m. and a grateful Terry possibly felt somewhat embarrassed, remembering Custer's words regarding being more use 'acting in the advance than elsewhere.' To prove this point was probably one reason Custer had been so anxious to carry out the scout. Bismarck *Tribune* reporter Mark Kellogg wrote a glowing report of Custer's scouting achievement.

What did Kellogg think three weeks later as Custer's troopers fell about him, his own death only minutes away?

The troops set up camp alongside the Powder River which has been described by one newspaper man as 'the filthiest stream in America or elsewhere' and 'too thick to drink and too thin to plough.' The stream derived its name not from the yellowish color of the water, but the dark, powder-like sand along its banks.

Terry decided to take charge of the *Far West* personally to make contact with Gibbon, scouts on horseback having failed to do so. It was vital that the two columns work in unison. Escorted by two companies of the 7th, Terry set out for the Yellowstone. He carried with him Custer's second report to the New York *Herald* which stated 'Terry's brief absence left Custer in temporary command of the expedition, Grant's positive orders to the contrary not withstanding.' No doubt Custer had smiled in grim satisfaction as he penned these mischievous words, imagining Grant's reaction when he read them.

Terry reached the *Far West* that evening. The vessel had been built in Philadelphia during 1870, and was powered by two steam engines. Her 190-foot long hull was graced by a steam capstan on either side of the bow, advanced for her time, to help pull her out of trouble spots such as rapids or shallow water. Her double-story superstructure, topped with two tall smoke stacks and the wheel house, was designed to give minimum wind resistance, with no officers' quarters and space for only 30 passengers. This made her one of the most stable river crafts afloat in blustery conditions. She was strong, quick and light, and skippered by the redoubtable Grant Marsh, was well suited to her current task.

Terry was pleased to find a detachment of troops under Major 'Grasshopper Jim' Brisbin from Gibbon's command already on board, having arrived by boat a few hours earlier. Terry heard Brisbin's account of Gibbon's actions, or lack thereof, and the actual size of the hostile village on the Rosebud. The ruffled general despatched two riders with orders for Gibbon's command to halt, and for the colonel himself to report onboard the steamer with all due haste.

The couriers rode through the night, reaching the Montana column before dawn the following morning. Gibbon learned from them that Major Brisbin had contacted Terry first, and Dr. Paulding wrote in his diary a revealing passage, 'Brisbin, of course, accomplished his object in getting in the first word with Terry, and Gibbon is very hot about it, apparently.'

Stokers fired up the boilers, and the *Far West* steamed upstream the following morning as Gibbon rode downstream with a small detachment. They sighted the steamer late in the morning and Gibbon went on board for a meeting with his commander. The boat chugged back upstream to Gibbon's camp where a no doubt chagrined Terry ordered the cavalry back to their former campsite opposite the mouth of the Rosebud. The infantry were to follow no later than the following dawn, and the hostiles camped on the Rosebud, if they were still there, were to be prevented from crossing to the north side of the Yellowstone at all costs. Terry, meanwhile, would return to the Dakota column, his strategy to be revised. Mitch Boyer, a prominent scout in Gibbon's employ, returned with Terry as he knew the Powder country like the back of his hand.

Thunder rumbled and lightning flashed as the general rode south with his escort through drenching rain and swollen streams, arriving at his command's sodden camp on the night of June 9th. His new plan called for converging columns against the hostile village on the Rosebud. But not yet. He ordered Major Reno to take six companies of the 7th and one Gatling gun under the command of Lieutenant Frank Kinsie, along with Mitch Boyer and eight Ree scouts, to move south searching the Powder River, then cross to the Tongue and ride north. He was to scout its banks back to the Yellowstone, then report back. Reno was to keep clear of the Rosebud to avoid alerting the hostiles, assuming, of course, that the nomadic Indians had not moved away. But why did Terry not simply march straight for the hostile village? Custer felt peeved at not being selected to lead this reconnaissance and protested to Terry, the issue becoming a subject of gossip amongst the troops. Terry evidently wanted to give Reno a chance at independent command, but there were tactical problems with his choice of action, as Custer wrote in a despatch to the New York *Herald*:

> Custer and most of his officers looked with little favor on the movement up Powder River, as, among other objections, it required the entire remaining portion of

the expedition to lie in idleness within two marches of the locality where it was generally believed the hostile village would be discovered on the Rosebud, the danger being that the Indians, ever on the alert, would discover the presence of the troops as yet undiscovered, and take advantage of the opportunity to make their escape.

Make their escape; a mistaken idea, influencing Custer's thinking that would have disastrous consequences in a few weeks time. But, with hindsight, had the column marched straight for the Rosebud, as Custer wished, they would likely have caught the hostiles between themselves and Crook's column coming up from the south. The unavoidable lack of communication would lead to the defeat of both columns in separate battles at separate times.

On June 10th Reno's battalion mounted up and rode out, and the following morning the remainder of the 'idle' command marched to the junction of the Powder and the Yellowstone. Custer led the way once again, scouting for a route passable by the wagon train. 'After passing through some perfectly terrible country,' he wrote his wife, 'I finally struck a beautiful road along a high plateau and instead of guiding the command within ten miles of here, we have all arrived and the wagon train besides.'

The *Far West* was at the mouth of the Powder, having transported stores from the Glendive depot. An enterprising sutler, James Coleman, had pitched his tent to sell a few luxuries to the travel-worn soldiers in the form of wide, shady straw hats and, of more importance, beverages to satisfy their thirst. He did a roaring trade as the soldiers shed the pay they had received shortly after leaving Fort Abraham Lincoln, a partition of canned food separating the officers from the enlisted men. The price was the same, however, for all who could afford to pay one dollar per pint of whiskey. Those who remained sober were detailed to stand guard over those who had not, after being moved out onto the open grasslands. As a result of this sale, stories would later be told of the troops being drunk at the Little Bighorn. The Ree scouts were limited to one glass each, selling 'fire water' to Indians being something frowned upon.

The morning of June 15th saw Custer's battalion ride out with the battery of Gatlings in tow, the band playing Garry Owen from a nearby bluff. He was headed towards the mouth of the Tongue for the rendezvous with Reno.

It has been argued by some that had Custer taken the Gatlings to the Little Bighorn the disaster may have been avoided. Dr. Richard Gatling had patented these early machine guns in 1862. Initially rejected by the army, General Ben Butler purchased 12 personally and his troops used them at the battle of Petersburg towards the end of the Civil War, but it was not until 1866 that they were officially adopted by the U. S. Army. For the next 40 years those manufactured in the United States came from the Colt gun factory, and various armies around the globe utilised them including the British against the Zulus in 1879. But it was not until 1898 that they saw serious American action in Cuba during the Spanish-American war. Despite improvements over the years, they were finally declared obsolete in 1911, the belated victim of more modern weapons such as the Maxim gun.

As Custer's battalion marched they found a Sioux campsite abandoned for some time. Amidst the ashes of an old fire they found the skull and bones of a cavalryman judging by his uniform buttons. Custer stood silently looking at the possible remains of one of his own men who went missing during a skirmish with the Sioux during the Stanley expedition of 1873.

Also discovered were the remains of a Sioux warrior on his burial scaffold. The body was thrown into the river and various articles like moccasins and buffalo horn spoons were claimed as souvenirs by the troops.

The *Far West* raised steam and moved off the afternoon of Custer's departure, Terry intending to join him before nightfall, but the industrial revolution suffered a minor pitfall in the form of the boat's machinery breaking down. Repairs were carried out, steam hissed once more, and Terry finally reached Custer's camp at the mouth of the Tongue at noon of the 16th. Here they cooled their heels and waited for Reno's return.—And waited.

Reno, his scouts, Gatling gun and six companies of the 7th explored along the Powder River with no result, then crossed rugged country to the banks of the Tongue. They saw no Indians, but the Gatling was overturned and the gun carriage damaged. On June 16th Mitch Boyer, having scouted in advance, galloped back with news of a large, abandoned campsite a short distance ahead; no doubt the one sighted by Lieutenant Bradley one month earlier before it moved to the Rosebud. An inspection revealed that 400 lodges had been there, representing a sizeable force. Reno was supposed to report back to Terry that same evening, but decided instead to extend his search. Despite orders to avoid the Rosebud, he followed Mitch Boyer across the divide where the scouts found another abandoned campsite on the riverbank. Also discovered was a wide, deep trail scoured by the Indians as they moved off to the south, upstream. The troops followed and Peter Thompson, a private of the 7th, later recalled that the 'trail was so wide and so torn up by teepee-poles that we found it difficult to secure a good camping place at night. This was especially so around watering places that were so necessary to us.' On the

17th Reno proceeded cautiously upstream, then called a halt for six hours. He ordered that no bugles be blown, and posted double pickets. While the soldiers and their horses rested, the hard-riding scouts pushed along the Rosebud for another 20 miles following the trail, then returned to camp. "What do you think of this trail?' Reno asked Fork Horn, in charge of the Ree scouts.

'If the Dakotas see us, the sun will not move very far before we are all killed. But you are the leader and we will go on if you say so.'

'Custer told us to turn back if we found the trail,' Reno replied, 'and we will return. Those are our orders,' he said, knowing he had, in fact, disobeyed his orders.

The trail when last seen by the scouts was heading southwest following the stream. If the hostiles kept moving in that direction, it would take them away from the winding Rosebud towards the Little Bighorn River. So where were they now? It was a question that could not be answered without Reno further violating his orders. The command mounted up and retraced their steps, camping that night on the site of the deserted village. Reno had gained vital intelligence, the Indians having moved out of reach of Terry's plan to trap them between himself and Gibbon. But if the hostiles were to learn of his presence he would be blamed for their movement, and a court-martial would be the best he could look forward to.

Next day, June 18th, Reno rode north to the Yellowstone and bivouacked opposite Gibbon's camp for the night. The following morning he marched for his belated rendezvous with Terry and Custer, his exhausted command camping a little short of their destination, but he forwarded news:

I am in camp about eight miles above you. I started this a.m. to reach your camp, but the country from the Rosebud here is simply *awful* and I had given orders to cache the gun, but Kinsie is coming in all right. I am sure you cannot take wagons to Rosebud without going some distance up Tongue River.

I enclose you a note from Gibbon, whom I saw yesterday. I can tell you where the Indians are *not*, and much more information when I see you in the morning. I take it the Tongue River is not fordable at the mouth and I will necessarily have to camp on this side. I have had no accident, except breaking the tongue of Kinsie's gun carriage. My command is well. I will be on Tongue River opposite your camp about 8 a.m. My animals are leg weary and need reshoeing. We have marched near to 250 miles.

Terry, furious with Reno, sent orders instructing him to stay put and await Custer's arrival. The reunited regiment would ride back to Gibbon's camp.

The sun was well up the following morning, June 20th, when Custer's battalion rode out, arriving at Reno's camp two and a half hours later. Shortly after midday the *Far West* steamed into sight with supplies and General Terry on board. His reunion with Reno was, no doubt, not a happy one. The Gatling gun was placed on board and fresh rations were distributed to Reno's men.

Terry wrote to his sisters back east on June 21st:

Here we lie in idleness until Monday evening, when to my great surprise I received a note from Colonel Reno which informed me that he had flagrantly disobeyed my orders, and that instead of coming down the Tongue he had been to the Rosebud…in the belief that there were Indians on that stream, and that he could make a successful attack on them which would cover up his disobedience...He had not the supplies to enable him to go far and he returned without justification for his conduct, unless wearied horses and broken-down mules would be justification. Of course, this performance made a change to my plans necessary.

The change was necessary because it demonstrated that Terry's plan was redundant. Perhaps this embarrassed the general, thus increasing his wrath. Custer also was happy to sink the boot in, accusing Reno of cowardice for not locating and attacking the village on one hand, and for possibly warning the hostiles of the troops' approach on the other. The New York *Herald* later quoted Custer as saying 'Few officers have ever had so fine an opportunity to make a successful and telling strike, and few have ever so completely failed to improve their opportunity.' Reno did not do a good job of defending himself, silence and sulkiness being his way of coping. And Terry seemed, on the surface, more interested in his disobedience than the information received. But Reno's news was vital to the campaign's next move.

Late that afternoon Custer led his reunited regiment up the Yellowstone, arriving at Gibbon's camp before nightfall. No doubt those who had been on Reno's trek groaned at having to retrace their steps over rough country, wishing they had stayed put.

When the steamer arrived the following morning, Terry was pleased to learn that Gibbon had already sent an infantry detachment up the Yellowstone clearing the trail in anticipation of their next march towards the mouth of the Big Horn River. He ordered Gibbon's troops to move out, then sent a despatch to Little Phil Sheridan disclosing his new plan:

No Indians have been met with as yet, but traces of a large and recent village have been discovered 20 or 30 miles up the Rosebud. Gibbon's column will move this morning on the north side of the Yellowstone for the mouth of the Big Horn, where it will be ferried across by the supply steamer, and whence it will proceed to the mouth of the Little Horn, and so on. Custer will go up the Rosebud tomorrow with his whole regiment and thence to the headwaters of the Little Horn, thence down the Little Horn.
I only hope that one of the two columns will find the Indians. I go personally with Gibbon.

It seems, however, that Terry thought the highly mobile Custer would be the strike force rather than Gibbon, saddled with slower moving infantry. Accordingly, he offered Custer the use of Brisbin's four companies of the 2nd Cavalry. Custer declined the offer, but accepted another; the pick of the scouts from both commands, as Gibbon's chief of scouts, Lieutenant Bradley, wrote:

> He is provided with Indian scouts, but the superior knowledge possessed by the Crows of the country he is to traverse, it was decided to furnish him with part of ours, and I was directed to make a detail for that purpose. I selected my six best men, and they joined him at the mouth of the Rosebud. Our guide, Mitch Bouyer, accompanied him also. This leaves me wholly without a guide, while Custer has one of the very best that the country affords. Surely he is being offered every facility to make a successful pursuit.

Grasshopper Jim, who had attended the conference, sent a despatch to the New York *Herald* which included:

It was announced by General Terry that General Custer's column would strike the blow and General Gibbon and his men received the decision without a murmur...The Montana column felt disappointed when they learned that they were not to be present at the final capture of the great village, but General Terry's reasons for affording the honor of the attack to General Custer were good ones. First, Custer had all cavalry and could pursue if they attempted to escape, while Gibbon's column was half infantry, and in rapid marching in approaching the village, as well as pursuing the Indians after the fight, General Gibbon's cavalry and infantry must become separated and the strength of the column weakened. Second, General Custer's column was numerically stronger than Gibbon's, and General Terry desired the stronger column to strike the Indians; so it was decided that Custer's men, as usual, were to have the post of honor, and the officers and men of the Montana column cheered him and bade them Godspeed.

And Lieutenant Bradley's wrote in his journal on June 21st 'it is understood that if Custer arrives first he is at liberty to attack at once if he deems prudent' but whatever discussion had taken place prior to Custer's departure, the written orders Custer received included the following:

The Brigadier General commanding directs that, as soon as your regiment can be made ready for the march, you will proceed up the Rosebud in pursuit of the Indians whose trail was discovered by Major Reno a few days since. It is, of course, impossible to give you any definite instructions in regard to this movement, and were it not impossible to do so the Department Commander places too much confidence in your zeal, energy, and ability to wish to impose on you precise orders which might hamper your action when nearly in contact with the enemy. He will, however, indicate to you his own views of what your action should be, and he desires that you should conform to them unless you shall see sufficient reasons for departing from them. He thinks that you should proceed up the Rosebud until you ascertain definitely the direction in which the trail above spoken of leads. Should it be found (as it appears almost certain that it will be found) to turn towards the Little Horn, he thinks that you should still proceed southward, perhaps as far as the headwaters of the Tongue, and then turn towards the Little Horn, feeling constantly, however, for your left so as to preclude the possibility of the escape of the Indians to the south or southeast by passing your left flank. The column of Colonel Gibbon is now in motion for the mouth of the Big Horn. As soon as it crosses that point it will cross the Yellowstone and move up at least as far as the forks of the Big and Little Horns. Of course, its future movement must be controlled by circumstances as they arise, but it is hoped that the Indians, if upon the Little Horn, may be so nearly inclosed by the two columns that their escape will be impossible.

According to latest intelligence reports the enemy they were facing, consisting of about 400 lodges, meant they would fight about 800 warriors. Either battalion should have the strength to prevail against those odds, but should they trap the Indians between them, the numbers would be with the troops. They did not take into consideration the addition of reinforcements for Sitting Bull from the reservations with the spring thaw, but even if they had, they could only use the troops at hand. Jim Brisbin later claimed to have been told by the scouts that they could face 3000 warriors, and warned Custer to 'be careful.'

Terry also had received word of a hostile village of 1500 lodges, meaning 3000 warriors, even before they left Fort Abraham Lincoln. The confusion over how many enemy were to be faced was a fatal flaw in the campaign. It seems there was an element of wishful thinking combined with a reliance on 'Custer's luck,' to see them through.

Terry's command had no contact with General Crook coming up from Fort Fetterman, and he was not considered in their plans. This was just as well, because as Reno had been following the Indian trail along the Rosebud on June 17th, Crook had been locked in combat about 40 miles to the south.

Having marched with a force of 1200 cavalry and infantry, Crook had followed the route of his previous expedition which had resulted in the humiliating retreat of his own troops after destroying the hostile village.

His men skirmished with warriors led by Crazy Horse on June 9th, then six days later nearly 300 Shoshone and Crow scouts, recruited by the invaluable scout Frank Grouard, reinforced his command. Leaving infantry to guard the wagons, Crook mounted the remaining footsloggers on pack train mules, then splashed across the Tongue River on June 16th, reaching the Rosebud the same evening. The troops moved out before daylight the next morning, following the stream, and arrived at a broad flat flanked by high bluffs. Believing the hostile village to be nearby, Crook ordered his scouts to fan out searching for any signs. A crackle of gunfire was soon heard, and the Crows and Shoshones came galloping back. 'Sioux! Sioux! Heap Sioux!' they shouted as hostiles, painted and ready for battle, appeared in large numbers on the surrounding hills. Crook ordered his men into line of battle, and a volley crashed out. Hooves thundered as Captain Mills led a cavalry charge against a hill swarming with Sioux, and Major Royall, to his left, bolted forward at the head of his battalion. Mills' men galloped at full speed across the flat and up the slope driving the enemy back a quarter of a mile to higher ground, and Royall had similar success, pushing the hostiles from their front. But then things began to change, the two detachments far in advance and dangerously exposed as the Indian numbers increased, Crazy Horse being reinforced by warriors under American Horse, and Little Hawk of the Cheyennes. Crook rushed reinforcements forward from the main command, no troops left in reserve, but then Crazy Horse ordered his warriors to take the offensive. With wild war whoops they charged and struck the bluecoat lines. A seething mass of entangled soldiers and troops struggled down the slopes amidst dust and smoke, then Lieutenant Vroom's company found itself cut off and surrounded, forming a defensive circle to hold the Indians back. Captain Henry's men came riding to the rescue, cutting their way through the redskin lines, then the troops beat a hasty retreat to a less exposed position. Henry was directing rearguard fire at the Indians, his back to the troops, when he was hit. He turned and the men behind were horrified to see his mangled face covered in blood. He swayed in his saddle and fell. Then the Indians charged once again, driving the troops back, overrunning the position where Henry lay. But then Shoshone and Crow scouts made a mad dash against the Sioux, pushing them back once more before they had a chance to kill the fallen officer and lift his scalp. Troopers galloped up and recovered Henry, still alive despite the severe wound which would not prove fatal. They carried him back as the hostiles charged, retaking the ground just lost.

Northeast of the broad flat held by Crook's troops, the Rosebud tumbled into a dismal gorge known as Dead Canyon. Crook believed this concealed Crazy Horse's village, and ordered Captain Mills' battalion to find and destroy it. But they had not marched far along the dark chasm, flanked by steep, rocky slopes, when they received orders to withdraw. The hostiles had withdrawn from the fight when Mills had entered the canyon, but not fought his advance. Crook, with dead and wounded, sent the order to pull back as he could not send effective support should the enemy attack. This was a wise move as fallen timber, rocks and debris from cascading floodwaters sometime in the past blocked Mills' advance. Had the Indians got above them and behind, it is unlikely any soldier would have escaped, and the Little Bighorn would not have been the white invader's first disaster.

Crook withdrew and returned to base for supplies, having lost eight killed and 23 wounded. His Indian scouts lost two dead and 11 wounded. The enemy loss is not known, but the Indian scouts took 13 Sioux and Cheyenne scalps. Crazy Horse, however, had defended his village and held his ground. Crook would not return, leaving the rest of this campaign to Terry, Custer and Gibbon.

'The news of the failure of the campaign in the other department was a death knell to our hopes,' recalled Libby Custer. 'We felt we had nothing to expect but that our troops would be overwhelmed with numbers, for it seemed an impossibility, as it proved to be, that our Indian scouts should cross that vast extent of country in time to make the warning of use.'

Ignoring Captain Fetterman's fate in 1866, and in ignorance of the way the Sioux had sallied forth in defence of their village against Crook, Terry's concern was that the enemy would flee when they saw their camp under threat. Crook's defeat was a tremendous boost to the self-confidence and esteem of the Sioux and Cheyenne. Their tribal way of life was under threat, their land was being stolen, but they still had plenty of ammunition. Should the bluecoats come again they would be ready for another big fight.

***

As only one newspaperman, Mark Kellogg, had ridden with the troops against the Sioux, only one newspaperman rode with the expedition against the Zulus.

Charles Norris Newman, known to his friends as 'Noggs,' a reporter for the London *Standard* and two Cape newspapers, emerged from the mist shrouding the Buffalo River at dawn on January 11th 1879. His horse splashed across the river and climbed the opposite bank, the first invader to enter a sodden Zululand, drenched from recent heavy rain. Major Cooper and his battalion of the Natal Native Contingent waded across close behind, along with men on horseback who quickly galloped up nearby slopes, taking posts as sentinels on the surrounding high ground.

Colonel Richard Glyn's No. 3 column, the central invading force, consisted of over 4,700 men; 1,890 European and 2,400 African troops plus staff officers and civilian back-up. Pulling a battery of the Royal Artillery and about 300 wagons and other vehicles were over 2,000 oxen and 67 mules. Most of the infantry crossed a short distance upstream, the Africans wading neck-high and the British using pontoon bridges. At this point the river was a swift 80 feet wide due to the rain, and several Africans were swept away to be drowned downstream.

The mighty host splashed across the river all day, and by nightfall most had made the crossing. A tent city arose along the riverbank, mounted patrols rode out, and sentries were posted in a protective arc over one mile into Zululand.

Next morning Chelmsford rode across one of the pontoon bridges to join the central column, effectively taking command, which sidelined Colonel Glyn. Major Francis Clery of Glyn's staff wrote to a colleague:

> That he should take command was of course to be expected, but it had the effect of practically effacing the nominal Commander of the Column and his staff. You know the general so well you will understand all this, and how his energetic, restless, anxious temperament, led him into very minor matters. For he used even to detail himself the patrols & constantly gave orders direct to commanders of Corps. Beyond placing one in an uncertain and sometimes anxious position in thinking what remained for one, as Staff Officer of the Column, to do, and what the General had left undone, or how far any orders one may issue would be running counter to those he may have issued etc. etc. I did not see any objection whatever to the General taking the whole thing in his hands. The only thing I thought of importance was that he should do so *thoroughly.*

Chelmsford, following the disaster to come, would claim that he was in no way involved with the column's daily routine, Colonel Glyn bearing that responsibility.

Cetshwayo's capital of Ulundi lay about 60 miles to the east of Rorke's Drift. Chelmsford ordered the troops to advance with caution as the kraal of Chief Sihayo was in the Batshe Valley to the left of the column's march. Sihayo was a favorite of Cetshwayo, and it was he, according to reports, who was to fight the British advance with 8,000 warriors.

The morning following the Rorke's Drift crossing, Chelmsford led a large reconnaissance force in advance. The 8000 warriors did not materialize, but a herd of cattle grazing peacefully beneath one of Sihayo's hilltop strongholds did. Chelmsford ordered four companies of redcoat infantry and a large detachment of native troops to take charge of the cattle. As the native troops approached in the van, guns cracked and smoke plumed from caves studding the hill. Several men fell, but their officers urged the others forward and, backed up by redcoats, about a dozen Zulus were killed as they were flushed out. Two of the Natal Native Contingent were killed and 20 wounded, including two officers. Sceptics had doubted the value of the native troops, but all agreed they had performed well this day.

Sihayo's main kraal rested beneath a rocky outcrop 200 feet above the valley floor. A combined force of redcoat and native troops under Colonel Henry Degacher clambered up the rocky mountain slope. Caves searched were found to be unoccupied, then they moved into the kraal itself. The Zulus had fled the day before to Ulundi, except for three old women and a girl. Clouds of smoke drifted skywards as the kraal was put to the torch, and Chelmsford, agitated by Sihayo's escape, rode back to Rorke's Drift, his men driving 500 head of Zulu cattle.

So much for Sihayo contesting Chelmsford's advance with a host of Zulu warriors. It had all been too easy, reinforcing Chelmsford's mistaken idea that the Zulus would have to be coaxed into battle.

Then Chelmsford received news of another success. Mounted troops had been ordered to secure a nearby hill, and as they ascended the slope a force of about 60 Zulu warriors opened fire. The troops, outnumbering the defenders, scrambled from their saddles, and returned fire. Ten of the Zulus were killed as they were driven off. One of the dead included Mkhumbikazulu, one of Sihayo's sons.

Chelmsford felt well pleased with his first day's work. By the light of a lantern that night he sat down and wrote to Sir Bartle Frere, anxiously awaiting news of his war:

> I am in great hopes that the news of the storming of Sihayo's stronghold & the capture of so many of his cattle...may have the salutary effect in Zululand & either bring down a large force to attack us or else produce a revolution in the country. Sihayo's men have I am told always been looked upon as the bravest in the country & certainly those who were killed today fought with great courage.

Chelmsford was certainly going to get his wish as regards the attack. But in the meantime the state of the sodden landscape was causing problems for the supply train:

> I do not know how we shall manage to get our wagons across the valley near Sihayo's Kraal. A large working party will start tomorrow to dig deep ditches on each side of the road which runs across a broad swamp—and I hope that under this treatment it may consolidate.

Lieutenant Colonel Anthony Durnford, meanwhile, had been waiting to play his part in the advance, possibly twirling his long moustaches and groping his hunting knife in frustration. He had returned to South Africa in 1877, his arm unhealed, after a stint at Queenstown, Ireland, where he was responsible for maintaining harbor forts. The climate had damaged his health, and with the help of an old and influential friend, General Charles Gordon, had retrieved his former post as Commanding Royal Engineer in Natal. Durnford had told Gordon of his desire to 'do great things' back in South Africa, and convinced him that he was one of the few British officers who understood native troops. It seems ironic that Gordon would meet a fate akin to that of Durnford and Custer, being surrounded and cut down by native hordes at Khartoum in 1885

Durnford, like Custer before him, had been demoted to play a secondary role in the invasion. The original plan had been for Durnford's No. 2 column to march across the Middle Drift with 3,000 black troops and the European rocket battery, covering the left flank of Colonel Pearson's southern column. But on January 1st he had received new orders from Chelmsford ordering him to hand over one of his Natal Native Contingent battalions to Pearson. Durnford was not allowed to cross the river into Zululand until Pearson had cleared the countryside in front of Middle Drift, near Durnford's position. As Durnford impatiently waited to proceed from his base at Kranskop, yet another infuriating order was received from Chelmsford. Durnford was to send his two strongest NNC battalions to Sandspruit to contest a reported Zulu counter-invasion across the Buffalo River. Those battalions could cooperate with Chelmsford's column if required, while Durnford and his depleted command remained idly waiting for Pearson to occupy Eshowe.

But the *Natal Mercury* of January 10th reported three Zulu regiments opposing Durnford's force at the Middle Drift, and on the 13th he received a written warning from Bishop Schreuder that Zulus were forming for an invasion of Natal at the same place. What to do? Chelmsford's instructions had given him some latitude in repelling any invasion, and here was a chance for action. He decided to ignore Chelmsford's orders, and instead instructed his men to form up for an advance on Middle Drift. They were preparing to march into the valley in the early hours of January 14th when a galloper arrived and handed Durnford a despatch. He hurriedly opened it and 'Suddenly he gave the word to retrace our way to camp,' recalled captain Dymes, 'and I well remember the look of disgust that crossed his countenance as he read the order.':

> Unless you carry out the instructions I give you, it will be my unpleasant duty to remove you from your command, and to substitute another officer for the command of No. 2 Column. When a column is acting *separately* in an *enemy's country* I am quite ready to give its commander every latitude, and would expect him to disobey any orders he might receive from me, if information which he obtained, showed that it would be injurious to the interests of the column under his command. Your neglecting to obey my instructions in the present instance has no excuse…If movements are to be delayed because report hints of an invasion of Natal, it will be impossible for me to carry out my plan of campaign. I trust you will understand this plain speaking & not give me any further occasion to write in a style which is distasteful to me.

It will be recalled that General Terry's orders to Custer stated that he did not 'wish to impose precise orders which might hamper your action when nearly in contact with the enemy.' Chelmsford shadowed this when he stated he would expect a commander to 'disobey any orders he may receive from me, if information which he obtained, showed that it would be injurious to the interests of the column under his command.'

In both cases it presented officers who had demonstrated a desire for independent action a great deal of freedom to move. With hindsight, too much freedom, perhaps, as both unfolding dramas would imply.

No counter-invasion occurred at any point, and the day following his rebuff Durnford was ordered to leave two battalions at Kranskop and march to Rorke's Drift with his Natal Native Horse, a battalion of infantry and the rocket battery. It seems that Chelmsford wished to keep tabs on his subordinate, but Durnford's excellent native horsemen could also help provide eyes and ears for the central column which, if reports were true, would see the brunt of the fighting. Chelmsford's strategy was for the three invading columns to 'push everyone slowly before us towards the King's kraal, or otherwise disarm the tribes and take their chief and some of their headmen as hostages for good behaviour.' Chelmsford's horsemen had scouted over 20 miles in advance but found the rutted track quite unfit for the supply train's passage. He needed somewhere to establish a base camp before the next push, a place with a good supply of both wood and drinking water.

Isandlwana was such a place.

From there Zulus could be cleared from the Qudeni Forest, Chief Matshana's domain, before the troops moved onto the treeless landscape between the Mhlabamkhosi and Siphezi hills. Chelmsford hoped to establish a base for Durnford's command at the mission station on Little Atala Hill, his final destination before pushing on to Ulundi. The general was attempting to oblige Cetshwayo to keep his warriors together, creating food shortages and discontent. 'we shall oblige him to attack, which will save us going to find him.'

Henry Francis Flynn was an influential advisor to Chelmsford, having grown up with the Zulus and speaking their language fluently. He was the magistrate of M'singa, the Natal district which bordered Zululand including Rorke's Drift. His knowledge of both terrain and natives was boundless, and he gained Chelmsford's ear when he claimed knowledge of the Zulu battle plans. Cetshwayo, he said, was to shelter his force in the Mangeni Hills till the central column had advanced to the point where the Zulus could move with stealth round behind them. He would cut them off from the border, then close in for the kill.

The proposed Zulu strategy made sense. Chelmsford's force could still head boldly for the Zulu capital, but fearful of the Zulus outflanking him and raiding into an unprotected Natal, he decided to clear the border area first. He laboured under the misapprehension, however, that Cetshwayo would avoid fighting a pitched battle if he could, thus his flawed assumption that he would have to starve them into attacking. The prime Zulu strategy was that of full-frontal aggression, the mass charge of thousands, the horns of the buffalo crushing the enemy into oblivion.

But first things first. A priority now for Chelmsford was to establish a base camp at Isandlwana. The Natal Pioneers were put to work levelling the rough, ten-mile trail between there and Rorke's Drift. On January 16th Major William Dunbar and his native troops were hard at work in the Ibashe valley repairing the wagon road when Chelmsford and his staff arrived, on their way to inspect Isandlwana. Dunbar had been ordered to pitch his camp alongside a stream in the midst of heavy scrub where he could easily be surprised by an enemy capable of moving with great stealth when required. He requested permission to move his camp to the other, clearer, side of the stream. 'If Major Dunbar is afraid to stay here,' said Colonel 'Wasp' Crealock, 'we could send someone who is not.'

Dunbar, who had one of the most distinguished war records in the 24th, stormed off in a fury and resigned his commission. Once the atmosphere had cooled, Chelmsford used his notable charm and talked him into withdrawing his resignation.

The road was prepared, and on the 20th the wagons began to roll. The track climbed from the sodden Batshe Valley, crossed a stream, then topped a broad saddle between Isandlwana to the left, and a stony koppie, or small hill, to the right.

What Last Stand Hill was to Lieutenant Colonel George Custer, the shoulder and stony koppie would soon be to Lieutenant Colonel Anthony Durnford.

But what exactly was Isandlwana? In Zulu the word meant 'something shaped like a small hut.' The New World Encyclopedia avoids the issue by calling Isandlwana a 'locality' while some sources call it a 'hill' and others a 'mountain.' Being too little to be a mountain, and too big to be a hill, the craggy mass of rock rises some 700 feet from the landscape, dominating the countryside like a well-worn rhinoceros horn.

At that time it was spelled in a variety of ways including; Insalwana, Isandlana, Isandwhlana, Sandula, Isandula, and so on. The name Isandhlwana eventually emerged to evolve further still into Isandlwana, as the Little Big Horn has evolved into Little Bighorn.

Some saw it the crag shaped 'like a *sphinx*, or Lion, and it is accessible, and that with difficulty, at one or two points only.' The sphinx had been part of the regimental badge of the British 24th Infantry Regiment since the celebrated victory over Napoleon's forces at the Battle of the Nile in 1800, thus it was seen by some as an omen. But what kind? The French had their revenge by capturing half of the First Battalion of the 24th and their colonel in 1810 when they took the British troop ships at sea. Then, during the second Sikh War in 1849, the regiment was bloodily decimated in a poorly executed assault at the Battle of Chilianwalla.

Major Francis Clery of Chelmsford's staff was given the task of selecting the precise camping ground, and asked Inspector George Mansel of the Natal Mounted Police to assist. As they trotted their mounts to the eastern slope where Isandlwana merged with the plain, Clery said 'I think this will do.' Mansel looked with concern at the terrain, noting that both the shoulder of Isandlwana and the stony koppie, which could provide cover to an advancing enemy, commanded the sight. He voiced his concerns, but Clery's mind was made up. 'No,' he insisted, 'this will do.'

Henry Flynn, also present, suggested open, flat ground two miles away where an advance could not be concealed, but Clery ignored him, only requiring endorsement of his chosen ground, apparently.

Mansel posted mounted sentinels at various posts along their front. These were up to five miles away on high ground, visible from the camp. He also posted more to the rear of Isandlwana, but the ones to the front were drawn in closer and those to the rear withdrawn on Clery's orders. 'My dear fellow,' the major said, 'those vedettes are useless there, the rear always protects itself.'

The flat to the east of Isandlwana became a hive of bustling activity as troops tramped in and the wagons were unloaded. Orders were barked, oxen unharnessed, and the camp began to take shape, 750 tents being neatly erected in an area nearly one mile square. There were two officers or 12 men to a tent, also hospital, messing, headquarters, and administration tents.

An old Zulu man was captured as the sentinels moved back on Clery's orders. He was questioned and replied that a big impi, or Zulu army, was on the trail from Ulundi, only to be ignored.

Flynn had told Chelmsford that the Zulus would gather in the Mangeni Valley to the southeast, so British infantry were deployed to hinder any advance from that quarter, and infantry pickets were placed about one mile from the camp. NNC detachments were also posted to the north and northeast, but several officers were not happy with the camp's protection. Crealock may well have been Chelmsford's 'evil genius' but he said to one major who complained about no sentries behind the hill, 'Well sir, if you are nervous we will put a picquet of pioneers there.' But his genius was lacking when he failed to send them. Sub-Inspector Phillips also approached the Wasp with misgivings, but it was Chelmsford who called out, 'Tell the police officer my troops will do all the attacking, but, even if the enemy does venture to attack, the hill he complains about will serve to protect our rear.' And Chelmsford ignored his own regulations which stated that all camps of a permanent nature were to be both entrenched and laagered; the wagons corralled creating a defensive wall. He would later state that the ground was too hard and the wagons were required elsewhere, but the real reason was his underestimation of the camp's danger. A defensive barricade could have been constructed of boxes and mealie bags as it was later at Rorke's Drift, but Flynn had said the Zulu impi would form in the Mangeni Valley, and Chelmsford was convinced that was where the action was going to be. His thoughts were preoccupied with marching there first and giving the enemy a hot reception when they arrived.

But Cetshwayo had other ideas. Supplied with intelligence from a large spy network, he knew the strength of his enemy and their likely intentions. He trod warily when the troops first crossed into Zululand, still hoping to prevent trouble by negotiation, and did not want to antagonize the invaders with a savage response. He wrote:

My troops, although many with me at my kraal, have not yet taken up arms, but are simply waiting for some settlement. The Zulus now, when they hear that the troops are laying waste their country, take the alarm and arm themselves…I am still telling my troops not to fire or throw an assegai; my people are simply firing and stabbing to defend themselves.

The young warriors, however, grew impatient as news arrived of the three advancing columns. They did not want to sit idle while redcoats and their native allies overran their country. Cetshwayo sent out messengers to call up those Zulu regiments to join others who had been with him since the First Fruits Ceremony on January 8th. A warrior of the iNgobamakhosi Regiment recalled, 'a special messenger came from Ulundi telling us to go there immediately as Cetshwayo, our King, had need of us. The white men were even then in their tents at Isandlwana.'

When the warriors arrived they were liberally feasted on beer and beef. Cetshwayo told those who did not possess firearms to bring 'a beast from his place' so they could buy guns. There was no shortage of firearms in Zululand. Gunrunners had been selling guns since the 1830s, and by the 1870s as many as 20,000 had been smuggled in, usually through Delagoa Bay, held by the Portuguese. But the now out-dated muzzleloaders were no match for the breech-loading Martini-Henry, and the Zulu tactics had not changed with the times. They still relied on the mass charge after firing a volley, and closing with the enemy for close combat with assegai and shield. The assegai, named after an African tree, was a spear carried in two different lengths; one of six feet for throwing, effective to about 70 yards, and a shorter, broad bladed weapon for stabbing at close range. The Zulu warrior could also carry a long, wooden club called a knobkerrie, or iWisa, along with his oval shaped, tough cowhide shield, the larger of two versions almost the height of a man and two feet six inches wide. As well as deflecting enemy arms, the shield could be a battering weapon in its own right.

Cetshwayo knew where the three columns had invaded Zululand, and he knew the central column, under Chelmsford, was the one to hit hardest. It was the strongest, so he knew his must strike while he had the numbers and his warriors were fresh. Once this was destroyed, he would unleash his main army on the other two. Captain Ruscombe Poole later wrote of Cetshwayo's tactics after hearing it from him first hand:

> Cetshwayo hoped to be able to crush the English columns, drive them out of the country, defend the border, and then arrange a peace. He knew the English in Natal could not bring a very large force into the field; but he had often been told by white men that they had a very large army beyond the sea. He knew that if the English had persevered in the war, he would get the worst of it in the end.

Cetshwayo had to hit hard and fast and overwhelm his enemy in a short time; his warriors needed to reap the harvest, tend cattle, and labor generally for the maintenance of tribal society. The Zulus could travel fast and light, not weighed down as the British were with supplies and wagons, but, unlike the British, could not keep up a sustained fight. The tribesmen of the North American plains had been in the same position.

At the military kraal of kwaNodwenga, on January 17th, 20,000 Zulu warriors formed into a massive circle to be sprinkled with the ashes of burnt medicines; a ritual of purification. According to one warrior, Nzuzi, Cetshwayo stood in the centre and boomed out this speech:

> I have not gone over the seas to look for the white man, yet they have come into my country and I would not be surprised if they took away our wives and cattle and crops and land. What shall I do? I have nothing against the white man and I cannot tell why they came to me. They want to take me? What shall I do?

There was a spontaneous cry from the massed warriors shouting their defiance. 'Give the matter to us!' they yelled. 'We will go and eat up the white men and finish them off. They are not going to take you while we are here. They must take us first!'

Then Cetshwayo said:

> If you come near the white man and find that he has made trenches and built forts that are full of holes, do not attack him for it will be of no use. But if you see him out in the open you can attack him because you will be able to eat him up.

But Cetshwayo later claimed that he was still open to negotiation. He said he instructed his commander, Chief Ntshingwayo kaMahole, 'not to go to the English troops at once, but to have a conference and then send some chiefs to ask the English why they were laying waste the country and killing Zulus...'

History has not clarified whether or not the Zulus planned to invade Natal, but one deserter claimed that Cetshwayo said:

> You are to go against the column at Rorke's Drift, and drive it back into Natal; and if the state of the river will allow, follow it up through Natal, right up to the

Drakensberg. You will attack it by daylight, as there are enough of you to eat it up, and you will march slowly, so as not to tire yourselves.'

It was late in the afternoon of January 17th when the main part of Cetshwayo's army marched from kwaNodwenga. Their target was the central column under Lord Chelmsford, who had inspected Isandlwana just the day before. Another smaller impi marched the following day under the direction of Chief Godide kaNdlela to engage the southern column, under Colonel Pearson.

The chastised Anthony Durnford, meanwhile, was at the head of his troops marching from Kranskop to Rorke's Drift. A courier appeared on the horizon, rode up, and delivered a letter from Chelmsford dated January 19th:

> No. 3 column moves tomorrow for Isalwana Hill and from there, as soon as possible to a spot about 10 miles nearer to the Forest. From that point I intend to operate against the two Matyanas (chiefs) if they refuse to surrender. One is in the stronghold on or near the Mhlazakazi Mountain; the other is in the Forest. Bengough ought to be ready to cross the Buffalo R. at the Gates of Natal in three days time, and ought to show himself there as soon as possible.
> I have sent you an order to cross the river at Rorke's Drift tomorrow with the force you have at Varmaarks. I shall want you to operate against the Matyanas, but will send you fresh instructions on this subject.

Durnford's command rode into Varmaark's farm and later that day he received orders to take the rocket battery, two companies of the NNC and his mounted troops across Rorke's

Drift. Major Bengough was also to be ready with his force of NNC to cross by January 22nd.

Durnford's column crossed the Buffalo at dusk and set up camp, having passed Otto Witt's Swedish Mission on the Natal side, the house now a hospital and the church a supply store for Chelmsford's column. Durnford wrote to the general requesting fresh orders, then wrote home, 'My movements are to operate against the two Matyanas and if they won't submit, make them.' But he added, 'I am "down" because I am left behind, but we shall see.' At least now that Durnford was in Zululand, he was getting closer to the action.

The two defiant Matshanas were reported to be in the vicinity of the Mangeni Gorge. On the afternoon of January 20th Chelmsford and his staff rode about 11 miles from the Isandlwana camp towards the gorge, moving across a hard, rolling plain dissected by dongas which, they observed, would not hinder wagon travel once some work by the pioneers had levelled the way. The Mangeni Gorge stronghold was a precipitous valley with rocky outcrops on each side, pock marked with caves. The Mangeni River flowed along the valley bottom, splashing over a precipice at the upper end. They saw no signs of Zulus except for a handful of women with bundles on their heads fleeing before their advance.

That night Chelmsford issued orders for a third of his force to march at dawn the following day, January 21st, for a reconnaissance in force. Although he had seen no sign of a Zulu impi that day, he and his party had been seen by the Zulus at a great distance as they closed in from the east. Still believing the threat to be from the Mangeni Gorge, Chelmsford ordered his men to thoroughly reconnoitre the rough terrain to the southeast. Commandant Rupert Lonsdale led out 1,600 Natal native troops to explore, while Major Dartnell and the Natal

Mounted Police followed the same route taken by Chelmsford. The two forces were to meet at the Mangeni Falls, then return to Isandlwana. They marched out without apprehension, and Captain William Penn Symons later wrote of the relaxed mood in camp:

> Every one turned in early that night, not dreaming even of what was in store for the morrow. Indeed so far the invasion had been as autumn manoeuvres in pleasant but hot weather in England. Officers with permission went out alone shooting and prospecting miles from camp, with no thought of risk or danger.

That morning Gamdana, a brother of Sihayo, arrived in camp with another chief to surrender their firearms. Chelmsford was not impressed with the collection of redundant muzzle-loaders and told him their best guns must be in the hands of Zulu warriors. Gamdana petulantly replied that Cetshwayo was sending an impi to eat him up for surrendering his firearms to the British. It had been expected that morning but had not yet arrived. Zulus were in force to the right of Siphezi Hill, to the east, Gamdana added, a vital piece of intelligence which should have prevented the looming disaster. Chelmsford ordered Gamdana to leave, then ordered Lieutenant Edward Browne to lead a small patrol of mounted infantry up the track towards Ulundi with orders to scout as far as Siphezi Hill. The detachment rode out and saw nothing, despite the Zulus main force being close by. As they returned to camp, however, about 30 Zulus on foot and another eight on horseback appeared to their front, blocking the track. Guns cracked and one Zulu fell dead while another was severely wounded. The soldiers galloped through and returned safely to camp. The incident was reported, but Chelmsford, still convinced the Zulus would arrive in the Mangeni Gorge, did not appreciate that Browne had just clashed with scouts of the main Zulu army. He did nothing to follow up with a more thorough reconnaissance, losing his best chance to avert the surprise Zulu attack.

The first night out from the military kraal of kwaNodwenga, the Zulu impi bivouacked on the west side of the White Mfolozi River. They had only marched seven miles, following Cetshwayo's orders not to tire themselves. Some may well have needed to conserve their energy, all ages being present through to their sixties, veterans who had fought the Voortrekkers back in the 1830s. The commander himself, Chief Ntshingwayo, was almost seventy, a short, muscular veteran with a large belly. He marched on foot with the rest, only flanking scouts being mounted. But on the whole the army consisted of the elite, young unmarried men in their twenties and thirties. Most had discarded their regimental ceremonial dress, wearing only headdresses and breechclouts. They exuded a restless energy, eager to smash the foreigners who had dared to invade their homeland. As the army marched, cattle and sheep were driven in at sunset, to be slaughtered, then cooked by thousands of boys, one to every three of four warriors, who followed carrying sleeping mats, dismantled shields and cooking utensils. As the 20,000 tramped towards Isandlwana they left a vast trail of flattened grass still visible five months later. Cetshwayo stayed behind at Ulundi protected by a couple of thousand reserves, older warriors in their fifties and sixties.

On January 19th the Zulu force split into two columns marching parallel and within sight of each other. Ntshingwayo commanded the left wing, and his second-in-command, Mavumengwana, the right. That day they covered nine miles before camping on tableland to the east of Badanango Mountain.

The following day they marched across open country before stopping for the night by Siphezi Hill, where Gamdana, while surrendering his guns the following day, told Chelmsford the Zulu impi had arrived. Cetshwayo later claimed that peace was still on the table, the Zulu leaders of his various regiments meeting to decide which chiefs should be sent to negotiate terms with the British.

Following Gamdana's departure, Chelmsford and his staff rode from the camp to reconnoitre the Nqutu Plateau to the northeast. At about 4 p.m. Major Gossett and Captain Buller, two of the general's aids, galloped up with urgent news. They had been out with Major Dartnell's patrol of Natal Mounted Police and observed a large body of Zulus, estimated at 1,500, moving to their front. Dartnell, with only 200 men, dare not attack until Commandant Lonsdale's 1,600 native troops came to his support. Dartnell intended to remain out that night and keep the enemy under observation. He had been following Chelmsford's route of the previous day towards Mangeni Gorge, so here was proof that Flynn's news had been correct. The general sent a courier to Dartnell with instructions to 'attack if and when he thought fit' and arranged for a pack train to be sent out with rations for the night.

Major Clery was not happy with this development, as he regarded Dartnell's force of Natal Mounted Police, Natal Carbineers and Newcastle Rifles to be mere amateurs when it came to soldiering:

> I had felt from the very first very much adverse to this movement of sending out irregulars under command of irregular officers, amounting to half the force, on a roving commission of this sort. And when word came that they were going to bivouac out, I could not help speaking

strongly to Colonel Glyn on the possibility of this sort of thing dragging the rest of the force into any sort of compromising enterprise that these people may get messed up in.

Glyn, however, did nothing to intervene, Chelmsford's presence having relegated him to a position of little power.

Chelmsford rode back to camp after completing his patrol, ignoring reports of their movements being observed by 14 Zulu horsemen four miles to the northeast of the camp. He also ignored news that Lonsdale's men had captured and tortured two Zulu warriors into revealing that they had left the main Zulu army near Siphezi Hill to visit their mother.

Shadows slowly stretched as day faded to night and a messenger rode into camp from Major Dartnell. He had not received Chelmsford's response to his first communication. The Zulus to his front were growing in strength, now several thousand, and he wanted to know if he should attack the next morning, Lonsdale's two battalions having reinforced him. Chelmsford sent word repeating that he should use his own judgement.

The combined force of Dartnell and Lonsdale had kept up a steady advance towards the Zulus who kept retreating at a distance of two or three miles. Finally the sun fell behind the western horizon amidst a crimson blush, and as twilight spread the elusive enemy could not be kept in sight. These Zulus had done their job well, having been detached from the main army near Siphezi Hill to decoy as many British troops from the Isandlwana campsite as possible.

Dartnell formed his command into a hollow square to wait out the night. Lonsdale's Natal Native Contingent formed three sides and his own mounted men the fourth. The horses were tethered in the centre, and fires were lit, while two companies of NNC were sent out as pickets to prevent any surprise attack. The campfires of the Zulus could be clearly seen glowing in the distance, so the enemy appeared a near and obvious threat.

Lonsdale's native troops were exhausted, their morale at a low ebb. They had marched, under a burning sun, over 20 miles of rough terrain that day, 'rather difficult to get through owing to the thickness of the thorns and the very broken country,' wrote Lieutenant Maxwell of the NNC. They had not eaten since morning and the Zulus, their feared enemies, though constantly falling back, had been growing in numbers throughout the day. And the NNC officers were not happy either, noted Captain Hartford of Lonsdale's staff. 'There was some grumbling among the officers of the Native Contingent, who were tired out, at having to bivouac without food, forage or blankets. Two young officers, Lieutenants Avery and Holcroft, went off without leave, evidently to ride back to camp, but were never seen or heard of again.'

Rations and blankets arrived along with Chelmsford's instructions on the back of four pack horses, but the tinned meat, tea and biscuits supplied were not nearly enough to feed all the troops.

The proposed dawn attack was no longer considered wise due to the increasing numbers of Zulu warriors to their front, so a detachment of Imperial Mounted Infantry were ordered back to camp with a request for British infantry support. The rest of the command attempted to sleep, but the outlying pickets, exhausted and nervous, were ready to shoot at any twig that snapped during the night. Shortly before 2 a.m. gunfire broke out and the camp became a scene of chaos as the outlying pickets retreated on the defensive square firing back into the dark. There was no Zulu attack, fortunately, as

'Not a man would have escaped,' wrote one policeman, 'for our natives were panic stricken and would have caused the greatest confusion in the dark.'

The officers and NCOs cursed and thumped the native troops back into order, but the remainder of the long night was spent in tense anticipation of a Zulu onslaught. The numerous enemy campfires in the distance, however, were a decoy, most warriors having slipped away under cover of dark to rejoin the main army to the northeast of Isandlwana.

The detachment of mounted infantry sent back to request support moved at a snail's pace, hampered by darkness and broken terrain. At 1.30 a.m. Major Clery was roused from his sleep and given Dartnell's request. By lamplight, he had trouble reading the pencilled note on the crumpled piece of notepaper 'that the enemy had shown in increased force and that it would not be prudent to attack them in the morning without some white troops.' Dartnell requested that two or three companies of the 24th Regiment be sent to his aid. Clery woke the general and read him the note.

'Order the 2/24th, 4 guns and all the mounted troops remaining, to get ready to start at daybreak,' replied Chelmsford with little hesitation. He then said, 'Order up Colonel Durnford with the troops, he has to reinforce the camp.'

Colonel Crealock, in the next tent, overheard and walked in. 'Is Major Clery to issue orders to Colonel Durnford?' he queried. Durnford was commander of an independent column, subject to orders directly from the general. 'No,' replied Chelmsford, 'but you do it,'

The order was quickly written out by the Wasp, then copied into his order book, to be lost during the chaos and slaughter to come. In early February of 1879 Crealock claimed his recollection of the order was:

> Move up to Sandhlwana at once with all your mounted men and Rocket Battery—take command of it. I am accompanying Colonel Glyn, who is moving off at once to attack Matyana and a Zulu force said to be 12 or 14 miles off, and at present watched by Natal Police, Volunteers, and Natal Native Contingent. Colonel Glyn takes with him 2-24th Regiment, 4 guns R. A., and Mounted Infantry.

But the 'evil genius' had not counted on his order book eventually being found on the battlefield, though the contents were kept under wraps for some time. The actual instructions to Durnford were:

> You are to march to this camp with all the force you have with you of No. 2 Column. Major Ben Gough is to move to Rorke's Drift as ordered yesterday. 2/24th, Artillery and mounted men with the General and Colonel Glyn move off at once to attack a Zulu force about 10 miles off.

The words 'take command of it' are conspicuous by their absence. Durnford was merely instructed to move to the camp. What was he to do then? Await further orders? Join Chelmsford's assault on the Zulus? Stay put and reinforce the camp? The vague orders were open to a variety of interpretations, especially considering Chelmsford's earlier words to Durnford regarding a commander having 'every latitude' when acting separately in enemy country, and his stated intension for Durnford to 'operate against the Matyanas.'

Lieutenant Horace Smith-Dorrien of the transport staff was given the task of delivering Durnford's orders. He galloped off at once, later recalling:

> It ought to have been a very jumpy ride for I was entirely alone and the country was wild and new to me, and the road little better than a track; but pride in being selected to carry such an important dispatch and the valour of ignorance (for I only realised next day that the country was infested with hostile Zulus) carried me along without a thought of danger.

Major Clery hastened to carry out Chelmsford's orders. Not wanting to give any warning to the enemy or disturb the camp, no bugle sounded and he went directly to each commander and issued instructions. The general was soon dressed and impatient to be on the march, and the troops hastily but quietly dressed, buckled on their ammunition pouches, and grasped rifles and bayonets. They assembled in relative silence, a ripple of excitement moving through the ranks, anxious to give the savage enemy a taste of British firepower.

Not wanting to bother a preoccupied Chelmsford, Clery took it upon himself to issue instructions regarding the camp's defence. Command of the camp would fall on the shoulders of brevet Lieutenant Colonel Henry Pulleine, commanding the 1/24th. Pulleine, born in 1838, had arrived in South Africa during 1879 with an excellent record in administration, but had never seen a shot fired in anger, let alone exercised command in the heat of battle. But, as Clery recalled, 'nobody from the general downwards had the least suspicion there was a chance of the enemy attacking the camp.' Clery later stated that he left these instructions with Pulleine:

> You will be in command of the camp in the absence of Colonel Glyn. Draw in your line of defence while the force with the General is out of the camp. Draw in your infantry outpost line, in conformity. Keep your

Cavalry vedettes still well to the front. Act strictly on the defensive. Keep a waggon loaded with ammunition ready to start at once, should the General's force be in need of it. Colonel Durnford has been ordered up from Rorke's Drift to reinforce the camp.

Pulleine received a visit from Clery in his tent shortly before the troops marched. The major repeated the substance of the orders verbally, Clery later claimed, 'laying stress on the point that his mission was simply to hold and keep the camp.'

Most Zulus had slipped away from their decoy fires near Dartnell to rejoin the main Zulu army, about six miles northeast of the camp in the Ngwebeni valley. Henry Flynn's original intelligence about the Zulus advancing through the Mangeni Valley had been correct. They had planned to move that way guided over the difficult terrain by Chief Matshana, then fall on the rear of the British column. When they arrived near Siphezi Hill, however, the British troops had been spotted in the Mangeni region by Zulu scouts. Realising the British had got wind of their plans, the Zulus knew this could be used to advantage. While the invaders probed the southeast, Ntshingwayo decided to attack from the northeast. He sent Matshana with a few thousand warriors, the force which decoyed Dartnell, to ensure British interest was maintained in the Mangeni region. The main Zulu army, meanwhile, left their position near Siphezi Hill in small detachments and moved with stealth to the Ngwebeni Valley to reform for the attack.

January 22nd was, to the Zulu's, the day of a 'dead moon' and as such not a suitable time for battle. One warrior explained, 'That day the moon had waned. It was not customary to fight at such a time…A young woman does not dance that day…A garden is not reaped, a hunting party is not sent out. It is our equivalent of Sunday.' The Zulus were preparing to rest through the following day, then attack at dawn the next morning, the 23rd, but Cetshwayo later claimed his chiefs were still allowing for consultation with the invaders before fighting.

But the Zulu strategy was working. As Dartnell and his force peered nervously at campfires kept alive by a small force of warriors, the British troops at Isandlwana assembled and prepared to march to their rescue at dawn, January 22nd 1879.

6
THE DIVIDED COMMAND

Morning, June 22nd 1876. The bugle sounded 'Boots and Saddles' and the troopers of the 7th U. S. Cavalry prepared to march. 'To horse' was sounded and each man stood at his horse's head, followed by 'Prepare to mount' then 'Mount.' Moving as one, the soldiers rose into their saddles, and the 'Advance' sounded across the plains. With a jangle of spurs and a muffled whinny of horses, the column of fours moved from the camp below the mouth of the Rosebud, the flags and company colors unfurled. The onlooking soldiers gave cheers of encouragement and waved their hats, as Terry, Brisbin, Custer and Gibbon reviewed the column. Terry had a kind word to say to each officer as he returned the salute, and wished them God speed. Custer shook hands with the three officers alongside him. As he turned his horse to leave, Gibbon suggested he not be greedy and leave a few Indians for the rest of them. Custer said he would not, then rode off after his men. 'Little did we think that we had seen him for the last time,' recalled Grasshopper Jim, 'or imagine under what circumstances we should next see the command, now mounting the bluffs in the distance with its guidons gayly fluttering in the breeze.'

The interpreter Gerard was detained briefly in camp, and later said he heard Terry say 'Custer is happy now, off with a roving command of fifteen days. I told him if he found the

Indians not to do as Reno did, but if he thought he could whip them to do so.'

The troopers carried fifteen day's rations and spare ammunition on pack mules, but there were no Gatling guns, no band, and only a couple of sabres taken along by Lieutenants De Rudio and Mathey; this column was to travel light. Custer said they would eat the mules if required to keep on the hostiles' trail. 'Custer takes no wagons or tents with his command,' he wrote in his despatch to the New York *Herald*, 'but proposes to live and travel like Indians; in this manner the column will be able to go wherever the Indians can.' And the Indian scouts felt that in Custer they had an officer who understood them, as Durnford's black troops felt he understood them. 'Custer had a heart like an Indian,' recalled Red Star, one of his scouts. 'If we left out one thing in our ceremonies, he always suggested it to us. We got on our horses and rode around, singing the songs. Then we fell in behind Custer and marched on.' One scout not marching just yet was Bloody Knife, having furtively sampled the sutler's liquid wares that morning. He would not be fit to catch the column until it had gone into camp that evening. The only other hint of trouble came from some irksome mules which kicked and bucked, throwing their packs. Perhaps these dumb animals were the only ones smart enough to have a hint of what was to come? The command consisted of 31 officers, 566 enlisted men, 35 Indian scouts; also white scouts; mule packers, interpreters, one newspaperman; grand total 647 men. Had Custer taken the 2nd Cavalry troops along, 196 soldiers, he would have had a total of 843 men, while Gibbon would have been left with only 356. What more proof is required that Custer was intended as the strike force? As it was, Gibbon's command would still only count 452 officers, enlisted men, packers etc., Custer having taken seven of his scouts.

The column rode two miles up the Yellowstone before turning south to follow the shallow waters of Rosebud Creek, deriving its name from the wild roses clustered along the grassy banks. It was a running stream, the gravely bed clearly seen through clear water three to four inches deep.

Custer's Indian allies galloped to the front and fanned out, disappearing into the hills to scout the column's advance. A group of Rees on one side of the stream was led by Bobtailed Bull, and another on the other side by Soldier. They were now leaving territory they knew well. Riding to their front were Mitch Boyer and six Crows who were well at home in this terrain. The troops rode on beneath a warm sun for 10 dusty miles alongside cottonwoods, sagebrush and small willows before stopping to bivouac at 4 o'clock. There had been no sign of Indians during that first afternoon's march.

A bugle sounded officers' call as the western sky turned red above the broad Montana horizon. The officers made their way in from their company bivouacs then gathered standing and squatting inside Custer's tent. He explained to them an outline of the campaign, and routine matters were discussed.

Lieutenant Edward Godfrey recalled that Custer said 'we might meet at least a thousand warriors; that there might be enough young men from the agencies, visiting their hostile friends, to make a total of fifteen hundred.'

Trumpet calls would cease from this point on, Custer instructed, except in an emergency. Stable guards were to wake their companies at 3 a.m., the column to march at 5 a.m. They were cautioned to conserve their mules and ammunition. There would be short marches of 25 to 30 miles per day to start with, getting longer as they moved further south. But he also urged cooperation and loyalty, attempting to inspire his men for the fight to come. 'I have perfect confidence in the officers and men of the Seventh,' he said, 'and I don't believe it would be of any use for anybody or any other regiment to try what we could not.' The Seventh was a regiment with factional rifts, however, and Custer said, 'I want it understood that I shall allow no grumbling, and shall exact the strictest compliance with orders from everybody—not only with mine, but with any orders given by an officer to a subordinate.' He also stated that he would listen to suggestions from any officer, providing it came in the 'proper manner'. He said that there had been complaints about him during the march to officers of the department staff, and such criticism must cease, or that the officers offending would be proceeded against as provided for in army regulations. Frederick W. Benteen, the regiment's senior captain and a brevet colonel, had a long-standing rift with Custer and took exception. 'It seems to me you are lashing the shoulders of all to get at some; now, as we are all present, would it not do to specify the officers whom you accuse?'

'Colonel Benteen, I am not here to be catechised by you, but for your own information, will state that none of my remarks have been directed towards you.'

The subject of the 2nd Cavalry and Gatling guns was raised. Benteen was not concerned about the Gatlings but the four companies of cavalry were a different matter. 'I, for one, am sorry you didn't take them,' he said, 'I think we will regret not having them.' He was well qualified to make such an observation. Although not a West Point man like Custer, he had served with distinction throughout the Civil War, being recommended for brigadier general of volunteers, not ratified due to the war's conclusion. He had actually fought Indians before Custer, having done battle with McIntosh's Confederate Indian brigade during the war. He joined the 7th in 1867 with a captain's commission, and was brevetted colonel the following year for defeating a large war party of Cheyenne with only 30 troopers in his command. Benteen and Custer did not blend; the serious, abrasive soldier who just got on with the job, but possibly jealous of the younger 'Boy General' who loved the limelight. One of the charges against Custer at his 1867 court-martial related to the shooting of deserters. 'I had taken the initiative to have Gen. Custer disciplined according with Army Regulations, which was done,' Benteen later wrote. 'It was like a buffalo hunt,' he testified at the Court Martial, 'The dismounted deserters were shot down, while begging for their lives, by General Custer's executioners...Three of the deserters were brought in badly wounded, and screaming in extreme agony. General Custer rode up to them, pistol in hand, and told them if they didn't stop making so much fuss he would shoot them to death.' The 7th was rife with desertion at that time and the regimental doctor testified that Custer later had their wounds tended, the cold-hearted approach being to impress upon the men that no quarter would be given to deserters.

The following year Benteen had been at the Washita, having a horse shot from beneath him, and a sarcastic letter, written to a friend, critical of Custer's abandonment of Major Elliot had found its way into St. Louis and New York newspapers. Custer, thumping his thigh with a whip, had demanded to know who wrote the piece, saying he would whip the offender. Benteen had stepped outside the tent for a moment, checked his revolver, then returned and said he was the man. Custer, stammering with rage, had glared at Benteen but did not raise the whip. 'Colonel Benteen, I'll see you again, sir,' he had said, then dismissed the gathering. Benteen later stated that he confronted Custer again with reporter Randolph Kein present, and that Custer 'wilted like a whipped cur.' During Stanley's Yellowstone Expedition of 1873 Custer refused Benteen compassionate leave when his daughter was dying. Benteen would later write in a personal letter that Custer was 'a murderer, thief and liar—all of which I can prove.'

Such was the relationship between them.

Lieutenant Gibson was unnerved by Custer's talk at the Rosebud campsite, writing in a letter to his wife after the battle 'finally he asked all officers to make any suggestions to him at any time. This struck us as the strangest part of the meeting, for you know how dominant and self-reliant he always was, and we left him with a queer sort of depression.'

Lieutenant Edward Godfrey later wrote:

> This 'talk' of his, as we called it, was considered at the time something extraordinary for General Custer, for it was not his habit to unbosom himself to his officers. In it he showed a lack of self-confidence, a reliance on somebody else; there was an indefinable something that was not Custer. His manner and tone, usually brusque and aggressive, or somewhat rasping, was on this occasion conciliating and subdued. There was something akin to an appeal, as if depressed, that made a deep impression on all present. We compared watches to get the official time, and separated to attend to our various duties. Lieutenants McIntosh, Wallace, and myself walked to our bivouac, for some distance in silence, when Wallace remarked: 'Godfrey, I believe General Custer is going to be killed.' 'Why, Wallace,' I replied, 'what makes you think so?' 'Because,' said he, 'I have never heard Custer talk in that way before.'

At five sharp the following morning Custer mounted and started up the Rosebud followed by two sergeants, one carrying the flapping regimental standard and the other his headquarters flag, a blue and red swallow-tailed guidon bearing crossed sabres.

With a rattle of trappings and a throb of hooves the troops started out after their buckskin-clad leader. They splashed across the Rosebud, following the meandering stream and recrossing five times in the next three miles. Then on the east bank scouts encountered the trail previously discovered by Reno. Following the ruts and traces of tepee poles and ponies' unshod hooves, they came across the abandoned campsite previously spotted by Lieutenant Bradley of Gibbon's command, then continued till they found the next site at Teat Butte. The pack train, always lagging behind, had time to come into view before the troops mounted and continued their march. At the mouth of Greenleaf Creek they rode into the third abandoned campsite located by Reno, spread along both banks of the stream. They continued on till a halt was called at 4.30, then bivouacked 42 miles from the mouth. At sunset the hard-pressed mule train finally made it into camp. Godfrey wrote, 'Everybody was busy studying the age of pony droppings and tracks and lodge trails, and endeavoring to determine the number of lodges. These points were the all-absorbing topics of conversation.'

Some of the men took advantage of this halt to bathe in the stream, and Captain Benteen even took time out to try a little fishing. His results, unfortunately, added nothing to the officers' mess. But the hard riding scouts had no time to share the good night's sleep enjoyed by the troops. Pressing ahead, they kept following the trail along the stream.

The early light of a sunny day rippled on the waters of the Rosebud as the command marched out at 5 a.m., June 24th. Custer would soon reach the point where Reno had abandoned the trail and turned back. Would it continue up the Rosebud, or turn, as was thought possible, towards the Little Bighorn?

This river rose in the foothills of the Big Horn Mountains, some always covered with snow, feeding clear, cold water to the stream's northwesterly, twisting journey. The water sparkled through cottonwood and box elder trees, willows, dogwood, wild roses and berry bushes before flowing into the Big Horn. At the campsite now occupied by Sioux, Cheyenne and some Arapahoe, the waters averaged three feet deep and sixty wide, and the grassy meadows alongside were colorfully splashed with wild flowers.

If the Indian trail stayed on the Rosebud and Custer were to catch his quarry, he would have his hands full fighting up to 1,500 warriors with less than 600 troopers of his own. If the hostiles were on the Little Bighorn there was a chance of support from Terry's column moving from the north. But Custer was, as he told his officers, confident that the 7th could whip any force of Indians they might encounter. But did he actually expect to meet that many hostiles? The campsites they had been examining indicated only about 800 warriors.

The column continued its march up the Rosebud, then scouts galloped back with news of another abandoned campsite to their front. 'The frame of a large "Sun-dance" lodge was standing,' wrote Lieutenant Godfrey, 'and in it we found the scalp of a white man, probably one of General Gibbon's command who had been killed some weeks previously.'

The Sun Dance was the most religious ceremony of the Sioux, the bravest warriors undergoing a torturous routine. Those taking part had their breasts cut by medicine men who wove skewer sticks into the flesh attached to long rawhide ropes running to the top of a long pole. They would dance, leaning back from the pole, the ropes taught, without food, drink or sleep. Finally the skewers would tear right through the flesh, ending the dance. This pain was inflicted to purify the entire tribe, and renew their faith and spiritual bonds. It often took place before unified and determined action, bonding the various bands, and the Indians of the plains now needed this more than ever. Most enlisted men would have been unaware of the significance of the sun dance, but Custer and some other officers with plains experience would have known. The Indian scouts, naturally, were also aware. Red Star later said of the discovery:

> Here was evidence of the Dakotas having made medicine, the sand had been arranged and smoothed, and pictures had been drawn. The Dakota scouts with Custer said this meant the enemy knew the army was coming. In one of the sweat lodges was a long heap or ridge of sand, on which Red Bear, Red Star, and Soldier saw figures drawn indicating by hoof prints Custer's men on one side and the Dakotas on the other. Between them dead men were drawn lying with their heads towards the Dakotas. The Arikara scouts understood this to mean that the Dakota medicine was too strong for them and they would be defeated by the Dakotas.

Sitting Bull had participated in this ceremony, which climaxed with his having a vision of soldiers tumbling upside down into the Sioux village. The desperate Indians saw in this great medicine; a great victory was about to be achieved. It gave them hope, it gave them confidence and high spirits for the fight to come.

A stiff breeze was blowing from the south. Custer's headquarters flag fell to the column's rear. Lieutenant Godfrey picked it up and placed the staff back in the ground, only to have it fall to the rear again. He shifted it to one side and bore it into the ground once more, with sagebrush for support.

Custer informed his officers that they were now penetrating beyond the territory covered by Reno's patrol, and ordered his scouts to fan out and search for signs of diverging Indian trails. His concern was that the hostiles would split up and head in different directions, a favorite tactic if they knew troops were close at hand. To help avoid detection he ordered that the regiment split into two parallel columns, thus reducing dust in the hot, dry conditions, while he rode ahead with two companies.

At 1 p.m. Custer called another halt just beyond the mouth of Muddy Creek. Scout George Herendeen had just informed him of an Indian trail diverging to the left up Lame Deer Creek, which the column had already passed. Custer immediately despatched Lieutenant Varnum and some scouts to check it out. While the troops rested, Varnum followed the trail only to find it swung back to rejoin the main trail, which had changed in character as they marched. Instead of one deep, well-defined trail, it appeared to spread over a wider area, less concentrated with numerous campsites. And the signs were fresher. Perplexed by the change, Custer discussed the possibilities with his scouts. Had the party of Indians they had been trailing broken into separate bands following the sun dance ceremony? The regiment rested for four hours while six Crow scouts were sent ahead on cavalry mounts, giving their own tired ponies a chance to rest. They were to ride ahead as far as possible allowing for a return to camp by sunset. Custer was vexed by the thought that the Indians may be splitting up; perhaps they would escape his grasp.

But it would transpire that the very opposite was happening. The trails were converging, not diverging. The fresh, diffused signs were reservation Indians travelling in bands of various sizes to join Sitting Bull, their tracks obscuring the older, original trail. The village was not scattering but growing larger by the day.

Who in the column realised the truth is hard to tell. Years later Private Henry Brinkerhoff wrote:

> About 2 p.m. we crossed a large Indian trail going directly north and coming from the south, and we then knew that the agency Indians were on their way to join the hostile Sioux camp. All signs pointed to the fact that there were a great many warriors in the bunch, as the trail in some places on the crossing of the Rosebud was a mile wide.

If Private Brinkerhoff knew this as he claimed, how come Custer did not? Perhaps Bloody Knife knew, however, as Brinkerhoff stated that Custer asked Bloody Knife how many Indians were on the trail, to which the scout replied, 'go count the spears of grass on the hills and he'd tell how many Indians there were there.' Custer, according to Brinkerhoff, told Bloody Knife he was crazy. Perhaps Custer, committed to a course of action, did not want to believe the truth, or still believed that no matter how many Indians were before him, they would scatter at his approach without a fight—a delusion shared by Terry, Custer—and later, Lord Chelmsford in Zululand, a mistake that was to cost them all dear.

One of the scouts named Stabbed, a 45 year-old leader of the Rees, rose from the fireside and dashed and darted from one side to the other, as though dodging bullets. 'I want you to tell Custer,' he said to Gerard, the interpreter, 'that I showed him how we fight, for when the soldiers go into the fight they stand still like targets while the Sioux are dodging about, so it is hard to hit them. But they shoot the soldiers down very easily.'

'I know your people,' Custer replied, 'you are truly like the coyote, you know how to hide, to creep up, and to take by surprise.' He probably wished the army-training manual had a section on 'How to fight like an Indian,' but they still preached European convention, as seen in the Civil War, with massed ranks standing and firing at one another, or skirmishers standing five yards apart on a firing line. The days of furtive commando units were yet to come. Custer told the Rees he did not expect them to fight alongside the bluecoats, but to target the enemy pony herd, running it off. They would be only too happy to do this, the wealth of an Indian being judged by how many horses he owned. It would also minimise the chance of Indian allies being taken out by 'friendly' fire.

The command moved out again at 5 p.m. A courier had arrived back an hour before from the Crow scouts with news of a fresh campsite. But as it transpired, this was an older site crossed by a fresh trail, creating confusion. A little further on was the crucial point where the trail diverged towards the Little Bighorn.

The march continued passing several large campsites, the trail now appearing fresh, 'the whole valley scratched up by the trailing lodge poles.' But Custer apparently was still preoccupied with diverging trails as scout George Herendeen recalled 'Towards evening the trails became so fresh that Custer ordered flankers out to the right and left and a sharp lookout for lodges leaving to the right or left. He said he wanted to get the whole village and nothing must leave the main trail without his knowing it.' The command arrived at Busby Bend on the Rosebud as per Terry's schedule, having covered 73 miles in two and a half days. The scouts had been kept very busy, but the pace had been so relaxed that Lieutenant Godfrey had cause to complain, 'The march during the day was tedious.

We made many long halts so as not to get ahead of the scouts, who seemed to be doing their work thoroughly...' Custer may well have wanted that first strike, but he did not needlessly tire men and horses in a rush as some later claimed.

The command halted and set up camp at 7.45 p.m. in a picturesque spot, almost like a man-made park. On their right was a high, steep cliff which helped conceal the regiment, and on the left numerous clusters of wild rose bushes were in full bloom, interspersed with leafy trees to the stream's edge. Fires were lit for cooking, and the troops made the best of a basic meal of bacon, hardtack and coffee. The flames were doused as soon as possible to avoid detection, and the soldiers turned in to get what sleep they could. It was to be a brief halt, the command to march again at 11.30 that same night.

As the sun set a blood red that evening, did any soldier have an inkling that it was the last sunset he would ever see?

At about 9.00 the Crow scouts returned with the news for Custer that was no real surprise; the trail veered away from the Rosebud and, following Davis Creek, headed towards the Little Bighorn. There was an observation point, they said, called the Crow's Nest, on the divide. The trail was so fresh that the village could possibly be spotted when the sun rose next day. Custer had been given freedom of action, but Terry had recommended his continuing along the Rosebud even if the trail did turn towards the Little Bighorn. But that was Reno's old trail. The overlaying trail was fresh; the enemy in striking distance. If he followed Terry's advice and continued south before crossing to the headwaters of the Little Bighorn the hostiles could well have moved away by the time he arrived, especially if they got wind of his presence. And what was the point of searching those headwaters when it seemed certain the village was just over the divide?

Lieutenants Godfrey and Hare lay down to sleep at 9.30. Someone approached through the dark. 'The General's compliments and wants to see all the officers at headquarters immediately.' They groped their way over sleeping men, between cavalry horses, and through thickets of bushes in an attempt to find Custer's tent. No one could tell them where it was, but eventually they saw a single, flickering candlelight in the dark. The officers straggled in from their various commands, then Custer informed them they were to march at once, as the trail led over the divide to the Little Bighorn. He was anxious to get as near the divide as possible before daylight, where the command would be concealed during the day, and give ample time for the country to be studied, to locate the village, and to make plans for a dawn attack on the 26th.

The officers made their way back to their companies and roused sleeping men to their feet. Saddles were hastily thrown on horses' backs, and the men mounted, only to be delayed for an hour and a half by a slow crossing of the pack mules across Mud Creek. But soon the 7th was marching across the divide with Custer in the lead. With him were scouts Bloody Knife, Half-Yellow-Face and interpreter Fred Gerard. Not wanting any Sioux escaping to the south, Custer told Gerard to be sure to have scouts follow any trail to the left, no matter how small. Custer asked the scouts for the latest estimate on the number of hostiles. Between 1500 and 2000 was the their reply.

Custer's written orders included his sending a scout to report to Terry the results of an examination of the upper reaches of Tullock's Fork, a stream flowing into the Big Horn between the two columns. Scout George Herendeen had been detailed to ride with this information, and on the night of the 24th Terry's column could easily be reached, being about 40 miles to the northwest. Had this occurred he would also have carried news of Custer crossing the divide following the fresh trail, the village believed to be close at hand on the lower Little Bighorn; vital news for the campaign commander.

But Tullock's Fork was never scouted, and Herendeen was never sent.

Lieutenant Bradley had written in his diary on June 21st, the day before Custer's departure, 'We have little hope of being in at the death, as Custer will undoubtedly exert himself to the utmost to get their first and win all the laurels for himself and his regiment.'

Although Custer had not pushed his troops, there would appear to be much truth in Bradley's observation. Custer was going to score a 7th Cavalry victory, come hell or high water, and the last thing he wanted was any chance of a forced march by Brisbin's 2nd Cavalry or anyone else interfering with his plans.

The 7th marched through a dusty darkness across the divide. Lieutenant Godfrey recalled:

> Because of the dust it was impossible to see any distance, and the rattle of equipment and clattering of the horses' feet made it difficult to hear distinctly beyond our immediate surroundings. We could not see the trail, and we could only follow it by keeping in the dust cloud. The night was very calm, but occasionally a slight breeze would waft the cloud and disconcert our bearings; then we were obliged to halt to catch a sound from those in advance, sometimes whistling or hallooing, and getting a response we could start forward again.

The eastern horizon had not yet seen dawn's first rays of June 25th when the command halted. Custer wanted news from scouts sent forward to the Crow's Nest high on the divide. The troops now had a substantial break of about 5 hours to nap and prepare breakfast, but despite this claims would be made that the troops were exhausted before the battle because of an all-night march. George Herendeen recalled

'I was not exhausted the morning of the 25th. We had slept until 11 the night of the 24th and then marched till about 2 and then laid down again. We marched again about 7.' They may have had time to rest, but the morning coffee had its shortcomings, the water of Davis Creek being so alkaline even the horses would not drink it.

At dawn's first glow, the scouts on the Crow's Nest scanned the landscape to the west for some sign of the hostile village. They told Lieutenant Varnum they could see a pony herd and smoke from a camp in the valley of the Little Bighorn, although the tepees themselves were obscured from view by intervening bluffs. Varnum wrote: 'we discovered the smoke of a village...The Crows said there were about two or three thousand ponies on the plains twelve miles off, but I could not see them, for their eyes were better than mine.' At 4.45 a.m. Varnum despatched a note to Custer with Red Star and Bull, but then the remaining scouts saw two Sioux warriors on horseback about half a mile to the west. Fearful they might see the smoke from Custer's camp or ambush the couriers, Varnum took Mitch Boyer, Charlie Reynolds and two Indian scouts to eliminate the menace, but they soon lost sight of them. Others saw the warriors from the Crow's Nest headed along Davis Creek towards Custer's command. The scouts spotted six other Sioux hunting buffalo in the distance, and others were seen not far from the base of the Crow's Nest. The chances of surprising the village at dawn the following day were beginning to look bleak.

Varnum's message was safely delivered to Custer who then held a conference with those scouts in camp. Custer squatted in a circle talking Indian fashion. Godfrey recalled:

> The General wore a serious expression and was apparently abstracted. The scouts were doing the talking, and seemed nervous and disturbed. Finally 'Bloody Knife' made a remark that recalled the General from his reverie, and he asked in his usual quick, brusque manner, 'What's that he says?' The interpreter replied, 'He says we'll find enough Sioux to keep us fighting two or three days,' The General smiled and remarked, 'I guess we'll get through them in one day.'

Custer rode bareback to the various companies instructing them to be ready to move at 8 o'clock, the hostile village having been seen 12 to 15 miles off. He then rode to the Crow's Nest to see for himself but, frustrated, had no more luck than Lieutenant Varnum in matching the Indian scouts' acute eyesight. Gerard claimed that he could see the Indians actually moving, kicking up a dust cloud, possibly the arrival of more Sioux. But then the scouts told Custer that they felt the command had been seen by the Sioux riders in the area, and would be riding back to camp to spread the news. Red Star recalled:

> Custer said: 'This camp has not seen our army, none of their scouts have seen us.' Big Belly replied, 'You say we have not been seen. These Sioux we have seen at the foot of the hill, two going one way, and four the other, are good scouts, they have seen the smoke of our camp.' Custer said, speaking angrily: 'I say again we have not been seen. That camp has not seen us, I am going ahead to carry out what I think. I want to wait until it is dark

and then we will march, we will place our army around the Sioux camp.' Big Belly replied: 'That plan is bad, it should not be carried out.' Custer said: 'I have said what I propose to do, I want to wait until it is dark and then go ahead with my plan.'

Custer rode back to the regiment to find it four miles closer than he expected, having advanced without his orders before halting again shortly after 10 a.m. He was irritated at this breach of discipline, but worse news was to come. Mitch Boyer reported seeing two Indians riding away 'as fast as they can go' and he had seen two others herding loose horses. Then Captain Tom Custer rode up to report that soldiers of Company F had returned down the trail to pick up a load of hardtack dropped along the way. They had found Indians breaking open the boxes, then exchanged shots before the hostiles galloped off into the hills. Custer could now no longer deny the truth; the regiment had been seen. He now thought he had little choice but to attack before the village could be struck and the Indians scatter.

Custer informed his company commanders that the order of march would be in accord with those who reported ready to move. Captain Benteen did not hesitate to say his troop was always ready, and he was given the advance. Custer then reminded the Indian scouts that it was their job to run off the Sioux ponies. The Ree scout, Stabbed, encouraged his fellow tribesmen to fight bravely. He had brought with him medicine to make their hearts strong, and proceeded to ceremoniously rub clay from their homeland on the warriors' chests. They were now ready to fight their ancient enemies on the other side of the divide. And appreciating the numbers they would be confronting, the Rees must have realised that not all would come back alive.

The order to mount up was given, then 'Forward' and the 7th Cavalry moved out under a rapidly warming sun towards the Little Bighorn. The column halted shortly after midday and Custer prepared his next move. The regiment, he decided, was to be divided into three fighting battalions with the pack train as a separate, fourth unit. Major Reno would command companies A, G, and M, and most of the scouts; Captain Benteen would command companies D, H, and K, and Custer would retain command of companies C, E, F, I, and L, the largest with 221 men. This included some scouts and Mark Kellogg, the newspaper man who had written in his last despatch that he would be with Custer *at the death*. 'How true' the editor would write when detailing the calamity. The 7th had no Company J, for fear verbal orders would be confused with Company A.

No doubt Captain McDougall was chagrined to be assigned to escort the pack train with Company B, thinking he would miss the action. But he would see more than enough bullets flying over the next few days. His slower command was to follow Custer's advance.

Custer, mounted on his fast and spirited Kentucky thoroughbred, Vic, was ready for action, dressed in buckskin trousers and a cool blue shirt, his buckskin jacket rolled up on the back of his saddle. Each trooper had 50 rounds of ammunition in his cartridge belt, another 50 in his saddlebag, and there was reserve ammunition in the mule train packs. He ordered Captain Benteen's battalion to veer off to the southwest, saying he did not believe the Indians were to their front; strange considering his scouts had reported seeing the village from the Crow's Nest, and they were now following the fresh trail towards it. There was no trail veering to the left for Benteen to follow, but he set out at 12.12 p.m. 'My orders were to proceed out into a line of bluffs about four or five miles away,' Benteen recalled, 'to pitch into anything I came across and to send back word to Gen. Custer at once if I came across anything.' He was to send an officer and six men in advance to scan the upper valley of the Little Bighorn. Lieutenant Gibson was selected and Benteen lent him his field glasses for the task. But if Custer seriously thought Benteen would encounter hostiles, why did he not provide any of the 35 sharp-eyed Indian scouts?

The march continued with the battalions of Reno and Custer, on the right, moving parallel. About one mile further on Custer sent a galloper instructing Benteen to move to the next line of bluffs if nothing was seen. After another mile's advance he sent yet another rider giving Benteen instructions to explore the valleys further on. And this is where Benteen's orders become blurred. Lieutenant Gibson was not present when Custer issued Benteen's verbal orders, but later wrote in a letter that they were to 'hurry and rejoin the command as soon as possible.' Benteen wrote in his report that after searching the bluffs, he carried out his other instructions, 'to return with the battalion to the trail the command was following.' And the following August he told a newspaper man that he was to 'join the main trail.' But over two years later at the Reno Court of Inquiry he said 'There was no plan at all. My orders were valley hunting ad infinitum...I consider that I violated my orders when I struck to the right.'

So when was Benteen telling the truth; after the battle, or at the inquiry?

Immediately after the disaster all were enraged and Custer was accused of disobeying orders, thus all surviving officers were anxious, no doubt, to be seen as having obeyed *their* orders. Benteen did not get within several miles of the

Little Bighorn, so it was in his interest that rejoining Custer's trail appeared to be in accord with his orders. Once the furore had abated and he had been hailed for the bravery which would eventually earn him a brevet to brigadier general, he apparently felt it was time to set the record straight. He had nothing to gain by doing this, and something to lose; his own credibility when it came to writing truthful reports. Despite this, he repeatedly emphasized the lack of any order to return to Custer's command. Other officers made statements tending to back Benteen: 'There was no plan communicated to us,' said Reno, 'if one existed the subordinate commanders did not know of it.' And Lieutenant Wallace stated, 'There was no announcement made to Reno as to junction with Benteen that I know of. There was no plan for the reuniting of the 3 battalions that I ever heard of.' Lieutenant Edgerly stated that Benteen was to 'move to the left at an angle of about forty-five degrees and pitch into anything he came to…those were all the orders I heard.'

Custer's own actions, or lack of them, would support these claims.

Reno and Custer lost sight of Benteen as they continued their advance, their scouts to the fore. At about 2 p.m. a lone tepee on a deserted campsite came into view with the army scouts clustered about. Inside was the body of a dead warrior who had been killed in the fight with Crook's column on July 17th.

'Here are your Indians, running like devils!' Custer looked up to see Fred Gerard waving his hat from the top of a nearby rise. What he had seen were tepees, a pony herd and a party of mounted Sioux riding along the right side of the river about three miles away. Also on the bluffs to their front were a small number of mounted warriors. They did not act as though surprised by the troops' appearance and kept far enough in advance to invite pursuit. But then trouble erupted with the Indian scouts who, not liking the odds, refused to pursue the Sioux. Custer gave them a tongue lashing, accusing them of being cowards. 'If any man of you is not brave, I will take away his weapons and make a woman of him.' One Ree replied through the interpreter, 'Tell him if he does the same to all his white soldiers who are not as brave as we are, it will take him a long time, indeed.' The scouts laughed at this exchange, but decided to do as Custer wished.

Custer beckoned Reno over to him and said,' You will take your battalion and try to bring them to battle and I will support you.' As Reno rode off he added, 'And take the scouts with you.' Custer had sent Benteen, a proven Indian fighter, off across empty bluffs with no scouts, and now ordered the inexperienced Reno to commence the attack.

The major led his column towards the river and at 2.43 p.m. the adjutant, Lieutenant William Cooke, rode up to confirm Custer's orders. 'Gen. Custer directs you to take as rapid a gate as you think prudent and charge the village afterward and you will be supported by the whole outfit.'

Custer had sent couriers with orders distancing Benteen's battalion, but now, at this vital time, failed to send orders to rejoin the command. Why was a 'Be quick,' message not sent now? The 'whole outfit' was unable to support Reno or anyone else, Benteen's battalion not coming into action for over one and a half crucial hours. 'If different parts of a command were expected to cooperate,' Benteen recalled, 'I should think it very necessary to communicate orders to other officers...'

Reno, taking the advance, did not gallop to the attack knowing the horses must be conserved for the coming fight. Both his battalion and Custer's moved forward three miles at the trot, with most Indian scouts to the front and flanks of Reno's command. The pony herd seen by Gerard was still kicking up a cloud of dust. Custer asked the Crow scout, White-Man-Runs-Him, what the haze meant. 'The Sioux must be running away,' he replied.

Reno led his battalion forward, cresting the bluffs above the Little Bighorn, then down the slopes to a natural ford across the stream. The scouts had positioned themselves on bluffs where they could see a vast number of tepees standing, not being struck for flight as was previously thought. Shrieking squaws, crying babies and the elderly, intermingled with barking dogs, quickly fleeing north on horse and foot, caused some of the dust cloud. But even more dust rose from ponies being driven into the village by young warriors eager for the coming fight. Despite Sioux having been seen near the column, it seems advance warning did not reach the village, or was largely ignored. But they now knew troops had arrived, and were moving to attack, not run, those days were over. Sitting Bull's vision had prophesised a great victory. 'A bird, when it is on the nest spreads its wings to cover the nest and eggs to protect them,' he said. 'It cannot use its wings for defence but it can cackle and try to drive away the enemy. We are here to protect our wives and children, and we must not let the soldiers get them.'

This was the day for the red man of the plains to make *his* last, angry stand against broken treaties and the theft of his land. Hokay hey! This is a good day to die! A scout galloped up to interpreter Gerard and gave him the news, 'Major Reno, 'said Gerard, 'the Indians are coming up the valley to meet us.' Gerard then rode up to Adjutant Cooke who was about to return to his commander and told him, as 'Custer should know it.'

Reno's battalion finished crossing the river once their thirsty horses had stopped to drink, then the men dismounted and tightened their saddle girths. As the troops mounted and moved into battle line, the major looked ahead and could see that Gerard was right, mounted warriors appearing to his front. He took action of his own to inform Custer. 'I sent back word twice,' recalled Reno, 'first, by a man named McIlargy, my striker, to say the Indians were in front of me in strong force. Receiving no instructions, I sent a second man, Mitchell, a cook...I still heard nothing to guide my movements and so proceeded down the valley to carry out my orders.' Custer and some of his battalion appeared on the bluffs across the river on Reno's right. They cheered and waved their hats, then rode off, disappearing from view. Unconfirmed stories abound regarding every facet of the Battle of the Little Bighorn, from sole survivors to supposed witnesses of the last stand. Trooper Theodore Goldin later claimed to have delivered a message, contents unknown, from Custer to Reno just before his retreat from the trees. But Reno denied receiving any communication from Custer and no one corroborated Goldin's claim.

Custer now had three separate combat battalions with no communication or battle plan between them, the most astonishing aspect the lack of any attempt to contact Benteen. If Custer seriously thought there were Indians to the south, Benteen could now be fighting a Sioux war party, attacking another village further upstream, or still searching through empty bluffs. A dust cloud, if visible, would have made finding him all the easier.

Two of Reno's companies formed across the valley in battle line while another was held in reserve. But as more warriors appeared, Reno realised reserves were a luxury he could ill afford. He ordered them forward to join the front line, then gave the order to advance. Private William Taylor recalled:

On our right was the heavily wooded and very irregular course of the river, flanked by high bluffs. On our left were low hills near which we could see a part of the pony herds, and as we came nearer, could distinguish mounted men riding in every direction, some in circles, others passing back and forth. They were gathering up their ponies and also making signals. We were then at a fast walk. Soon the command was given to 'trot.' Then as little puffs of smoke were seen and the 'Ping' of bullets spoke out plainly, we were ordered to charge.
Some of the men began to cheer in reply to the Indians war whoops when Major Reno shouted out, 'Stop that noise,' and once more came the command, 'Charge!' 'Charrrge!'

The trotting horses leapt forward into a gallop. The Battle of the Little Bighorn had begun.

***

The sun was barely shimmering over the eastern hills on January 22nd 1879, when Chelmsford and his staff, with a small escort, led the relief column from Isandlwana. Imperial mounted Infantry, six companies of redcoats from the 2/24th, four pieces of artillery, and a company of the Native Contingent followed them. The infantry carried one day's rations and, being in light marching order, no greatcoats or blankets. Each man had only 70 rounds of ammunition instead of the 100 normally carried when action was expected.

Lieutenant Henry Hartford remembered seeing 'a more-or-less low-lying dark cloud' hanging over the camp like some ill omen, 'And there it hung for the best part of the morning, frowning as it were, over the fated camp. I have never forgotten it.'

At about 6.30 that morning Chelmsford joined Major Dartnell's command in the Hlazakazi Hills. The Zulus, so prominent the day before, were now nowhere to be seen, and Dartnell was instructed to send out mounted scouts to locate their strength. But soon that strength seemed to make itself apparent as black lines of warriors appeared on distant heights. Most of the Zulus who had confronted Dartnell were returning to the main impi, but Chief Matshana's men had remained behind as a distraction, which worked as they moved to occupy a projecting spur commanding the plateau beneath.

Convinced the main Zulu force was confronting him, Chelmsford ordered Lonsdale's two battalions of NNC to move forward and occupy the spur before the Zulus could get there. Colonel Glyn was instructed to march with the four 7-pounders and the redcoat reinforcements up a valley which lay to the left of the spur. The Mounted Infantry were ordered to cover the left flank, the Natal Mounted Police and mounted volunteers the right.

The Zulus then started withdrawing without firing, deliberately luring the command forward. But due to rough terrain about 300 of their number were cut off from the main force. They took refuge in several caves but the Natal Carbineers and a large detachment of the Native Contingent flushed them out, killing 50 in the process. The main force of Zulus moved off unscathed to Isipezi Hill, about six miles from the advance of the mounted troops. Captain Penn Symons of the 2/24th recalled:

> We marched twelve miles. We then saw the enemy in scattered bodies of from 10 to 500 dispersing and retreating in front of us in all directions. We followed them. It was like hunting a shadow, or worse than a shadow, as men, who well knew the Zulus, their character and tactics, declare that the cattle which had been seen,

and the retreating bodies of men, were simply a decoy to entice us away from the camp.

Chelmsford became frustrated as the Zulus played will-o-the-wisp, unable to bring about any form of decisive combat. He was disappointed that 'we were going to have our day's work for nothing,' Major Clery recalled. Any thought of the Zulu retreat being a ruse did not enter Chelmsford's head.

But then something did happen which should have sent alarm bells ringing. At 9.30, as Chelmsford watched a party of Zulus being chased towards Siphezi Hill, a courier galloped up. He handed Captain Hallam Parr of Glyn's staff a piece of pale blue paper which read:

'Staff Officer—Report just come in that the Zulus are advancing in force from left front of the camp. (8.5 a.m.). H. B. Pulleine, Lt. Col.'

The note was handed to Major Clery who read it, then handed it to Chelmsford who appeared quite unperturbed as his eyes scanned the lines.

'What is to be done on the subject?' Clery asked.

'There is nothing to be done on that,' Chelmsford replied.

Clery later wrote, 'I said nothing more; but the fact is, whether from over-work or other causes, the General has got rather irritable since we knew him, and particularly touchy about suggestions being made to him.'

Chelmsford issued some orders regarding troop deployments, then turned his glass on the camp, visible 12 miles away. Seeing nothing of consequence, he despatched two officers up the slope of a nearby hill armed with powerful telescopes for a better look. He then ordered Captain Alan Gardner of Glyn's staff back to the camp with orders for Pulleine 'to send on the camp equipage and supplies of the troops camping out, and to remain himself at his present camp.'

But the next important thing on the agenda was food. While some troops in the field had not eaten for 24 hours, the staff enjoyed a leisurely hot drink and a hearty breakfast. An exhausted Commandant Hamilton-Browne and his hungry battalion of Natal Native Contingent intruded on the scene:

> I shall never forget the sight of that peaceful picnic. Here were the staff quietly breakfasting and the whole column scattered over the country! Over there the guns unlimbered, over the hills parties of mounted infantry and volunteers looting the scattered kraals for grain for their horses, a company of the 24th one place and another far away.

Chelmsford did, however, order Lieutenant Colonel Harness to get his four guns limbered and march with two companies of redcoats to the Magogo Valley. Hamilton-Browne was told to return to the Isandlwana campsite and, on the way, search through the ravines to flush out any Zulus close to the camp. On the return trip he encountered two Zulu warriors, killing one and capturing the other, who admitted scouting for the main Zulu impi located to the northeast of the vulnerable camp. A message was sent back to Chelmsford who later denied its arrival.

The two officers, Symons and Milne, who had ascended the heights to view Isandlwana through powerful telescopes, 10 miles away, could see nothing out of the ordinary; tents pitched and all peaceful. But they did note some large bodies of Zulus in the vicinity, and other dark patches they took to be oxen. One group of Zulus near the base of Siphezi Hill withdrew as Mounted Infantry commanded by Colonel Russell approached in pursuit of fugitives. Russell later reported that the 'hill was covered with the enemy in very large numbers.'

Symons and Milne, having spent the best part of an hour at their task, scrambled back down and reported their observations to Chelmsford at about 11 a.m. Convinced there was no threat to the camp, Chelmsford, having finished breakfast, moved out with his staff towards the Mangeni Valley to choose a suitable location for the column's next campsite. They rode through the hills for an hour, quite out of touch with the troops. But had they been with Lieutenant Colonel Harness and his four guns, they would have heard the boom of distant gunfire erupt from the direction of Isandlwana. Lieutenant Mainwaring, part of Harness' escort, galloped to a hilltop and 'distinctly saw the firing and the shells bursting on the western slopes of the range.' As he headed back, he saw swarms of Zulus on the plain below. Captain Hugh Church volunteered to ride and investigate, and Lieutenant George Banister peered towards the camp through his field glasses. He could see, 'where our lines of skirmishers were by the puffs of smoke and could also distinguish kaffir lines.' They all peered with envy at the distant battle never doubting who was getting the worst of it, 'cursing our luck being out of it.' But then Captain Church galloped back, the alarmed look on his face anything but one of envy. He had encountered a British sergeant at the base of the hill with an urgent message from Commandant Hamilton-Browne: 'For God's sake send every man back to the camp, it is surrounded and will be taken unless helped at once.' Hamilton-Browne and his battalion of NNC, six miles from Isandlwana, had seen three massive columns of Zulus cutting off his march towards the camp. Recognising the looming disaster, he had dug in and sent the message for help. 'How very amusing,' said a sceptical Crealock, 'Actually attacking our camp! Most amusing!'

Perhaps the Wasp's staff did not take Hamilton-Browne too seriously because he was a volunteer officer with a reputation for being an adventurer fond of creative yarns, especially about his own past. He claimed to have been a Papal Zouave, and fought not only Maoris in New Zealand, but Indians in the USA. Perhaps he was one of the many who would, in years to come, claim to be the sole survivor of Custer's Last Stand?

Colonel Harness, however, took the threat seriously. He had in his charge four guns and two companies of escorting redcoats. He 'at once turned back, and the men of the 24th on being told that the camp was in danger, and that they must push on with all speed, gave a cheer, and set off home with a will.'

But the spirited dash was short-lived. Major Gossett of Chelmsford's staff rode up demanding to know 'what we meant by moving,' said Lieutenant Bannister. A hurried explanation of the camp's plight made no difference. Gossett 'utterly ridiculed the idea of any assistance being necessary.' He warned Harness that he would have to take the responsibility of disobeying orders if he continued marching back to camp. Harness complied and sent Lieutenant Parsons of the artillery galloping off to locate Chelmsford and inform him of the predicament. So Harness sat fidgeting in frustration while the crash of desperate gunfire continued.

Parsons soon returned with orders from Chelmsford to withdraw towards the Mangeni River. One can only imagine Harness' disgust. Chelmsford would later deny having ever received either of Hamilton-Browne's messages regarding the threat to the camp, and never admitted ordering the withdrawal of Harness. But he ascended the Mdutshana hill at about 1.15 and peered back towards Isandlwana.

Noggs wrote:

Every field glass was levelled at the camp. The sun was shining brightly on the tents but all seemed quiet. No signs of firing or any engagement could be seen and although bodies of men moving about could be distinguished, yet they were not unnaturally supposed to be our troops.

Chelmsford began his return from the location of the proposed next campsite after 2 o'clock that afternoon, having ordered his infantry to bivouac there the following night. He claimed that at this time he had no fears for the camp's safety, but Colonel Crealock of his own staff was told of cannon fire being heard from Isandlwana at 1.15, then:

> About 1.45 p.m., however, a native appeared on a hill above us, gesticulating and calling. He reported that heavy firing had been going on around the camp. We galloped up to a high spot, whence we could see the camp perhaps 10 or 11 miles distant. None of us could detect anything amiss; all looked quiet. This must have been 2 p.m. The General, however, probably thought it would be well to ascertain what had happened himself, but not thinking anything was wrong, ordered Colonel Glyn to bivouac for the night where we stood.

Chelmsford mounted and, with staff officers and forty mounted volunteers, set out for Isandlwana. There would be a rude shock awaiting him on his arrival.

Following Chelmsford's march from the Isandlwana campsite that morning, Colonel Pulleine, following Clery's instructions, had sent orders for the infantry sentinels to be drawn back in closer to the camp. Some lookouts were sent scrambling to the top of Isandlwana, however, and others were left on the Tahelane Ridge to the north. Cavalry outposts, each consisting of two Natal Carbineers, were also left in their forward positions, the farthest being over six miles to the east on Nyezi Hill.

Troopers Villiers Hawkins and Walwyn Barker were stationed on a low ridge along the track to Mangeni Gorge. Horsemen were seen approaching from the east, first taken for British, but soon recognized as mounted Zulus. Hawkins and Barker galloped down the slope back towards the camp and soon encountered their commander, Lieutenant Scott, and reported the sighting. They started out for Isandlwana and Zulus appeared on the ridge they had just left, and two more Carbineers rode up reporting 'thousands' of Zulus to the left of the camp. Trooper Whitelaw was sent back to camp on the double, and it was his report that prompted Colonel Pulleine to send the warning message to Chelmsford at 8.05 a.m. of Zulus 'advancing in force from the front left of the camp.' Perhaps Pulleine should have mentioned Whitelaw's 'thousands' as this may have enticed more interest than Chelmsford's 'There is nothing to be done.' Pulleine may have thought Whitelaw's report an exaggeration, but in Zulu terms 'in force' could well mean thousands.

Pulleine ordered Whitelaw to return to Scott, watch the Zulus, and send back reports of their movements.

A bugle sounded Column Alarm and men moved from their tents, rifles in hand, and formed up. Pulleine's command consisted of five companies of the First Battalion, 24th Regiment, one company of the Second Battalion, four companies of the 3rd Natal Native Contingent, two 7-pounder guns; a squadron of mounted troops, and a small detachment of Natal Native Pioneers; grand total, 1241 of which 891 were European and 350 African. But some of these were cooks, bandsmen, blacksmiths and farriers. Wagon drivers and other civilians brought the overall number to almost 1,600 men.

The troops saw between 1000 and 2000 warriors on hills about two miles off. Many were elated at the thought of some action at last. 'We congratulated ourselves on the chance of our being attack,' recalled Lieutenant Henry Curling, 'and hoped that our small numbers might induce the Zulus to come on.' Curling noted the paucity of redcoats actually available for the firing line at that time. 'The companies were very weak, no more than 50 in each, and there were only six of them in all...I suppose that no more than half the men left in camp took part in its defence as it was not considered necessary and they were left as cooks etc.'

Pulleine did not take the threat seriously at this early stage. One soldier said the men were 'marched below the Native Contingent Camp where they waited for orders for about half an hour. They were then sent back to their own Camp where they stood under arms about three quarters of an hour.'

While the troops marched to and fro reports of many Zulus to the left of Isandlwana kept arriving from various outposts. Lieutenant Chard arrived in camp from Rorke's Drift at about 9.30, and later recalled seeing 'the enemy moving on the distant hills, and apparently in great force.' Trooper Arthur Adams of the Buffalo Border Guard was on sentry duty with others on a high hill overlooking a deep valley. A massive Zulu army moved into sight which they estimated at 'between 25,000 and 30,000.' The troopers moved with all haste back to camp and reported their sighting to a British officer who was still in bed. He 'pooh-poohed the idea that the Zulus would attack the camp.' Finding no heed being taken, Adams and his comrades resolved to ride back towards Natal if the Zulus attacked.

Oxen were spread about the camp, so Pulleine ordered that they be inspanned; tied to the yokes so as not to hinder troop movements through the camp, but he still did not take the threat seriously enough to laager the wagons, or strike the tents to allow an unimpeded line of fire.

At 3 a.m. that morning Lieutenant Colonel Durnford had received the message from Crealock stating, 'You are to march to this camp with all the force you have.' He read it and said, 'Just what I thought, we are to proceed at once to Isandlwana. There is an impi about eight miles from the camp, which the General moves out to attack at daybreak.' But what exactly he was supposed to do following his arrival was uncertain. He had been out on a foraging mission when the order arrived, but quickly returned to his command. There was a bustle of activity as horses were saddled, weapons and ammunition checked. Durnford led the column out mounted on Chieftain. Dressed in his usual cavalier's outfit; blue jacket, slouch hat with red crown, leather belts, hunting knife, revolver, boots and spurs, he must have looked every bit as impressive as the buckskinned Custer setting out for the Little Bighorn. But unlike Custer his moustaches flowed, this long hair not cut short. Behind Durnford were five troops of the Natal Native Horse, the rocket battery, then two companies of the Natal Native Contingent; a total of 526 men. In their dust plodded the ox-wagons carrying supplies.

As the command neared Isandlwana a horseman approached; Lieutenant Chard of the Royal Engineers riding back to his post at Rorke's Drift. He informed Durnford that Zulus on hills to the north of the camp appeared to moving towards Rorke's Drift. Durnford was concerned for the safety of the slow moving ox-wagons, far to the rear. The NNC were also some way behind the horsemen, and Durnford asked Chard to take a note to them instructing Captain Nourse's D company to escort the rocket battery and Captain Stafford's E company to protect the supply train.

At 10 a.m. Durnford rode at the head of his column into the bustling campsite alongside Lieutenant Charles Raw of the Natal Native Horse. Raw had been one of those courageous five who had volunteered to stand with Durnford at Bushman's River Pass. 'We found the troops drawn up in front of the camp and the oxen inspanned,' Raw later wrote, 'There were a few Zulus on the ridge in front of the camp about two miles off.' Durnford ordered his men to dismount, then walked with some of his officers towards the headquarters tents at the rear, backing onto the massive bulk of Isandlwana. As he arrived, Durnford noticed a body of about 400 Zulus on a ridge to the right, then a sentry brought word that they appeared to be moving away. Durnford immediately despatched six scouts to see if a larger body was anywhere in sight.

He entered the tent to be greeted by Lieutenant Colonel Pulleine who quickly gave a summary of the troops at hand and his orders to defend the camp. Lieutenant Francis Cochrane of Durnford's command later said:

> The news was that a number of Zulus had been seen since an early hour on top of the adjacent hills, and that an attack had been expected. In consequence the following disposition of troops had been made: the natives of Lonsdale's contingent were on outpost duty on the hills to the left; the guns were in position on the left of the camp; the infantry were turned out, and formed in column in the open space in front of the General's tent. The wagons etc. were inspanned. Constant reports came in from the scouts on the hills to the left, but never anything from

the men on top of the Isandhlwana hill, that I heard. Some of the reports were: 'The enemy are in force behind the hills on the left,' 'The enemy are in three columns,' 'The columns are separating, one moving to the left rear, and one towards the General,' 'The enemy are retiring in every direction.'

Lieutenant Walter Higginson of the NNC had made this last report. He had sent lookouts to the top of Isandlwana at Durnford's request. The Zulus are 'retreating' they reported.

'Here are your Indians, running like devils!' Gerard had called to Custer from his vantage point. Durnford was about to make the same mistake of believing what he was told.

'Ah! Is that so?' said Durnford. 'Well we will follow them up.' Durnford said he wanted to prevent the 'retreating' Zulus from joining up with those opposing Chelmsford. In marked contrast to Custer, he now sought reinforcement, asking Pulleine if he would give him two companies of redcoat infantry to back him up. Pulleine objected, saying that he did not think he would be justified in that course of action, his orders being to 'defend the camp.'

Durnford outranked Pulleine, but knew they must both abide by Chelmsford's orders. 'Very well,' he said, 'perhaps I had better not take them. I will go with my own men.'

This is where the delineation of Durnford's responsibilities became obscure. Did he as the senior officer present inherit Pulleine's orders to stay and defend the camp? He had received no such instruction directly, and Chelmsford, on the 19th, had informed Durnford his command, a separate column, was required for action 'against the Matyanas.' But Durnford's decision to go on the offensive would lead to his being charged with having disobeyed orders, as Custer would be charged with disobeying orders for his decision to follow the Indian trail and attack the Sioux village before Terry's arrival.

Durnford's current command consisted of only four companies of Natal Native Horse, having despatched part of his force to protect the rocket battery and supply wagons. He sent Captain William Barton, an Irish adventurer who had seen much action in South America, with two companies to the Nqutu Plateau, northeast of the camp. It was his task to drive the enemy back into the valley below the plateau. Durnford planned to march to his right with the remaining two companies up the Ulundi road to strike the Zulus if they attempted to move from the valley onto the easterly plain. The plan bore a marked resemblance to Reno's orders to charge the village while Custer attacked from the right flank.

'If you see us in difficulties you must send and support us,' said Durnford to Pulleine, who readily agreed, thus arranging for reserves to be brought up if required, unlike Custer who had ignored Benteen's battalion when ordering the attack.

Major Russell arrived in camp with the rocket battery and the escorting native troops. Durnford quickly explained the situation and issued his orders. Durnford and his two companies, 102 men, mounted up and rode smartly up the Ulundi track, leaving about 20 minutes after Barton, having less ground to cover. Russell's rocket battery, carried by mules, followed, but were not able to keep pace with the faster moving horsemen. Durnford's force was divided, like Custer's; Barton's command on the left to strike the Zulus, his own native horse and the rocket battery on the right to hit them in the flank. Unlike Custer, he had deployed all available men to fight, but even this would be to no avail, Durnford's detachments and those troops in the Isandlwana camp looking at odds of about fourteen to one, far less favorable than those encountered by the 7th Cavalry.

As Durnford rode he could still see Zulus retreating along the Nqutu Plateau. 'If they are going towards the General we must stop them at all hazards,' he said. Then the sound of galloping hooves approached from the rear. A breathless Carbineer caught up with startling news; the enemy retreat was a ploy, and the great Zulu army had been seen not far from the camp. A small patrol of Natal Carbineers had been scouting several miles to the northeast of Isandlwana when they encountered massed Zulu warriors squatting, hidden in a valley.

No doubt Durnford felt much the same as Custer when told by Adjutant Cooke that the Indians were not running, but standing to fight. Realising he had been outfoxed, Durnford made some choice remarks about the scouts he had deployed before leaving camp. He wheeled Chieftain about and gave the order to ride back, but just as the troops turned, a crash of gunfire was heard a few miles away on the left. As the Little Bighorn had commenced with Reno's attack to Custer's left, so now did Isandlwana commence with Barton's attack to Durnford's left.

Captain Barton's two companies, following Durnford's orders, had moved from the camp up onto the Nqutu Plateau by a wide spur that joined the northern end of Isandlwana. He had 107 men under company commanders Lieutenants Charles Raw and Joseph Roberts. The two companies separated, Barton staying with Roberts, doing a circuit to the left quite reminiscent of Benteen's southern excursion, then moving back towards Raw as he advanced, the two columns converging. Raw's men, crossing rugged country and weaving their way through a rock and boulder myriad, stayed in pursuit of retreating Zulus, who were driving cattle as they went. At about 11.30 both animals and warriors disappeared over a ridge. The troop galloped to the crest and Commissariat Officer James Hamer recalled 'On coming up we saw the Zulus, like *ants* in front of us, in perfect order, quiet as mice and stretched across in an even line. We estimated those we saw at 12,000.' The Zulus were several hundred yards off, and Raw ordered his men to dismount. They scrambled from their saddles, took aim, then unleashed one volley into the Zulu centre.

The bullets smashed home, the Battle of Isandlwana had begun.

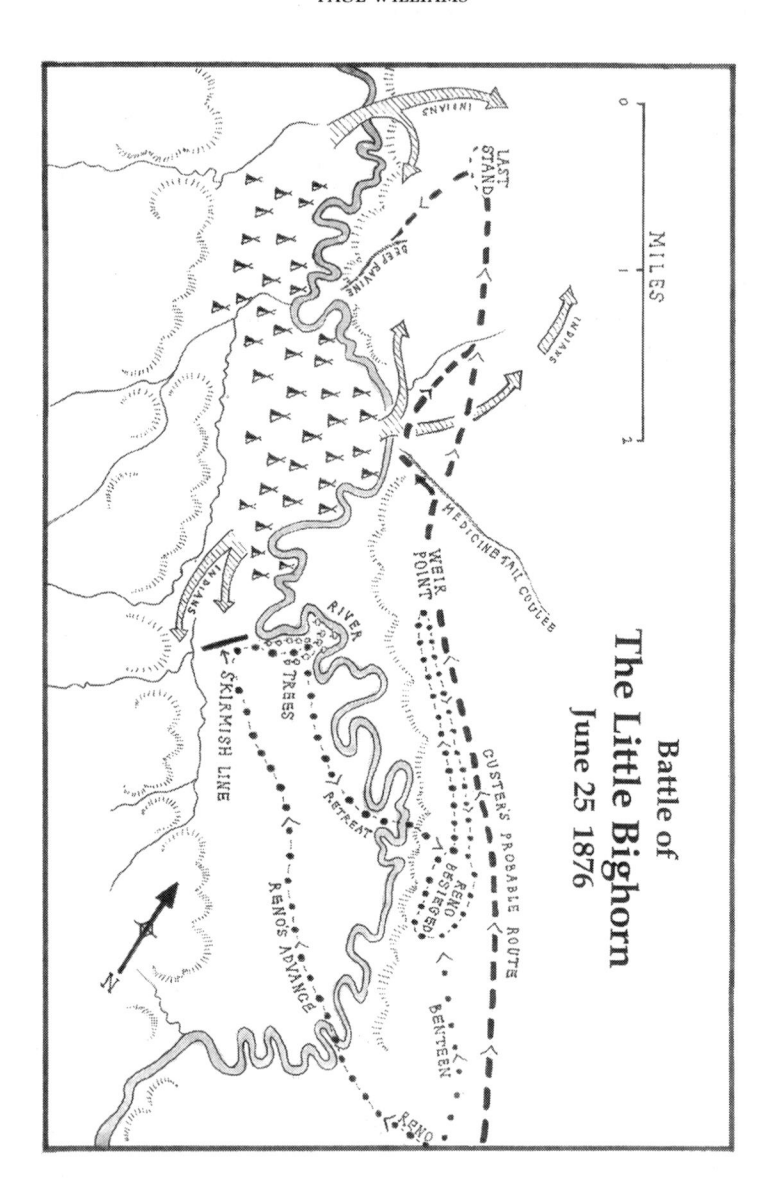

Battle of
The Little Bighorn
June 25 1876

LITTLE BIGHORN & ISANDLWANA; KINDRED FIGHTS, KINDRED FOLLIES

Battle of Isandlwana January 22 1879

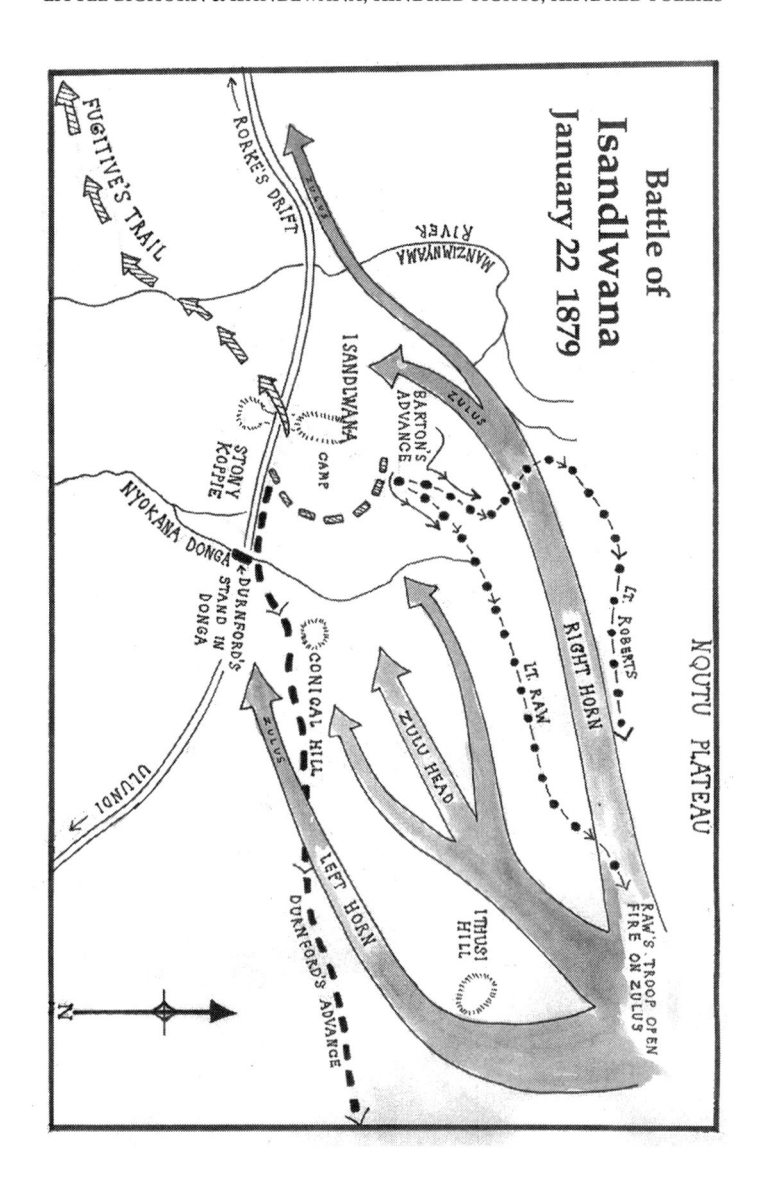

7
THE LAST MAN, THE LAST BULLET

The hooves of scores of cavalry horses thundered, guidons streaming, as Reno's battalion charged along the final two-mile stretch towards the Indian village in the valley of the Little Bighorn. Some Indian scouts stayed with the troops on the left flank but most followed Custer's orders and veered off in an attempt to drive away the Indians' pony herds. The closer the troopers got, the more warriors appeared between them and the tepees nestled amidst the trees. Custer had said he would support Reno with the whole outfit, but there was no sign of him now. Yet more warriors appeared; too many for the command to handle. A repetition of the disastrous Charge of the Light Brigade was not what Reno had envisioned. 'Of course,' recalled Reno, 'ten men could be ordered to charge a million; a brilliant illustration was the battle of Balaklava.'

'Halt!' he ordered, 'Prepare to fight on foot!' Every fourth man from the right remained in his saddle, the others dismounting and tying their horses together. But four men could not control their mounts and they kept on towards the Indian lines. Troopers Meyer and Rullin succeeded in turning their horses, but Smith and Turley disappeared into the Indian lines, never to be seen again.

Each of Reno's dismounted men handed the reins to the fourth man, then sprang forward to their places in the skirmish line. The U. S. Cavalry of the 1870s had developed into mounted infantry in reality, a man on foot with a rifle being more formidable than a man on horseback swinging a sabre. Lieutenant Hare, in charge of the led horses, ordered them taken into the cottonwoods along the river bank on the command's right for greater safety from enemy bullets.

The kneeling troopers on the skirmish line, spread across the valley floor, returned fire as bullets sent up puffs of dust around them. Indians on horseback moved from the west side of the village and started riding around to the left of the troops. Reno could see they risked being outflanked and attacked from at least three sides on open ground. The right flank of the skirmish line ended against trees where the horses sheltered. He ordered his men to disengage and take cover in the timber. They rushed in, seeking their horses, then, sheltering amidst the brush and foliage and along an old, dry section of riverbank, returned fire.

Reno shouted orders amidst the din as Bloody Knife fired alongside him. Then puffs of smoke belched from the other side of the river. Some braves had splashed their ponies through the water to the flat opposite Reno's position. The 50 rounds carried by each man dwindled and they hurriedly pulled more ammunition from pouches on their mounts. A number of Sioux entered the timber and fired a volley into the troops from about thirty feet. Trooper Lorentz cried 'Oh, my God, I have got it,' and fell from his saddle. The major suddenly found himself splattered with blood and brains as another bullet ripped into Bloody Knife's head, killing him instantly.

Reno dashed into a clearing within the grove and gave the order for the men to mount for what he would later call a 'charge' to the high bluffs on the other side of the river. Many men spread amidst the trees did not hear the order, especially those of G Company fighting some distance away. As men started mounting, Reno changed his mind and ordered them to dismount. 'All was the greatest confusion,' recalled Private Taylor, 'and I dismounted twice and mounted again, all in a few moments, but why, I do not know, unless because I saw the others do it and thought they had orders to.' Reno, still seeing the promised support nowhere in sight, again ordered the command to 'mount and get to the bluffs.' The blood spattered major leapt onto his horse and led the way, with no attempt to organise a rear-guard action. More warriors infiltrated the timber as the troopers remounted, all chaos and confusion. Then Reno galloped from the trees at the head of those who had managed to mount. The tattered column galloped back the way it had come, the yelling braves on fresh mounts riding after it, clad in their normal fighting apparel, 'a breech-clout at one end, a feather at the other, a whip hanging from their wrist and a gun in their hand.' There was at least one exception, however, recalled Private Taylor, 'he wore a magnificent war bonnet of great long feathers encircling his head and hanging down his back, the end trailing along the side of his pony.' The warriors shot the fleeing troopers or their horses from under them, and pulled others from their saddles as they rode alongside. Taylor recalled:

> a whooping, howling mass of the best horsemen, the most cruel and fiercest fighters in all our country, or any other…Talk about the 'Thin Red Line' of the English. Here was a thick Red line of Sioux and growing thicker every moment. Out of the clouds of dust, anxious to be in at the death, came hundreds of others, shouting and racing towards the soldiers, most of whom were seeing their first battle, and many, of whom I was one, had never fired a shot from a horse's back.

Lieutenant Donald McIntosh was killed during this headlong flight. 'He was pulled from his horse, tortured and finally murdered at the pleasure of the red devils,' the Bismarck *Tribune* would report, a comforting thought for his widow at Fort Lincoln. But the writer had embellished the story, there being no evidence of McIntosh having been tortured. Lieutenant Varnum's orderly had his horse shot from under him and was wounded, but Varnum and a few others caught a riderless horse and saw him remounted before continuing the retreat. Lieutenant Wallace also tried to save a dismounted trooper, but the man was cut down by the hostiles before Wallace could reach him. Trooper Davern's horse stumbled and fell, leaving the soldier on foot. Nearby two dismounted men from Company G were also under attack by two mounted braves. Their horses clashed together and in the confusion Davern retrieved his mount and made his escape, but the other two were cut down.

Reno emptied his revolvers and his straw hat blew off, disappearing in the dust. The galloping hostiles crowded in on the fleeing troops, forcing them to the left blocking access to the ford they had used on their approach, but they struck another and began splashing across where a pony-trail led to a ravine giving access to the bluffs on the opposite side. They splashed across the Little Bighorn, the Sioux braves uttering victorious war whoops after them. 'I saw a struggling mass of men and horses,' recalled Taylor, 'from whom little streams of blood was coloring the water near them.' Lieutenant Hodgson's horse leaped from the bank and into the river as a bullet hit home. Hodgson, his leg wounded by the same bullet, landed in the water as retreating troopers splashed by. 'For God's sake don't abandon me!' he cried. A trooper paused long enough for Hodgson to grasp his stirrup and the horse splashed across with the officer in tow. But as Hodgson made it to dry land another bullet struck and he released his grasp, dying where he lay.

The survivors scrambled up steep slopes to gain high ground. Dr. De Wolf was killed as he attempted to make it up, his skills a great loss to the command on such a day as this. Private Taylor's exhausted horse, Steamboat, 'a poor, broken-winded beast at the best,' refused to ascend the bluffs. The trooper dismounted and trudged up on foot, bullets sending up 'little puffs of dust rising from the ground all round.' He was overtaken by another dismounted soldier, 'Tinker Bill' Meyer. They slogged up the bluff alongside each other until Meyer cried out and 'pitched forward face down to the ground. I bent over him but he was dead, shot between the left ear and eye.' Another mounted trooper came along with a riderless mount, Old Dutch, in tow. Though not much better than Steamboat, Taylor gratefully scrambled into the saddle and rode up the grassy slope where a hatless Lieutenant Varnum was attempting to rally the troops. 'For God's sake, men,' he cried, 'don't run. There are a good many officers and men killed and wounded and we have to go back and get them.' But no one seemed interested as they made for the crest.

Reno dismounted and the others followed. They opened fire on the hostiles as stragglers from the command came up the hill behind them. Dr. Porter made it to the top where he saw Reno. 'Major,' he said, 'the men were pretty well demoralized, weren't they?' 'No,' retorted Reno, 'that was a charge, sir.' Reno's defence at the Court of Inquiry would compare the civilian Dr. Porter with a watchmaker who 'might understand tic-tacs, but certainly did not understand tac-tics.'

The Sioux did not pursue the bluecoats to Reno's new position, but galloped about on the river flat amidst smoke and dust hunting the tail end of his command. At least the cavalry's Springfields had a greater range than the rifles carried by the Indians. Forty men had been either killed outright or left behind to die. Reno's report would play down the numbers. Thirteen of the wounded had managed to make it up to the top, but there were still many men missing, scattered between the hilltop and the trees. Most of the Indian scouts had dispersed over the surrounding terrain in pursuit of Sioux ponies.

The best Reno could hope for now was to keep the savages at bay while Custer's battalion rode to their rescue. Or Benteen. But where were they?

After leaving Custer, Captain Benteen's column had marched over rough terrain; steep hills and valleys 'wandering among hills without any possibility of accomplishing anything,' recalled Lieutenant Godfrey in his diary. The view from their point of departure had not revealed the true nature of the country, and the further they advanced the rougher it became. At one point they saw Custer's battalion at a considerable distance, distinguished by the grey horse troop, advancing with a rapid gait. Lieutenant Gibson, in advance, signalled seeing no enemy from various vantage points. In a letter to Godfrey written 32 years after the battle, Gibson said that he scanned the Little Bighorn valley to the south, then seeing 'not a living thing,' reported to Benteen, causing his decision to turn right, back towards the trail. Benteen, however, gave the impression that a successful scan of the valley was not achieved, 'I did not get to any valley, and did not see the valley of the Little Big Horn...' and as his column veered right several miles from the river, it would not seem possible for Gibson's scan to be conclusive, the river twisting and turning amidst trees and bluffs off towards the distant Big Horn Mountains. Lieutenant

Godfrey wrote of riding over rough country and, 'The obstacles threw the battalion by degrees to the right until we came in sight of and not more than a mile from the trail. Many of our horses were greatly jaded by the climbing and descending, some getting far to the rear of the column.'

At the inquiry Benteen said he felt he was disobeying orders and 'My going back was providential or accidental or whatever you may be pleased to term it.'

Benteen came upon the trail left by Custer and Reno's battalions and followed their course towards the Little Bighorn. Had he continued on to properly reconnoitre the upper river valley, Reno as well as Custer could well have been wiped out. The reconnaissance had achieved nothing that could not have been accomplished far more quickly by a few good scouts on good horses.

Benteen came upon a morass, the source of a small stream, and while the grateful horses drank their fill, gunfire was heard in the distance. Captain Weir, chafing at the bit, moved his troop out in advance despite his proper place being second in the column. The rest of the battalion moved out just as the lagging pack train arrived, then delayed as the parched mules plunged into the water and drank, despite curses from their masters, not having had water since the previous evening. Men riding in advance came across the lone tepee, the dead brave's last resting place. They dismounted, peered inside, then the warrior was cremated as they set it ablaze.

Sergeant Kanipe of Tom Custer's Company C rode up with a message from General Custer for Captain McDougall of the pack train, far to the rear, to hurry it along. After talking with Benteen he rode past the column and said 'We've got 'em, boys,' giving the impression to some that Custer had attacked and captured the village.

Benteen quickened his pace and about 15 minutes later a second rider, Trumpeter John Martin, appeared. He was a member of Benteen's own Troop H, and Custer's orderly for the day. He handed Benteen this message:

Benteen.
Come on. Big
Village. Be quick.
Bring packs
W. W. Cooke.
P.S. Bring pacs

The message, brief to say the least, says nothing about Custer splitting north from Reno and does not say the battle is under way.

'I asked Martin,' Benteen recalled, 'after reading the note, about the village. He said the Indians were all "skedaddling," therefore there was less necessity for me to go back for the packs.'

'Capt. Benteen asked me where Gen. Custer was,' recalled Martin, 'I said I supposed that by that time he had made a charge through the village. I said nothing about Maj. Reno's battalion. He did not ask about it.' Benteen, who later described Martin as a 'thick headed, dull witted Italian,' did not ask because 'When I left I did not know that Reno had any command; the division had not been made yet; and I don't think Reno knew anything about it at the time I left.' And Reno recalled 'Capt. Benteen had started to the left up the hill. I had no instructions as to him and asked him where he was going and what he was going to do. His reply was to the effect that he was going to drive everything before him on the hill. That was all that passed between us.' Custer had divulged no battle plan to his subordinates, each not knowing what the other was doing.

Lieutenant Edgerly overheard Martin, elated and laughing, telling an orderly that they had found the Indians all asleep in the biggest village he had ever seen. Major Reno was charging it, he said, 'killing everything, men, women and children.'

As Martin had delivered his message the sound of gunfire had been heard again; firstly straggling shots, then it grew in volume as the command moved at an increased pace. Benteen ordered pistols drawn and to advance at the gallop. He expected to meet Indians fleeing from Custer's command. But as they approached, Lieutenant Godfrey recalled:

> We were forming in line to meet our supposed enemy, when we came in full view of the valley of the Little Bighorn. The valley was full of horsemen riding to and fro in clouds of dust and smoke, for the grass had been fired by the Indians to drive the troops out and cover their own movements. On the bluff to our right we saw a body of troops and they were engaged. But an engagement appeared to be going on in the valley too. Owing to the distance, smoke, and dust it was impossible to distinguish if those in the valley were friends or foes. There was a short time of uncertainty as to the direction in which we should go, but some Crow scouts came by, driving a small herd of ponies, one of whom said 'Soldiers,' and motioned for the command to go to the right.

Benteen assumed Custer was also engaged in the fight. The picture he recalled seeing was clearer than that seen by Godfrey:

> I then noticed our men in large numbers running for the bluffs on the right bank of the stream. I concluded at once

that those had been repulsed, and was of the opinion that if I crossed the ford with my battalion, that I should have it treated in like manner; for, from long experience with cavalry, I judge there were 900 veteran Indians right there at the time, against which the large element of recruits in my battalion would stand no earthly chance as mounted men.

As they arrived, Reno, a handkerchief tied around his head, 'appeared to be much excited,' It was claimed he was firing at hostiles far out of range with his revolver. Benteen's men dismounted and deployed as skirmishers along the western edge of the bluffs overlooking the river valley below. Lieutenant Hare walked up to Godfrey and shook him heartily by the hand. 'We've had a big fight in the bottom, got whipped, and am I damned glad to see you.'

Benteen has been accused of being deliberately tardy in riding to the rescue. Had there been any desire on his part to delay, he could simply have followed Custer's orders to 'Bring packs,' the pack train being some way behind. It was only by disobeying these instructions that he arrived to reinforce Reno at a critical time.

Benteen's troopers shared their ammunition with Reno's men, and while they awaited the arrival of McDougall with the pack train, Reno made plans to recover the body of Lieutenant Hodgson, a personal friend, lying near the riverbank. He led Dr. Porter and a party of soldiers down to the river where they found Hodgson and several other bodies, but due to the zip and thud of bullets being fired from a few Indians on the bluffs and in the valley, no attempt was made to move them. The party filled their canteens and on the trudge back up found a dismounted trooper from company G hiding in the brush. They made it back to the top to find the pack train still nowhere in sight, and Reno despatched Lieutenant Hare to hurry it along.

But where was Custer? By now Benteen had learned of his separation from Reno, and all were puzzled at his disappearance. 'What's the matter with Custer that he don't send word, what shall we do?' was typical of comments made. 'Wonder what we are staying here for?' There was a certain uneasiness at the lack of contact, but no one doubted the ability of Custer and his five companies to look after themselves, just as Chelmsford had no doubt about his camp's ability to look after itself.

Benteen's men heard from those who had seen Custer and others wave their hats and cheer encouragement from the bluffs before riding out of sight. Captain Moylan, looking at the throng of hostiles in the valley below, however, remarked, 'Gentlemen, in my opinion General Custer has made the biggest mistake of his life by not taking the whole regiment in at once in the first attack.'

But then, as if at a signal, the feathered horsemen turned their ponies' heads and galloped off downstream, back towards the village. Within a few minutes there was scarcely a hostile to be seen, and volleys of gunfire were heard to erupt from the north.

Following Reno's advance towards the Little Bighorn, Custer had followed for a short distance before leading his battalion to the right, staying to the east of the river. He no doubt wanted to 'support' Reno by striking the village a little further to the north, taking the hostiles by surprise as they were concentrating on Reno's attack, a valid ploy, especially if your subordinate knows the plan. But the time it took for Custer to come into contact with the enemy, Reno's repulse and no timely 'Be quick' message to Benteen would prove a fatal combination.

The thirsty horses lapped up water from the North Fork, then moving on, Custer and others caught sight of Reno's men preparing to charge, waved their hats and cheered them into battle. At this point the full extent of the village could not be seen, the southern end still downstream to Custer's right. But even now he had probably been informed by Cooke that the village was not fleeing as reported earlier by the scouts. The command trotted for another one and a half miles along the bluffs northward until reaching the slope of a knoll which would provide a bird's eye view of their surrounds. Custer rode up and saw more of the huge village along the Little Bighorn; a village not in flight. He may well have felt a sickening lurch when he suspected how many hostiles they confronted. 'Courage, boys!' he cried, with a wave of his hat, 'we will get them, and as soon as we get through, we will go back to our station.'

Did Custer now recall his own words from *My Life on the Plains* '...experience only confirmed me in the opinion that Indians seldom, if ever, permit hostile parties to stumble upon them unless the stumblers were the weaker party.'

Stumbling back to his command, Custer ordered Sergeant Kanipe to head south with the message for Captain McDougall with the pack train. Kanipe recalled 27 years later, 'bring the pack train straight across to high ground—if packs get loose, don't stop to fix them, cut them. Come quick. Big Indian camp. If you see Capt. Benteen, tell him to come quick—a big Indian camp.'

If you see Captain Benteen? Even now Custer did not send out a rider specifically to locate the missing battalion, and if that last part of the message ever existed, Kanipe did not seem to deliver it. Benteen testified 'The C Company sergeant who came to me had verbal orders to the Commanding Officer of the Pack Train, and I did not consider that an order to me. The pack train was not a part of my column or command.' Lieutenant Edgerly endorsed this, 'Capt. Benteen said he thought Custer had made a mistake—that Captain McDougall was in charge of the packs, and he showed him the place and he went on.' It made no sense for Benteen to tell Kanipe he had made a mistake if the message also applied to him.

Custer's battalion moved on for another mile, then he and the scouts ascended the hill later called Weir Point, affording an even better view. What he needed was a suitable ford to cross and make his attack. Looking to his left he saw the alarming sight of Reno's skirmish line falling back into the trees, the attack beginning to fail. He told the Crow scouts and Mitch Boyer they could ride back to the pack train, their scouting jobs complete. Mitch Boyer chose to stay; he wanted to see this thing through to the finish, no matter what the odds. Three Crows lingered for a short time before riding off. One, Curly, stayed and would later claim being the command's sole survivor, having stayed till near the end. A few troopers' lives had been saved as their worn horses fell back, the men eventually rejoining Reno's command.

About 50 minutes after ordering Reno forward to attack, and over three hours since the regiment split, Custer finally instructed his orderly trumpeter to ride back with the message 'Benteen. Come on. Big Village. Be quick. Bring packs. W.W. Cooke. P. S. Bring pacs.'

Giovanni Martini, or John Martin, an Italian, was not fluent in English, and Adjutant Cooke quickly wrote out the note. Martin rode off, the last surviving member of the 7th Cavalry to see Custer alive. He looked back to see the command already coming under fire from a few braves in an attempt to halt its advance, his own horse receiving a bullet wound. He passed Boston Custer riding from the pack train to join his brother's command. He would bring Custer first news of Benteen's whereabouts, having ridden past his battalion.

Why had Custer sent Benteen away exploring empty bluffs to the south? When George Herendeen had located a trail to the left up Lame Deer Creek, Custer had sent Lieutenant Varnum and some scouts to check it out. Such action would have covered Terry's orders to 'feel to your left.' But Custer had abandoned Terry's recommended course of action anyway.

'I understood it as a rather senseless order,' Benteen stated at the inquiry, 'We were on the main trail of the Indians; there was plenty of them on that trail...Why I was sent to the left I don't know. It was not my business to reason why; I went.' Custer had sent two couriers after Benteen ordering him to keep going, distancing him from the central command, then, when the village was seen and Reno's attack order given, sent Benteen no orders of any kind. Whether more troops were just behind or miles away any commander would, naturally, do his utmost to make sure they were brought forward to support the attack, as Durnford had requested support from Pulleine before moving against the Zulus.

'I consider that I violated my orders when I struck to the right,' Benteen said, 'If I carried them out I would have been at least 25 miles away. I don't know where I would have been. As it was, I was certainly too far to cooperate with Custer when he wanted me. He could have found out what was behind that line of bluffs by following the trail he was on.'

Custer had been assuming all along, of course, the Indians would not stand and fight, but flee to protect their women and children. Gerard saw the village and said the Indians were 'running like devils.' Eight companies should be sufficient to cut the fleeing red devils down, apparently. 'The three orders I got from Custer,' Benteen testified, 'did not indicate that he expected me to cooperate in any attack on the village.' Custer's own actions validate this. After ordering Reno to attack, Custer led his battalion north away from Benteen whose whereabouts were becoming more obscure with every minute, with no attempt to communicate. Custer saw Reno go into action and realised the village was not in flight. If the enemy stood and fought, perhaps the 100 rounds of ammunition per man would not be sufficient? 32 minutes after ordering Reno in he sent word with Sergeant Kanipe to McDougall. The pack train and Benteen were separate commands, not necessarily near each other, but still, even now, no courier expressly seeking Benteen.

Had Custer found a ford to attack a village in flight before this time, it must be assumed no message would have been sent to Benteen or the pack train, thus excluding one third of the regiment from the fight.

Obviously Benteen's command was not intended to have a share in this 'victory' any more than Terry's column approaching from the north. Custer had sent no scouts, white or Indian, with Benteen because they were needed to pinpoint the village and run off the Sioux ponies in support of those troops he expected to be in the fight.

At Weir point, however, Custer could no longer deny the horrible truth. Here, at 3.30, he could see not only the vast number of tepees shimmering in the sunlight along the Little Bighorn, but also Reno's skirmish line being outflanked and drawn back into the timber. The 7th was going to need not only every bullet but also every man. Probably through clenched teeth, he finally ordered Trumpeter Martin back to fetch the detested Benteen.

But where was Benteen supposed to go? The note made no mention of Custer moving north, and Martin was given no instructions to guide Benteen back to Custer's command. At the time of writing Custer's men were not engaged and had not fired a single shot; they did not know they would soon be wiped out.

It was Reno who was in trouble.

The major's command had been firing for some time and was being driven back. It was obvious that Benteen, following the trail, would arrive at Reno's beleaguered command first, and they were the ones who needed more men and ammunition at this time.

The 'Be quick. Bring packs' message was intended to reinforce Reno whose success was vital to Custer's plan to effectively attack from the flank. He needed those hostile braves to remain occupied at the southern end of village. The *P. S. Bring pacs* reinforces this. Reno needed more ammunition, not Custer. Was Benteen supposed to ride straight past Reno's embattled command and deliver unneeded ammunition to Custer? Obviously not. Benteen would later be criticised for not delivering the packs to Custer as ordered, but he did, in fact, carry out his orders when he reinforced Reno and the packs arrived. Because Custer was wiped out, a hindsight view made it appear that the packs were for him.

Following the Washita, Benteen's letter had publicly criticised Custer. 'Colonel Benteen, I'll see you again, sir,' Custer had said, before the second confrontation when Long Hair 'cringed like a whipped cur.'

'Now all this kind of business was apt to result disastrously for me when Custer could so work it...' Benteen recalled. He had 'taken the initiative' to have Custer charged for shooting deserters in 1867, then testified against him at the court-martial. Following the Washita his letter had ridiculed Custer in the press. Custer had attempted to 'banish me to Fort Dodge in the Spring of '69,' Benteen recalled, 'rendered nugatory' by Colonel Mitchell of General Hancock's staff.

But now, with an independent command, there was nobody to prevent Custer from banishing Benteen to empty bluffs in the south, a more effective whipping than anything done with a quirt.

It had been eight years since the Washita. Indian campaigns were few. This was the Boy General's last chance for an untarnished, pure Custer victory.

The time lapse between Adjutant Cooke instructing Reno to attack and sending Benteen's 'Be quick' order, about 50 minutes, was critical to the outcome of the battle.

Benteen increased speed after he spoke to Kanipe, then moved faster again after receiving Cooke's message. Had Custer sent word when he ordered Reno in, Benteen's battalion would have arrived to join Reno in the valley fight before the rout. Reno's command had lost few men before the disastrous flight from the trees. Opinion among white survivors was divided as to whether they could have maintained the fight there or not. Some said they would have been wiped out, but Lieutenant DeRudio, who remained in the trees till the night of the 26th, giving ample time to assess the area, was to say 'Maj. Reno could have held his position in the timber three or four hours by careful use of ammunition.'

Reno is said to have asked the advice of Captain French, who advised getting out of the river valley, but in a letter written to Lieutenant Cooke's widow in 1880, French said he was tempted to shoot Reno when he ordered the retreat, and had since come to the conclusion he would have been justified in doing so.

George Herendeen, one of those left in the timber, testified, 'In my judgement 100 men with 6 or 7 thousand rounds of ammunition could have held that timber against the Indians; and they couldn't have got them out of there at all, if they had water and provisions.' And Benteen later said it 'was an A-1 defensive position, and could have been held five or six hours, depending on the size of the attacking force.' All this depended, of course, on good leadership. Had Custer sent word to his subordinates of the proposed flanking attack they would have understood what he had in mind. Considering Benteen's later coolness and command on the bluffs, it is hard to believe the same rout would have taken place, especially with more than twice as many troops on hand, and the pack train supplying ammunition. The Indians would have still been hotly engaged at the southern end fighting Reno and Benteen when Custer attacked the village from the flank. Given an equal distribution of warriors, this would have reduced the odds Custer's battalion fought by more than half. How exactly this would have altered the battle's outcome is not known, but a dignified retreat or even a victory were possible. And, of course, had Grasshopper Jim's four companies of the 2nd Cavalry been present, yet another battalion would have been in the fight.

With the exception of sending no courier, Custer did not disobey Terry's orders at the Little Bighorn. His decision to follow the *fresh* trail across the divide was within the latitude granted, and made sense if the hostiles were not to escape. But other aspects of his judgement were fatally flawed by personal ambition, oversight and paranoia.

Exactly what happened to Custer's command after Martin

rode off will forever remain obscure, despite Indian testimony and archaeological surveys begun in 1956. Indian accounts are contradictory and confusing, and how many artefacts were carried off before 1956 by souvenir hunters and the Indians themselves? But a probable scenario follows:

As the trumpeter rode off, Custer entered a dry watercourse which joined what is now known as Medicine Tail Coulee, providing a suitable approach to a ford opposite the village. The Crow scout Curley stated that he and Mitch Boyer delayed at Weir Point after the command moved off. From here they witnessed the beginning of Reno's galloping retreat. They caught up with the command and reported the bad news. Custer then sent another courier *north*; Terry being the only possible objective in the vain hope his column would be close enough to give support. If so, the rider never made it.

Custer divided the command again into right and left wings. The right wing, Companies C, I, and L remained on the bluffs while the left wing, companies E and F, moved down towards the ford, either as the advance of an attack or a feint to draw the hostiles away from Reno's beleaguered command until he could be reinforced by Benteen. It has been argued that troops did not approach this ford, but it was, in fact, a logical place for a flanking attack. If Custer was not going to cross here, where? Those Indians who said he did not make this approach may well have only seen the troops on the hill behind, those moving down Medicine Tail Coulee obscured from view, or arrived from the Reno fight after the bluecoats had retired from near the ford.

Custer possibly stayed with the troops on the bluffs from where he could survey the whole picture, and moved them along the ridge where a mounted skirmish line was formed.

But by now more Indians were arriving to fight the troops approaching the ford. They opened a heavy fire and the troops were forced to retire to the northeast over rough ground. Sitting Bull recalled 'Our young men rained lead across the river and drove the white braves back.' Sitting Bull's 26 year-old nephew, White Bull, also took part in the fight. 'We all raced downstream together,' he recalled, 'Some rode through the camps and crossed the river north of them, but I and many others crossed and rode up a gully to strike the soldiers on the flank.'

Seeing the two companies beating a retreat from the ford, Custer ordered two volleys fired at the Indians on the opposite bank. These volleys may also have been fired as a signal of their location to the other troops. By now hundreds of Indians were arriving in force splashing across the ford and sweeping up Deep Coulee, cutting off retreat to the south where Reno's command lay. Under increasing fire, the command was pushed north along the ridge top and reunited with the retreating left wing. White Bull continued:

> After a while I could see five bunches of soldiers trotting along the bluffs. I knew it would be a big fight. I stopped, unsaddled my horse, and stripped off my leggings, so that I could fight better. By the time I was near enough to shoot at the soldiers, they seemed to form four groups, heading north-west along the ridge.

Here Custer's brother-in-law Lieutenant James Calhoun with Company L fought a rear-guard action, with Captain Myles Keogh's Company I held in support immediately to his north along the ridge. Tom Custer's company C was placed on the slope to the west of Calhoun. Companies E and F continued along the ridge towards Last Stand Hill, while hundreds more warriors swarmed up from the north of the village to cut them off in that direction. Thus Custer was being surrounded on his right and left, the Indians inadvertently forming the 'horns of the buffalo', while those warriors between himself and the village formed the head.

White Bull recalled:

> All the Indians were shooting. I saw two soldiers fall from their horses. The soldiers fired back at us from the saddle. They shot so well that some of us retreated to the south, driven out of the ravine. Soon after, the soldiers halted and some got off their horses. By that time the Indians were all around the soldiers, but most of them were between the soldiers and the river, trying to defend the camp and the ford. Several little bunches of Indians took cover where they could, and kept firing at the white men.

Lame White Man of the Cheyenne led a charge against Tom Custer's Company C. They were the first to fall under an onslaught by hundreds of braves, although some, including Tom, retreated to temporary safety joining Calhoun's and Keogh's companies on the ridge. Lame White Man died in the attack, killed by a Cheyenne who mistook him for a Crow scout. The warriors now turned their fury against Calhoun's Company L. Soldiers holding the horses of the dismounted troops were picked off under a withering fire and the animals stampeded, the position soon overrun. When Custer had helped secure a commission for Calhoun in the 7th, the young officer had written 'I shall do my best to prove my gratitude. If the time comes you shall not find me wanting.' Calhoun's body was found at the rear of the 1st platoon where he died directing the rear-guard action.

White Bull continued:

> I rode south and worked my way over to the east of the mounted bunch of soldiers. Crazy Horse was there with a party of warriors and I joined them. The Indians kept gathering, more and more, around this last bunch of soldiers. These mounted soldiers kept falling back along the ridge, trying to reach the rest of the soldiers who were fighting on foot.

Keogh's Company I was now the southernmost fighting unit. The Indians charged, cutting off Keogh from the rest of the command to the north.

White Bull recalled:

> When I saw the soldiers retreating, I whipped up my pony, and hugging his neck, dashed across between the two troops. The soldiers shot at me but missed me. I circled back to my friends. I thought I would do it again. I yelled, 'This time I will not turn back,' and charged at a run the soldiers of the last company. Many of the Sioux joined my charge and this seemed to break the courage of those soldiers. They all ran, every man for himself, some afoot and some on horseback, to reach their comrades on the other side. All the Indians were shooting.

Hemmed in by warriors to the north, west and south, Custer established a holding position on the slope of Last Stand Hill. He possibly avoided using the crest as the intense Indian fire from the many braves between himself and the village would rake any Indians who attempted to attack from that quarter, thus the Indians themselves provided the covering fire for his rear. Perhaps this was Major Clery's logic at Isandlwana when he said 'the rear always protects itself.' Had Custer positioned himself on the crest, he would have been open to fire from all sides. But was it still possible at this time for Custer to have escaped with some of his command by continuing over the crest and charging through the fewer warriors to the east? Did he deliberately choose to dig in and die, rather than live with the disgrace of his last campaign having been a shocking defeat?

Whitebull saw a handful of soldiers 'some afoot and some on horseback,' from the defeated companies to the south make it to Custer's command post. 'The survivors of these two bunches of soldiers moved up and joined those in the north and west, about where the monument stands now. Another bunch of soldiers was down the hill nearer the river. The air was full of dust and smoke.'

Custer had sent Lieutenant Smith's Company E in a charge, southwest, towards the river and a cleft today known as Deep Ravine. Kate Bighead, a Cheyenne who had crossed the stream to watch the battle, recalled:

> A band of soldiers on the ridge mounted their horses and came riding in a gallop down the broad coulee towards the river, towards where were the Cheyennes and Oglallalas. The Indians hidden there got back quickly into the deepest parts of the gulch or kept on going away from it until they got over the ridge just south of it…The soldiers who had come galloping stopped and got off their horses along another ridge, a low one just north of the deep gulch.

They formed a skirmish line and opened fire while Custer

and Captain Yates' Company F shot long range from the slope above. This sent the Indians into temporary retreat, but they rallied, and as they closed in the rapid fire of their Henrys and Winchesters began to tell. The Springfield used by the troops was a better long-range weapon, but much slower to load and fire. The Indians charged amidst dust and smoke to cut off Smith's men on the slope. Men died as fugitives were forced down into Deep Ravine where 28 soldiers were killed by arrows and bullets fired from above. 'They were undoubtedly fighting and retreating,' recalled Captain Moylan after viewing their bodies, 'The marks were plain where they went down and where they tried to scramble up the other side, but these marks only extended half way up the bank.' Possibly the last to die were here, it will never be known. Custer, meanwhile, was under attack on Last Stand Hill where survivors from the various companies gathered around him. Some cavalry mounts were deliberately shot, forming an arced breastwork, a disciplined action which, along with volley firing distinctly heard by many upstream early in the battle, disproves claims of a complete rout. 'By this time,' recalled White Bull:

> all the soldiers up the hill had let their horses go. They lay down and kept shooting. The horses turned loose by the soldiers—bays, sorrels and greys- were running in all directions. Lots of Indians stopped shooting to capture these horses. I tried to head some off, but other Indians were ahead of me. I caught just one sorrel. Now that the soldiers were all dismounted their firing was very fierce. All at once, my horse went down, and I was left afoot. For a while the Indians all took cover and kept shooting at the soldiers.

Below the crest the last of Custer's men fought, their eyes no doubt glancing south in hope of rescue. One can imagine the trepidation resonating in Custer's mind as his men fell, having distanced both Benteen's and Terry's commands. Relying on 'Custer's luck,' the Boy General had gambled and lost.

There are accounts of some charging from this position on foot. Iron Hawk recalled 'We saw soldiers start running down the hill right towards us. Nearly all of them were afoot, and I think they were so scared they didn't know what they were doing.' If these soldiers ran as a unified group, perhaps they did know what they were doing, a charge to either break out or die trying, bringing the ordeal to an end.

Stories are told of arched barrages of arrows being sent into the air, but if this tactic was employed, why was it not later used on Reno's men in their entrenched position where Indians got close enough, in ravines, to throw clods of dirt and arrows by hand?

The fire from Last Stand Hill dropped off under a barrage of lead from below. Wounded men cried in pain. Some, seeing the end was near, shot themselves according to some accounts. 'The chances of being wounded and captured were many,' recalled Private Taylor of Reno's command. 'One's fate in such a case was easy to imagine, so I reserved one of the six bullets that my revolver contained for the "last resort" myself.' But White Bull scoffed at reports of mass suicide: 'The soldiers looked tired,' he said, 'but they fought to the end. There were few cartridges left in the belts I took off the soldiers.' White Bull recalled his fight with one soldier towards the end:

> I charged in. A tall, well-built soldier with yellow hair and moustache saw me coming and tried to bluff me, aiming his rifle at me. But when I rushed him, he threw

his rifle at me without shooting. I dodged it. We grabbed each other and wrestled there in the dust and smoke. It was like fighting in a log. This soldier was very strong and brave. He tried to wrench my rifle from me. I lashed him across the face with my quirt, striking the coup. He let go, then grabbed my gun with both hands till I struck him again. But the tall soldier fought hard. He was desperate. He hit me with his fists on the jaw and shoulders, then grabbed my long braids with both hands, pulled my face close and tried to bite my nose off. I yelled for help: 'Hey, hey, come over and help me!' I thought that soldier would kill me. Bear Lice and Crow Boy heard me call and came running. These friends tried to hit the soldier. But we were whirling around, back and forth, so that most of their blows hit me. They knocked me dizzy. I yelled as loud as I could to scare my enemy, but he would not let go. Finally I broke free. He drew his pistol. I wrenched it out of his hand and struck him with it three or four times on the head, knocked him over, shot him in the head, and fired at his heart.

There was a final rush through the battle haze as warriors on horse and foot dashed in for the kill. They had seen their friends killed that day too, and some squaws and children had died from overfire into the village. The braves slashed and clubbed the last few soldiers into oblivion. There was a chorus of victorious war whoops as braves rode about firing into the fallen bluecoats, then the smoke and dust shrouded battlefield calmed. The squaws, some wailing for the loss of loved ones, moved up from the village and, with the warriors, began stripping, scalping and mutilating the dead.

Who exactly killed Custer will never be known, several braves being mentioned in tribal folk law of having the honor, but White Bull said his cousin Bad Soup knew Custer by sight, having spent time at Fort Abraham Lincoln. He viewed the body of the tall soldier he had killed. 'Long Hair thought he was the greatest man in the world. Now he lies there,' he said.

The warriors collected the weapons and ammunition of Custer's dead, then mounted their ponies and rode south to renew their attack on Reno's troops, still licking their wounds a few miles away. Reinforced by Benteen's command, they dug in on the bluffs preparing to make their stand.

***

As the smoke cleared from the volley fired by Lieutenant Raw's company of Native Horse, the uMcijo Regiment, having received the blast, leapt to their feet in a spontaneous rage and charged without orders. The regiments on either side of the uMcijo, following their lead, uncoiled, a fearsome sight as thousands of shields rose in unison, and rushed to join the attack. The indunas were unable to stop the charge to organise a more orderly advance, but managed to hold two regiments back to form a reserve.

As Major Reno had retreated after opening the Battle of the Little Bighorn, Captain Barton now did likewise with his two companies of Natal Native Horse, but in much quicker time. Even if there had been sheltering trees as in Reno's case, the 107 men would have been overwhelmed by the Zulu thousands in a matter of minutes. Durnford's political officer, Captain George Shepstone, and Commissariat Officer James Hamer galloped back to warn Colonel Pulleine of the advancing threat. A supporting company of NNC under Captain Barry, mostly armed only with shield and assegai, could see they had no hope of survival against the rushing horde. They turned and fled, their officers moving on foot alongside Barton's native horsemen who, being well armed, paused to fire back as they made an orderly retreat. The Zulu masses surged forward, the British camp their ultimate objective.

A few miles to the right, Durnford and his two companies of Natal Native Horse looked towards the sound of firing from the Nqutu Plateau. Within moments they were also confronted by warriors of the Zulu left horn flowing like a mighty black wave from the valley to their front and left flank. They were 'in skirmishing order but ten or twelve deep, with supports close behind.' The Zulus delivered a ragged volley at about 800 yards. There were no casualties and the troopers returned fire as they executed a disciplined withdrawal in stages. Jabez Molife of Durnford's command recalled: 'we remounted and retreated 20 yards, always in a long thin line, then we dismounted and fired, up again for another ten yards, dismounted and fired again, and so on ten yards at a time, firing always, slowly back towards the camp.'

It had not been Chief Ntshingwayo's intention to fight on this day, the day of the dead moon, but ancient beliefs were put to one side when the British had split their force, inviting attack. Dartnell and Lonsdale's columns had marched out the day before, and at dawn that morning Chelmsford had accommodated Ntshingwayo by taking out most of his force in their support. The chief's ploy, luring the troops away from their vulnerable base camp, had worked to perfection. Durnford's reinforcements had arrived, but had also been lured out, dividing into three separate commands; Captain Barton's two companies, Durnford's two companies, and the rocket battery.

And the young warriors were impatient for action, and did not want to wait for the pre-battle rituals which normally took place. Natal settler T. E. Newmarch said he was later told by an iNgobamakhosi warrior:

> their scouts had been out early and had returned to report to the leaders that the White People were scattered about the hills around the camp like a lot of goats out grazing and they were convinced that the spirits of the Zulu nation had put them into their hands to be killed and that they should attack whether they had been doctored or not that day. In the end the young men prevailed against their more cautious leaders and were given the order to attack, especially as they knew that the greater part of the British forces had gone further into the country.

So Ntshingwayo decided to attack. On the morning of January 22nd he moved his regiments to a valley alongside Nqutu Plateau, within striking distance of Isandlwana. Wanting to avoid detection, and awaiting the return of those warriors used to lure Chelmsford, he did not rush the movement. It was here they were discovered by Barton's command who opened fire, which was like throwing a stone into a massive hornets' nest, the Zulus stung into the attack, regardless of Ntshingwayo's planning.

While Barton and Durnford both executed fighting retreats, the rocket battery with its escort of NNC arrived at the Conical Hill, about two miles to Durnford's rear. Here they encountered a Natal Carbineer scout. He informed Major Russell that the Natal Native Horse were fighting on the ridge to their front and offered to lead them through a steep and rugged opening to the top. As they struggled up the slope a mass of Zulu warriors appeared along the ridge. 'Action front!' shouted Russell. His men hastily pulled the iron troughs from the mules, erected them, lit a fuse, and one poorly aimed missile shot off, crashing harmlessly against a rock face. Then the Zulus opened fire at about 100 yards. Balls sliced into the command, killing three of the eight gunners and Russell receiving a mortal wound. The NNC escort fired a few shots in retaliation, but then bolted along with most of the horses and mules. Those gunners still standing also fled, and would have been cut down but for the arrival of Durnford's command as they fought their retreat. The Zulus dashed back to cover, then Durnford resumed his defensive withdrawal eventually arriving at a deep, dry, watercourse; the Nyokana Donga. It formed a natural defensive breastwork, and here Durnford decided to make his first stand, about one mile southeast of the camp.

Shortly after Durnford's march from the camp that morning, Pulleine had decided to send a company of redcoat infantry along the Tahelane spur in support of Captain Barton's command. This represented a change in attitude, having previously told Durnford his orders were to remain on the defensive. Presumably he despatched these troops because the Zulus 'retreating' ploy too had taken him in, and no one took seriously the notion of a Zulu attack. The remaining infantry, standing to arms, were dismissed, but just in case were told to leave their straps and ammunition pouches on, and 'to be in readiness to fall in at any moment.' Lieutenant Curling of the artillery joined infantry officers in their mess:

> Not one of us dreamt there was the least danger, and all we hoped for was the fight might come off before the General returned. In the meantime our dinner had been cooked and as there seemed no chance of our being attacked, we broke off and went into our tents.

But then there was the distant rattle of gunfire as Barton's native horsemen fired into the massed Zulus. The camp came to a standstill as all stopped and looked towards the Nqutu Plateau. Very soon Shepstone and Hamer galloped in from Barton's retreating command with news of the massed Zulu advance. As a breathless Shepstone was shown into Pulleine's tent, another rider, Captain Alan Gardner, arrived with orders from Chelmsford to strike part of the camp in preparation for its removal, and to entrench the remainder. What Pulleine had expected was news of Chelmsford's return in response to his 8.05 a.m. warning that Zulus were threatening the camp.

'I'm not an alarmist, sir,' said Shepstone, keeping his calm, 'but the Zulus are in such black masses over there, such long black lines, that you will have to give us all the assistance you can. They are now fast driving our men this way.'

Pulleine hesitated. Orders were orders. But then Gardner, a member of Chelmsford's staff, spoke up. 'The General knows nothing of this. He is only thinking of the cowardly way the Zulus are running before our troops over yonder.' Gardner later recalled:

> The men of the 24th Regiment were all fallen in, and the Artillery also, and Colonel Pulleine sent two companies to support Colonel Durnford, to the hill on the left, and forming up the remaining companies in line, the guns in action on the extreme left flank of the camp, facing the hill on our left. Shortly after, I took the mounted men, by Colonel Pulleine's direction, about a quarter of a mile to the front of the camp, and left them there with orders to hold the spriut.

Two messages were despatched to Chelmsford. One from

Pulleine said 'Staff Officer. Heavy firing to the left of our camp. Cannot move camp at present.'

Gardner sent his own by separate courier. 'Heavy firing near left of camp. Shepstone has come in for reinforcements and reports that Zulus are falling back. The whole force at camp turned out and fighting about one mile to our left flank.'

Zulus are falling back? Where Gardner got this idea is a mystery. He must have misconstrued something Shepstone said. As Chelmsford read these words at about two o'clock that afternoon, his troops in camp were being slashed and stabbed to death. The mistake made no real difference; it was already too late for a rescue to take place.

When Pulleine heard gunfire from the Nqutu Plateau he despatched troops to support Durnford as requested, then spread most of the remaining troops around in a loose, large defensive line vulnerable to easy attack. This closely resembled Chelmsford's own written instructions regarding deployment of troops in case of Zulu attack, a copy of which would later be found on Durnford's body. It recommended 'British Infantry to the front line, deployed or extended, with one or both flank companies thrown back.' Artillery would be slightly forward of the centre, and the infantry reserve well to the rear. The native troops were to support the infantry in the rear 'well clear of each flank.' The Mounted Infantry were to be behind each flank, prepared to 'move around the flanks, and rear, of the enemy.'

But, of course, no one set of instructions can cover different situations. History is full of 'ifs.' *If* Pulleine had pulled his troops back into a tight defensive position, the camp may well have survived. The action at Rorke's Drift later in the day would prove this. Pulleine could have improvised breastworks from wagons and other materials at hand and, with Isandlwana protecting his rear, an effective defence could have been maintained until Chelmsford finally moved to the camp's relief.

As the Zulus closed in, however, the threat was not taken seriously. Transport officer Captain Edward Essex, writing in his tent, was not at all perturbed when he went outside to see what was going on. 'I had my glasses over my shoulder and thought I might as well take my revolver; but did not trouble to put on my sword as I thought nothing of the matter and expected to be back in half an hour to complete my letters.'

The advancing centre of the Zulu buffalo head formation moved quickly over Nyoni Ridge and into the depression between there and Conical Hill. The right horn bypassed Barton's retreating horsemen and came into the view of Lieutenant Cavaye's infantry, sent by Pulleine in support, deployed at five-yard intervals along the crest of Tahelane Ridge. A volley crashed out from the redcoat line and they continued firing as 2nd Lieutenant Dyson moved with a detachment to the left. From here they fired on the enemy as they emerged from behind a small ridge. Zulus fell under fire from both parties, but the warriors moved inexorably on over rough terrain to the camp's north.

Captain Essex arrived with another company of redcoats, and detachments of native troops on both horse and foot. He recalled:

> On arriving at the far side of the crest of the hill, I found the company in charge of Lieutenant Cavaye, a section being detached about 500 yards to the left, in charge of Lieutenant Dyson. The whole were in extended order engaging the enemy, who was moving in similar formation towards our left, keeping about 800 yards from our line. Captain Mostyn moved his company into space

between the portions of that already on the hill, and his men extended and entered into action. This line was then prolonged on our right along the crest of the hill by a body of native infantry. I observed that the enemy made little progress as regards his advance, but appeared to be moving at a rapid pace towards our left.

Captain Stafford's company of Natal Native Contingent, and Lieutenant Vause's company of Natal Native Horse were now to the right of Cavaye's infantry. George Shepstone had led them to the Tahelane Ridge after they had safely escorted Durnford's wagons into camp. The troopers had dismounted and taken a defensive line alongside the NNC. Then Captain Barton with part of his command arrived, the rest having retreated back to camp. Lieutenant Roberts was killed during the withdrawal, possibly by British artillery fire.

The troops found themselves confronted by 2,000 steadily advancing Zulu warriors, part of the Zulu right horn. Stafford fired a few shots, getting their range at 700 yards, then ran over to Barton and suggested sending word to Durnford. A rider soon thundered off, then the lines were closed up, the firing becoming a constant chatter through the hills and valleys. 'The Zulu impis continued their steady advance,' Stafford recalled 'splendidly the savages pressed forward and when within 300 yards the native Contingents began to waver and bolted.' But not for long. They reformed a little to the rear and were reinforced by company of redcoats under Captain Reginald Youghusband of the 24th. Then orders arrived for Mostyn and Cavaye's companies to withdraw closer to camp. Hard pressed by the Zulus, the survivors scrambled to the rear barely avoiding annihilation, but Lieutenant Dyson's isolated party on the left never received the order. They stood and fought at their post firing and reloading with well-drilled precision. They stayed and fought on, only to fall under a rush of Zulu assegais and shields.

The defensive line reformed with the NNC and NNH filling the spaces between the three companies of redcoats. Volleys of fire and smoke crashed out on the advancing horde and Zulus fell. The warriors retreated back over the crest of the hill, but then reformed for another push.

Major Stuart Smith, meanwhile, had returned to camp in company with Captain Gardner. From high terrain on the camp's left his two 'bye and byes' convulsed on the Zulu centre which lay about 1000 yards to their front. The Zulus used this name because in 1836 they had inquired of a naval officer what cannons were for. 'You shall see bye and bye,' he had replied. 'Bye and bye' was here and now as the gunners rammed shells down the barrels, then stepped back as each projectile plunged into the massed ranks and burst, warriors, dirt and smoke flung all about. The two remaining companies of redcoat infantry joined the artillerymen, lying down in skirmish order, ten yards between each man on each flank of the guns. Their Martini-Henrys cracked as they opened fire sending out plumes of smoke obscuring the advancing ranks. But the Martini-Henry did not always work flawlessly, suffering a similar problem to the Springfields at the Little Bighorn; cartridges sometimes not ejecting after firing. The fault with the British rifle was attributed to the thin brass cartridge melting in an overheated weapon, the extractor system lacking the strength to eject.

Another infantry company under Lieutenant Pope was 800 yards to the right defending the camp's centre, and firing over Durnford's men defending the Nyokana Donga. Captain Essex recalled:

> I was surprised how relaxed the men in the ranks were despite the climatic tension of the battle. Loading as fast

as they could and firing into the dense black masses that pressed in on them, the men were laughing and chatting, and obviously thought they were giving the Zulus an awful hammering.

Lieutenant Curling of the artillery later wrote:

The Zulus soon split up into a large mass of skirmishers that extended as far around the camp as we could see. We could get no idea of numbers but the hills were black with them. They advanced steadily in the face of the infantry and our guns, but I believe the whole of the natives who defended the rear of the camp soon bolted and left only our side of the camp defended.

The Zulus were quick to learn. Seeing the artillerymen standing to one side of the gun before unleashing another shell, they flung themselves to earth, avoiding much of the explosion's savage blast, then rose again to continue the advance. But the Zulu line began to waver under the withering fire as warriors fell. The Zulus took shelter in any depression or dip as the bullets whined overhead. Their indunas berated them, saying their king had not ordered this. 'Go and toss them into Maritzburg,' one cried. Many of the advancing warriors held their shields at an angle, the belief being that this would deflect the British bullets. This ploy may well have been partially effective 300 yards or more from the firing line, but no closer. Many of those who rose to the attack dropped again as hot lead ripped through hide shields only tough enough to deflect savage thrusts with a spear or bayonet. Those who were not hit fell to earth again to avoid the same fate.

A grey haze of gunsmoke hung over the Nyokana Donga where Durnford made a long stand. Here the left horn of the

Zulu advance had also become bogged down beneath the storm of lead fired by his command, now about 150 men. His Native Horse had been joined by Captain Bradstreet's volunteers, about 30 in all, some Natal Mounted Police, and a handful of Natal Carbineers.

Durnford rode up and down the line encouraging his men. 'Fire my boys,' he cried. 'Well done my boys!'

Jabez Molife recalled 'He was calm and cheerful, talking & even laughing with us.' Durnford sometimes dismounted and stood on the edge of the donga completely exposed to enemy fire as he shouted encouragement to his men.

> Some of us did not like his exposing himself so much to the enemy, & wanted him to keep behind us, but he laughed at us, & said, 'All right! Nonsense!' Sometimes as he passed amongst us one of the men brought him his gun with the old cartridge sticking, & he dismounted &, taking the gun between his knees, because of him only having one hand with the strength in it, he pulled the cartridge out and gave the gun back.

Such was his bravery that Lieutenant Alfred Henderson thought he had lost his head, and doubted he was fit to command. But perhaps sheer bravery was something beyond Henderson's grasp, as he was not only to escape Isandlwana, but also leave the courageous garrison at Rorke's Drift to their fate later the same day.

One of Sihayo's sons, Mehlokazulu, later said 'We could not advance against their fire any longer. They had drawn their horses into this donga, and all we could see were their helmets. They fired so heavily we had to retire. We kept lying down and rising again.'

But then ammunition began to run low. Not only for

Durnford's men, but the infantry along the British line began to call for more after they had been firing for about half an hour. The supply of ammunition to the firing line was awkward at best, reserve ammunition for the 1st Battalion infantry stored one mile away. The timber boxes each containing 600 rounds for the Martini-Henrys would be opened and loaded upon mule-carts for transport to the firing line. Here the ammunition was placed in haversacks and distributed by carriers to the various platoons, but the 70 rounds each man carried was running out. More ammunition was sent to the firing line as Lieutenant Smith-Dorrien recalled:

> I, having no particular duty to perform in camp, when I saw the whole Zulu Army advancing, had collected camp stragglers, such as artillerymen in charge of spare horses, officers' servants, sick, etc., and had taken them to the ammunition-boxes, where we broke them open as fast as we could, and kept sending out the packets to the firing line.

The lieutenant had to break the boxes open by smashing them with rifle butts because screwdrivers were in short supply, the sliding lid being fastened by a single two-inch screw. And then he struck another problem; 'For heaven's sake, don't take that, man, for it belongs to our battalion,' he was told by Quartermaster Bloomfield of the 2nd Battalion. 'Hang it all,' replied the officer, 'you don't want a requisition slip now, do you?' Others like Quartermaster London of the Natal Carbineers were more interested in survival than correct paperwork and readily doled out ammunition to all who asked. Captain Essex recalled 'I had some boxes placed on a mule cart and sent it off to the companies engaged, and sent more by hand, employing any men without arms. I then went back to the line, telling the men that plenty of ammunition was coming.' When returning Essex noticed that the redcoat companies of the 1st Battalion had 'retired within 300 yards of that portion of the camp occupied by the Native Contingent. On my way I noticed a number of native infantry retreating in haste towards the camp, their officers endeavouring to prevent them but without effect.'

Durnford despatched a rider back to camp for more ammunition, but when none came he sent Lieutenant Henderson. He located Durnford's supply wagons on the other side of the saddle bridging Isandlwana and the stony koppie, but by that time it was too late. With his ammunition running out, Durnford could see the Zulu left horn was moving around to outflank his position, as Reno had seen the Sioux warriors outflanking his skirmish line on the river flat. Durnford gave the order to pull out, then his command mounted up and galloped back to camp. Henderson met Durnford and led his native horsemen to their supply wagons while the volunteers and police went to their own ammunition supplies. Trooper Sparks of the Natal Mounted Police said later:

> There still seemed to be a great deal of confusion, no kind of information being made for the defence of the camp, and it was only after some considerable time that we were able to procure any ammunition, as the boxes in which it was packed were all screwed down, and we had no tools to open them. I noticed Quartermaster London, of the Natal Carbineers, opening one of these boxes, and he was killed by a bullet wound in the head while doing so.

The Zulu movement had made Durnford's position untenable, but his withdrawal from the Nyokana Donga had the same effect as Reno's retreat from the timber alongside the Little Bighorn. The Zulus now advanced at a rapid rate taking control of the field. Durnford's retreat coincided with Lieutenant Pope's infantry company moving forward to his support, a fatal mistake. This left Pope too far forward and dangerously exposed. Pope's men delivered withering blasts into the advancing horde, only to be swamped and crushed like blades of grass beneath an avalanche. Lieutenants Pope and Godwin-Austen both wore monocles, and a Zulu induna recalled seeing two officers with pieces of glass in their eye. One fell by rifle fire but the other continued the fight with his revolver. The induna was wounded in the leg and grazed by another bullet, but hurled his long assegai into the officer's chest. As he attempted to pull it out, the Zulu rushed in and cut him down with the shorter assegai.

As Pope's company G was cut down, Durnford attempted to find Colonel Pulleine, his intention being to consolidate the camp's defences by ordering the troops in closer, thus reducing the length of the firing line, but Pulleine was not to be found. Durnford asked Captain Essex to take as many men as possible to the right of the British line to keep the Zulu left horn at bay. Pulleine, elsewhere, finally appreciated the deteriorating situation and ordered the defence line to withdraw closer to their ammunition supplies. 'Then at the sound of a bugle,' recalled the warrior uMhoti, 'the firing ceased at a breath, and the whole British front rose from the ground and retired on the tents. Like a flame the whole Zulu force sprang to its feet and darted upon them.' A massive wave of shields moved forward at frightening speed, the warriors charging in a mad rush across open ground through the dense pall of smoke. They shouted the war cry 'uSuthu! uSuthu!' the name of Cetshwayo's faction in a previous war, but both Chiefs kaMvundlana and Biyela, who had rallied them, were killed in the charge.

Trooper Sparks continued:

> By this time the Zulu Army had thrown out wings on our flanks, so that we were hemmed in on three sides and in a very short time the camp was invaded by vast numbers of Zulus, and owing to every one of us being more or less in skirmishing order it was impossible to make any effective defence.

The two 7-pounders each fired one round of caseshot, the mass of metal balls cutting a killing swath through the attackers, then Major Smith ordered the guns pulled back. The Zulu line continued its determined rush forward, and Lieutenant Curling later wrote:

> At this time, out of my small detachment, one man had been killed, shot through the head, another wounded, shot through the side and another through the wrist. Major Smith was also shot through the arm but was able to do his duty. Of course, no wounded man was attended to, there was no time or men to spare. When we got the order to retire, we limbered up at once but were hardly in time as the Zulus were on us at once and one man was killed as he was mounting in a seat on the gun carriage. Most of the gunners were on foot as there was not time to mount them on the guns.

Major Smith and Lieutenant Curling rode back towards the camp as the artillery horses pulled the clattering and bouncing gun carriages over the rough ground behind. They arrived to find utter chaos and confusion, the camp already overrun with fighting Zulus who had dashed through a defence gap to the camp's right. The artillery train continued its mad scurry right on through the camp, the gunners alongside being hacked down by the livid warriors as they ran. Only a couple survived the horrific gauntlet to emerge near the road to Rorke's Drift.

Quartermaster Pullen of the 1st Battalion was handing out ammunition as the British line crumbled. He rallied some men around him 'Come on, men, rally here, follow me. Don't be running away like a parcel of women. Let's try and turn their flank.'

He asked a man on horseback to get Pulleine to send help as they were being outflanked on the right. Pullen led his rallied party of soldiers off towards the stony koppie, only to perish amidst the smoke and slaughter of the ongoing fight.

The Zulus pressed home the attack on the camp's left flank, as Lieutenant Raw of the Natal Native Horse recalled:

> The enemy attacked in great force in front of the camp or should I say to the left. I turned my troop and engaged them, the troops drawn up in camp firing over us. We took up the left of a company of the 24th Regiment having on our left a troop of Lonsdale's men. The company of the 24th then retired towards the tents and the enemy followed close after cutting them up before they could rally, killing them close to the tents. We were driven through the camp and found the right had also been driven in and the camp surrounded.

But Raw's company managed to escape. As the infantry retired at the run, the swift Zulus catching and tangling with them, the whole picture became blurred amidst a maelstrom of dust and smoke. Horsemen, redcoats, Zulus and native troops struggled, fighting hand to hand and bayonet to assegai, men screaming as they were cut down. The Zulu warrior Muziwento recalled 'Some covered their faces with their hands, not wishing to see death. Some ran around. Some entered into their tents.

Others were indignant; although badly wounded they died where they stood, at their post.' The redcoat infantryman, weighed down with uniform, boots, rifle, straps and pouches had no chance in a race against the fleet-footed and almost naked Zulu carrying only his shield and weapons in hand.

As soldiers fell beneath the Zulu onslaught panic set in. The camp was full of teamsters, furriers, clerks and others who had not come to fight. Those who could made for the neck between the stony koppie and Isandlwana, beyond which lay the road to Rorke's Drift, Natal, and hopefully safety. Commissariat Officer James Hamer was fighting alongside George Shepstone on the left flank when the thin red line fell back and disintegrated amidst a mass of shields and assegais. Deciding it was time to beat a hasty retreat, he rode through the struggling confusion, dust and smoke of the camp towards the neck. 'The scene at the top of the camp baffles description, oxen yoked to wagons, mules, sheep, horses & men in the greatest confusion, all wildly trying to escape.' He saw the Zulus there being held at bay by a company of redcoats and 'good old Colonel Durnford making a heroic & most gallant stand to cover the retreat.'

Survivor Trooper Richard of the Natal Mounted Police recalled:

> I stopped at the camp as long as possible, and saw one of the most horrid sights I ever wish to see. The Zulus were in the camp, ripping our men up, and also the tents and everything else they came across, with their assegais. They were not content with killing, but were ripping our men up afterwards.

Zulus believed that bodies swelling after death was the soul trying to escape, thus they disembowelled the fallen to avoid being haunted by the victim's spirit, which would cause his own stomach to swell, leading to insanity.

The head of the Zulu buffalo had advanced on the camp from the northeast, the centre striking the left of the camp, the left horn sweeping over the donga defended by Durnford before he fell back on the camp. This horn, sweeping in a southerly arc, then struck the right of the camp, the warriors infiltrating the tents. The right horn, meanwhile, swept from the north around the rear of Isandlwana. The left and right horns would meet on the neck, thus surrounding the camp and cutting off retreat down the road to Rorke's Drift. It was here that Durnford fought, keeping the horns from meeting, thus holding the escape route open, and George Shepstone took a detachment of NNC around to the back of Isandlwana in an attempt to hold back the Zulu right horn. Shepstone's men fought hard, according to the Zulus, but were overwhelmed by weight of numbers and died where they stood.

As the Zulus closed in, Captain Younghusband's Company C of the 1st Battalion retired in good order from the left of the British line. They took position on a rocky shelf above the neck and here held off the Zulu attack. "They fought well,' said one warrior, 'and the Zulus could not get at them at all; they were shot or bayoneted as fast as they came up.' But then their ammunition ran out. The redcoats, hemmed in, made a desperate charge towards another seat of resistance along the neck, the officer leading them with 'a long flashing sword which he whirled around his head as he ran—it must have been made of fire.' They never made it; every man hacked down as they fought, reminiscent of Indian accounts of some of Custer's men in a suicidal charge near that fight's end.

How exactly Colonel Pulleine died is not known, but his body was found in the 1st Battalion's camp area where he had been seen by Captain Gardner shortly before Durnford retreated back into camp. One claim is that he died in his tent while writing a last letter.

Durnford and the Natal volunteers, all having horses, could have made their escape, but saved the lives of many by holding their ground. He had ordered his native horsemen to retire earlier and they made their escape along the Fugitive's Trail. But a lot of those who made it through the neck did not survive, as described by one Zulu warrior of the right wing.

> We worked round behind Isandhlwana under cover of the long grass and dongas, intending to join with the iNgobamakhosi on the neck and sweep in upon the camp. Then we saw white men beginning to run away along the road to Rorke's Drift; many of these were cut off and killed, down in the stream which flows along the bottom of the valley. More and more came over, some mounted and some on foot. When they saw that the valley was full of our warriors, they turned to the left and ran off along the side of the hill towards the Buffalo; those who had not got horses were soon overtaken. The uNodwenga pursued the mounted men, numbers of whom were killed along the thorns and dongas, but I heard that some escaped.

Major Smith's battery had rattled through the camp and over the neck. Lieutenant Curling reported:

> When we got on the road to Rorke's Drift it was completely blocked up by Zulus. I was with Major Smith at the time, he told me he had been wounded in the arm. We saw Lieutenant Coghill, the ADC, and asked him if we could not rally some men and make a stand, he said he did not think it could be done. We crossed the road with the crowd, principally consisting of natives, men left

in camp, civilians, and went down a deep ravine heading towards the river. The Zulus were in the middle of the crowd, stabbing the men as they ran.

The battery only clattered a further 400 yards before the guns ground to a halt in a deep rut across the road. By this time only one gunner was still clinging to a gun carriage, but both guns were covered with other men trying to escape. The Zulus leapt upon them, hacking and stabbing, and dragged the drivers off their horses. Seeing the hopelessness of the situation, Curling rode off in a desperate bid to make his own way, joining the throng of escapees heading over rough, steep ground towards the Buffalo River six miles distant. Those attempting escape on foot had little chance, being overtaken by fast Zulus and struck down as they ran. There were mules, oxen, horses and men all entangled in a mad, ghastly scramble for survival 'man and beast, apparently all infected with the danger which surrounded us,' recalled interpreter James Brickhill. Mounted, he caught a riderless horse and gave it to an exhausted soldier who climbed into the saddle just to be dropped by a Zulu bullet, the horse running off. Brickhill soon came upon Band Sergeant Gamble, staggering across the stony ground, who begged him for a lift. "My dear fellow, it is a case of life or death with me,' he replied, then kept riding towards the Buffalo.

There was no clear trail, the fugitives having to blaze their own as they wove their way in a mad scramble through boulders, scrub and stunted trees. Those coming after tripped over shields, assegais, guns, ammunition belts, clothing; all types of debris, as the fast Zulu warriors swooped like angels of death.

Brickhill saw Lieutenants Melville and Coghill of the 24th

Regiment riding alongside each other. Melville held the queen's Color of the 1st Battalion, mounted on an eight-foot staff and furled in its leather case. Whether these officers were heroes saving the regimental colors from the enemy, or were merely using them as an excuse to desert, would be debated for years to come. Neither survived, and officially their deed would be recognised as that of heroes; the British Empire needing all the heroes it could this day.

Harry Davies recalled a Zulu catching hold of his bridle. He attempted to kill the warrior with a bayonet thrust, but the Zulu grasped his carbine and pulled it out of his hand, which at the same time made Davies' horse rear, clearing him. He then had only his revolver, and he saw a Zulu right in his course, and rode at him and shot him in the neck. His horse was wounded but Davies escaped and rode on.

The blood-soaked fugitives' trail led to the Manzimnyama, a marshy tributary of the Buffalo. A party of about 60 redcoats under Lieutenant Edgar Anstey struggled to this river's banks before being caught, surrounded, and cut down.

Some survivors managed to make it along the stream's banks to arrive at the Buffalo, where a scene of carnage reminiscent of Reno's flight across the Little Bighorn ensued. But there were more fugitives here, and the Buffalo was high due to the recent rains. High cliffs lined the river, and the crossing at one point could only be reached by a narrow path, causing a panic-stricken crush at the top. Lieutenant Smith-Dorrien dismounted amongst the terrified throng and made a tourniquet for a bleeding infantryman's arm. 'For God's sake get on, man,' he heard the wounded Major Smith say, 'the Zulus are on top of us!' Smith-Dorrien was in the act of mounting when his horse 'a broken kneed old crock' was struck by an assegai and plummeted over the precipice. In the next few moments Major Smith and the wounded infantryman died under a hail of assegais along with other wounded. 'With the help of my revolver,' Smith-Dorrien recalled, 'and a wild jump down the rocks, I found myself in the Buffalo River, which was in flood and eighty yards broad.' Swept away by the current, he saved himself by grasping the tail of an unmounted horse which towed him to the other side. Unlike Lieutenant Hodgson at the Little Bighorn, Lieutenant Smith-Dorrien lived to tell the tale of his horse-borne crossing.

Captain Barton and Lieutenant Raw rallied their native horsemen to provide covering fire from the Natal bank as fugitives swam for their lives. Both Barton and Reno's commands, which had opened their respective battles, had retreated to survive mostly intact while other companies were wiped out to a man.

Private Sam Wassall of the Mounted Infantry was crossing the churning waters when he heard a cry for help from Private Westwood, caught by the current and drowning. Despite Zulus swarming towards the riverbank, Wassall turned his horse back to dry land where he tied his mount to a branch, then waded out to rescue Westwood. He pulled him to shore, they mounted up and made it safely to the Natal bank, Zulu bullets splashing about them. Wassall would receive the only Victoria Cross to be awarded for Isandlwana, until nearly 30 years later when Lieutenants Coghill and Melville would receive posthumous Victoria Crosses for saving the regimental colors.

Lieutenant Curling of the Artillery was another lucky survivor, as he wrote in a letter to his mother:

> We rode for about 5 miles, hotly pursued by the Zulus, when we came to a cliff overhanging the river. We had to climb down the face of the cliff and not more than

half those who started from the top got to the bottom. Many fell right down among others, Maj. Smith and the Zulus caught us here and shot us as we climbed down. I got down safely and came to the river which was very deep and swift. Numbers were swept away as they tried to cross and others shot from above.
My horse, fortunately, swam straight across, though I had three or four men hanging on his tail, stirrup leathers, etc. After crossing the river, we were in comparative safety, though many were killed afterwards who were on foot and unable to keep up. It seems to me like a dream, I cannot realise it all.

Lieutenant Smith-Dorrien found, on the Natal bank, numerous native allies and amidst them one European, James Hamer, who was lying on the ground, having been kicked by his horse. Smith-Dorrien helped him remount and lent him his knife, on the understanding that Hamer would catch for him one of the untended horses that had made it across. But Hamer simply galloped off into the distance leaving the officer on foot. He moved up a hill along with friendly natives, but then some fell as bullets began to thud amongst them, the Zulus getting their range from the far bank. Smith-Dorrien reached the crest to see some Zulus had forded the river and were running to cut him off. He dashed to the left and for three miles had about 20 warriors chase him, but was eventually saved by the arrival of some Natal Native Horse. They dismounted and opened fire on the Zulus, driving them off.

While Smith-Dorrien and a few others made their escape, Durnford fought on, rallying others around him; about 30 redcoat infantrymen and 40 white horsemen of the Natal Mounted Police, Newcastle Mounted Rifles, Buffalo Border Guard, and Lieutenant Scott with 14 of his Natal Carbineers.

In their last fight together, old wounds over Bushman's River Pass were forgotten. Being expert horsemen, the Carbineers may well have escaped, but they stood with Durnford on the neck just below the stony koppie. With his crippled arm in his coat, and flowing moustaches, this Long Hair was easily identified by the Zulus who attacked his position. A Zulu said that a one-armed officer had his men in disciplined order, and took his wounded with him. He killed four Zulus with his revolver as they were forced up the slope. 'It was a long time before they were overcome. They threw down their guns when their ammunition was done, and then commenced with their pistols,' said Mehlokazulu, 'and then they formed a line, shoulder to shoulder, and back to back, and fought with their knives.' Durnford was an inspiration to those around him as he fought this last time, as he had been in Nyokana Donga.

> Some Zulus threw assegais at them, others shot at them; but they did not get very close—they avoided the bayonet; for any man who went up to stab a soldier was fixed through the throat or stomach, and at once fell. Occasionally when a soldier was engaged with a Zulu in front with an assegai, another Zulu killed him from behind.

One warrior, Kumbeka, described his attack on an officer.

> Dum! Dum! went his revolver as he was firing from right to left, and I came alongside him and stuck my assegai under his right arm, pushing it through his body till it came out between his ribs on the left side. As soon as he fell I slit his stomach so I knew he should not shoot any more of my people.

One of Chief Sihayo's sons, Muziwento, later said:

> They made a desperate resistance, some firing their pistols and others with swords. I repeatedly hear the word 'fire' but we proved too many for them, and killed them where they stood. When all was over I had a look at these men, and saw an officer with his arm in a sling and with a big moustache, surrounded by Carbineers, soldiers and other men I did not know.

As Durnford's men fought this desperate last stand, the sky darkened as the moon's shadow passed over the sun, causing a partial eclipse. One Zulu recalled 'the sun turned black in the middle of the battle; we could still see it over us, or should have thought we had been fighting till evening.'

The Zulus had won the day, but their victory was costly in lives and blood, at least 1000 being killed, and possibly many more dying of their wounds in the weeks to come. And the humiliated British would want their revenge.

The last fighting man was said to a redcoat from Younghusband's command. He took refuge in a 'deep ravine' of his own—a small cave on the southern slope of Isandlwana. Zulus who attempted to enter died where they stood. Finally a well-directed volley was fired through the entrance, no gun barked in return, and the fight was over. The moon's black shadow moved on and the sun shone once more, casting an eerie, ghostly glow over the smoke and dust that hung over the carnage of Isandlwana.

At sundown Smith-Dorrien arrived at Helpmekaar, having walked 20 miles from the Buffalo. Here he joined about 30 Europeans who had survived the rout to help the townspeople form a wagon laager. They sat up nervously all that night 'momentarily expecting attack,' an attack which never came. Smith-Dorrien would be only one of five British regular army officers to survive Isandlwana, probably, like the other four, because of his blue uniform jacket. Three others were also mounted transport officers, Captains Gardner and Essex, and Lieutenant Cochrane. Lieutenant Curling of the Royal Artillery, mounted, had also lived to tell the tale. Cetshwayo had told his warriors to target the redcoats, and no officer wearing one survived. Figures vary as to the number of survivors, but the usual is 55 European, a few hundred native, with 854 Europeans killed. 1,329 dead soldiers and civilians of both races were scattered about the camp and along the Fugitives' Trail. Six infantry companies of the 24th Regiment had been wiped out with a loss of 52 officers. Waterloo and Quatre Bras had seen fewer officers killed in 1815.

On the material side, 132 wagons, hundreds of oxen, horses and mules, and 60,000 pounds worth of ammunition and supplies had been lost.

Durnford's horse, Chieftain, was amongst the survivors. Durnford's servant rode him to the Colenso's, where Frances's sister, Agnes, cared him for till he died in 1883.

Captain Frederick W. Benteen
(Little Bighorn Battlefield National Monument)

PAUL WILLIAMS

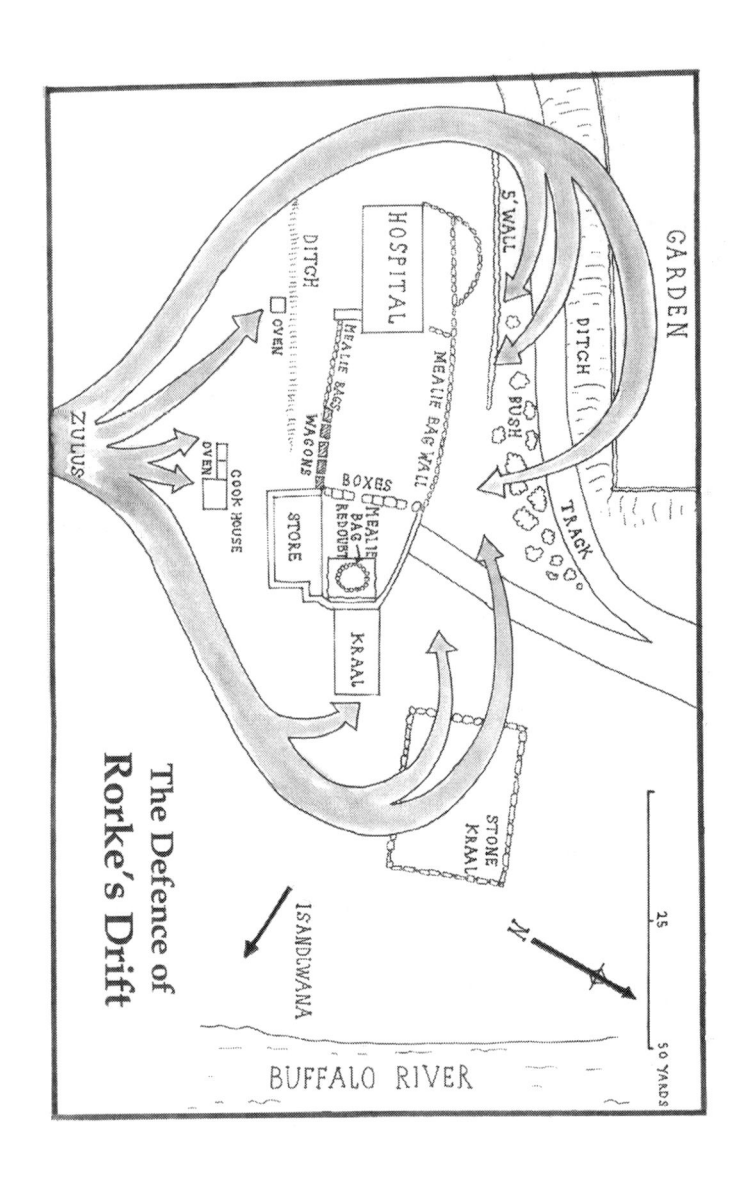

The Defence of Rorke's Drift

8
BESIEGED

'Our command ought to be doing something or Custer will be after Reno with a sharp stick,' was the general consensus amongst the soldiers on the bluffs overlooking the Little Bighorn. The rattle of gunfire echoing from the north satisfied everyone that Custer was engaged with the enemy, but not a single soul envisaged his plight. Two volleys were heard. Soldiers smiled. 'Custer is giving it to them for all he is worth,' one man said.

'I have but little doubt now,' wrote Lieutenant Godfrey years later, 'that these volleys were fired by Custer's orders as signals of distress and to indicate where he was.'

Private Taylor recalled:

> We heard firing off in the general direction Custer was supposed to have gone, 'Why don't we move?', was a question asked by more than one. The three Troops that had been engaged in the valley were it is true somewhat demoralized, but that was no excuse for the whole command to remain inactive. A few of our men had been wounded, but none so seriously that they could not ride with the pack train.

Captain Weir, commander of Troop D, could also hear the firing and peered irritably along the bluffs to his north. His company had driven the Indians away along his perimeter, and now he was impatient for orders to ride to the sound of the guns; orders which never came. He rode to a high point and peered through his binoculars to the north while his second-in-command, Lieutenant Edgerly, moved the troop out, thinking he had received permission to move. Orders or no orders, the captain joined his company and led them to the north.

Reno, meanwhile, sent Lieutenant Varnum down the slope with a party to bury Lieutenant Hodgson. They encountered more survivors coming up the slope, a party of 12 men who had been left behind in the trees. The scout George Herendeen was one, and later described how, having been thrown from his falling horse, he found 13 others sheltering amidst the trees. They heard firing from downstream as Custer was engaged, then moved from the timber to rejoin Reno's command on the bluffs. Two men refused to move, despite Herendeen's urging, but the others moved towards the ford only to encounter five hostile braves on horseback. Shots were exchanged, then the Indians rode off. The soldiers waded across the river, 'heart deep,' then made it up the bluffs to the relative safety of Reno's command. The dead and mutilated bodies of the two troopers who stayed behind were later found.

The mule train with the packs finally arrived, and Captain Benteen moved out following Weir with Companies H, K, and M, also without orders from Major Reno, who was supposed to be in command. But their march would be too little too late; no more effective than Colonel Harness' attempt to ride to the sound of the guns at Isandlwana over two years later.

Captain Weir and his company, meanwhile, reached the height later called Weir Point. They saw, about two miles further on, through the dust cloud 'many Indians riding around and shooting at objects on the ground.' Even then they did not guess that the dead bodies of Custer's command provided the targets.

Reno finally started marching the remainder of the command after the others, but encumbered with wounded and the pack train, he did not move far. Lieutenant Godfrey, with Benteen, recalled:

> The advance went as far as the high bluffs where the command was halted. Persons who have been on the plains and seen stationary objects dance before them, now in view and now obscured, or a weed on the top of a hill, projected against the sky, magnified to appear as a tree, will readily understand why our views could be unsatisfactory. We could see stationary groups of horsemen, and individual horsemen moving about; from their grouping and the manner in which they sat their horses we knew they were Indians. On the left of the valley a strange sight attracted our attention. Some one remarked that there had been a fire which scorched the leaves of the bushes, which caused the reddish-brown appearance, but this appearance was changeable; watching this intently for a short time with field-glasses, it was discovered that this strange sight was the immense pony-herds of the Indians.

It was here that Trumpeter John Martin first told Benteen which side of the river he had left Custer on, and pointed out the place he was sent back. In the distance they could see many mounted warriors. Some of those closest reacted to their presence, and distant shots were heard. They assumed Custer had been driven off and these were fired by his rear guard. But the firing ceased and dust clouds rose as the mounted warriors started racing towards Weir's position. The order to dismount was given and the troops deployed to fight on foot. Companies K, D, and M lined the crest of the bluffs at right angles to the river while the remainder of the command retired to the rear. Lieutenant Godfrey, Company K, was startled when they disappeared from view rather than hold a supportive position. As the other two companies came under attack, Godfrey received orders to pull back and join the main command. The troop mounted up and turned back but had not gone far when the other two companies came galloping down the slope behind them. One wounded man had been left behind to face the horrific mercy of the Indians. Lieutenant Edgerly was almost left as well when his skittish horse would not let him mount. He vaulted into the saddle and galloped down the bluff, then hostiles appeared along the crest and opened fire on the retreating troops. One man dropped from his saddle, killed, and others were wounded along with some of the horses. Then the Indians launched an assault, galloping, howling down the slope. Godfrey gave the order for his troop to fight on foot 'deploying as rapidly as possible without waiting for the formation laid down in tactics.' They opened fire, but then he received a second order to join the main command. As the Indians broke to take cover from the fusillade, Godfrey's men commenced a fighting retreat. The Indians were reinforced and their fire intensified, causing the troopers to move too quickly and bunch up, providing a better target for hostile bullets. Godfrey recalled 'the "ping-ping" of the bullets overhead seemed to have a more terrifying influence than the "swish-thud" of the bullets that struck the ground immediately about us.' He called a halt and respaced his men back across the skirmish line, and the fighting retreat continued. As they approached Reno's position he ordered Lieutenant Hare and 10 men to occupy an overlooking hill, but then a third order came calling his company back with all haste. Hare's mission was aborted, and they all fell back, rejoining Reno. The Indians quickly occupied the contentious hill and other crests, keeping up a constant fire, the command effectively besieged on the same bluffs overlooking the river they had climbed after the valley fight.

Despite flying bullets, Dr. Porter established a hospital of sorts in a sheltering depression with the horses and mules. The men given the task of holding the animals cringed as close to the ground as possible to avoid long-range bullets from the east. Godfrey recalled 'I was horrified to find myself wondering if a small sagebrush, about as thick as my finger, would turn a bullet.'

Private William Taylor recalled:

> Our company was considerably scattered and then I saw Sergeant Feihler near the low end of the herded horses and pack mules. I approached him and said to him. 'What are we going to do, stay here all night, or try to move away?' Major Reno was then standing quite near, and heard my question. He turned at once, with the remark, 'I would like to know how in Hell we are going to move away?' I was quite surprised at his words and manner, but as I had certain ideas in my mind, I continued to Sergeant Feihler that 'If we are going to stay here we ought to be making some kind of a barricade, for the Indians would be at us first thing in the morning.' Major Reno, who was still there, spoke up at once, saying, 'Yes, sergeant, that is a good idea. Set all the men you can to work, right away.' Sergeant Feihler then began to order men to take boxes of hardtack, packsaddles, sides of bacon, dead mules and horses, in fact anything they could use, and make a barricade across the lower part of the depression.

To conserve ammunition, orders were given for only the best shots to return fire, the others to load rifles, and remove cartridges stuck in the breach, a similar problem to that experienced with Martini-Henrys at Isandlwana. Godfrey recalled:

> When cartridges were dirty and corroded the ejectors did not always extract the empty shells from the chambers, and the men were compelled to use knives to get them out. When shells were clean no great difficulty was experienced. To what extent this was a factor in causing the disaster we have no means of knowing.

Private Edward Pigford of M company recalled talking to a soldier named Pat Golden alongside him on the firing line:

> We had been talking at intervals during the battle that afternoon, and when the fighting stopped shortly after dark I started to talk to him again. He didn't answer as I rattled on, and at last when I reached out my hand and touched his head it was covered with blood.

That afternoon another five men were killed and six wounded, but when night fell, the firing ceased. The hilltop force now consisted 367 men and officers, and 14 others, including 13 wounded men. The weary troopers were able to move freely about, many muttering and speculating as to Custer's whereabouts. Why did he not communicate by courier or signal? The feeling amongst many was that he had been defeated and driven down the Little Bighorn to join Terry's column. It would not be long till they arrived, they hoped, lifting the siege. But, on the other hand, had he merely ridden off, abandoning them to their fate, as he had done to Major Elliot's detachment at the Washita? Some felt angry and betrayed. Custer's orderly, John Burkman, claimed he heard Reno say to another officer, 'I wonder where the Murat of the

American army is by this time?' Both officers laughed in a sneering manner.

It was not a case of all quiet along the front during the night, as Godfrey recalled:

> The long twilight was prolonged by numerous bonfires, located throughout the village. The long shadows of the hills and the refracted light gave a supernatural aspect to the surrounding country, which may account for the illusions of those who imagined they could see columns of troops etc.... Their camp was a veritable pandemonium. All night long they continued their frantic revels; beating tom-toms, dancing, whooping, yelling with demoniacal screams and discharging firearms. We knew they were having a scalp dance.

Bugle calls were also heard from the village, an Indian who had learnt its basic use at an army post, apparently. But the troops were far from silent. It was imagined by some that they could see a relief column on the hills, and shots were fired and bugles blown to attract their attention. A civilian packer galloped along the line, 'Don't be discouraged boys,' he yelled, 'Crook is coming!'

Once it was realised that troops on the horizon were a figment of the imagination, the command did all they could to ensure their own survival. There were only three or four spades in the whole command, so all set to work digging rifle pits in the hard, dry ground with knives, mugs, axes, spoons, and any other object they could lay their hands on.

Scouts moved stealthily out seeking some sign of Custer's command, but returned in short order saying the countryside was swarming with Sioux. Darkness provided an opportunity to redeploy the troops, and the animals were relieved of saddles and packs. They were secured to lariats picketed to the ground, men no longer required to hold them.

Dawn's first glimmer in the eastern sky brought a few scattered shots from the Indians, but as more warriors recovered from the night's revelry their lines were reinforced. Reno later reported:

> We could see, as the day brightened, countless hordes of them pouring up the valley from the village and scampering over the high points towards the high places designated for them by their chiefs, and which entirely surrounded our position. They had sufficient numbers to completely encircle us, and men were struck from opposite sides of the lines from where the shots were fired. I think we were fighting all the Sioux Nation, and also all the desperadoes, renegades, half-breeds, and squaw men between the Missouri and the Arkansas and east of the Rocky mountains, and they must have numbered at least twenty-five hundred warriors.

The Indians would jump up in full view for an instant, fire, then drop to the ground causing the troops to waste ammunition as they attempted to hit an impossible target. And the Indians amused themselves by exposing hats and blankets on sticks, enticing yet more useless fire. Horses and mules dropped, being visible to riflemen on the eastern heights, and Benteen's Company H took several hits, their position on a bluff to the south being exposed to long-range shots from the north. Private Windolph of H Company recalled:

> Corporal Lell…was fatally wounded (in the abdomen) and dragged to the hospital. He was dying and knew it. 'Lift me up boys,' he said to some of the men, 'I want to see the boys again before I go.' So they held him up in a sitting

position where he could see his comrades in action...then they laid him down and he died soon after...I will never forget Corporal Lell.

Benteen's line was the key to the command's defence, and the Indians mounted several charges against his men. He quickly dashed over to Reno's position and requested reinforcements for his troop. While he was gone a young brave shot one of his troopers, then boldly ran up to the line, touching the victim with his coup-stick. He turned and started running back just to be brought down by one of many bullets that blazed from the line. Other Indians sheltered by ravines were so close they were 'amusing themselves by throwing clods of dirt, arrows by hand, and otherwise, for simply pure cussedness among us' recalled Benteen.

While Benteen conferred with Reno, Private McDermott dashed across with an urgent message from Lieutenant Gibson, Benteen's second-in-command. He urgently needed the reinforcements and more ammunition, his position being in danger of being overrun. Reno finally agreed for Company M to move across to the southern position. Benteen also collected several men who were skulking with the horses and rejoined his troop with the reinforcements. Deciding the best form of defence was attack, he told his men to prepare for a charge. With a rallying cry he led them down the slope, firing as he went. The Indians retreated before this bold and unexpected move, dragging their dead and wounded with them.

The Indian gunfire slackened off, then stopped. Everyone breathed a sigh of relief. Perhaps they'd given up? But then there was a deafening blast as flashes erupted from the surrounding bluffs with increased fury. And there was more movement amongst the Indians at the base of the bluffs. Benteen suspected something was up, the enemy possibly preparing for a major assault. He scrambled back to Reno's position where he voiced his concerns, but Reno was indecisive.

'You've got to do something here pretty quick,' Benteen said impatiently, 'this won't do, you must drive them back.'

Reno gave the order to prepare for a charge. The preparations were made, the Springfields loaded, and every able man poised for the assault. 'All ready now, men,' yelled Benteen, 'Now's your time. Give them hell. Hip, hip, here we go!' Reno and the troopers leapt from behind their improvised breastworks with a hearty "Hurrah,' and rushed down the slope. All except one who lay in his rifle pit, weeping. The others commenced shooting without orders as the Indian line erupted in a crescendo of rifle fire. The bullets zipped and thudded about them, but not one found its mark, the moving targets proving elusive. At the foot of one hill a large body of braves broke off in retreat. They had probably been preparing to charge the lines, as Benteen feared.

'Get back, men,' yelled Reno when they were about 90 yards down the slope, 'Get back!' The charge halted and the troopers scrambled back to their positions, lying low as bullets flew about them. Not one exposed trooper had been hit, but the weeping man fell silent as a bullet smashed into his head. Earlier, he had told a comrade of his premonition that this was to be the day of his death.

The scout George Herendeen was impressed with Benteen's performance:

> I think in desperate fighting Benteen is one of the bravest men I ever saw in a fight. All the time he was going about through the bullets, encouraging the soldiers to stand up to their work and not let the Indians whip them; he went amongst the horses and pack mules and drove out the

men who were skulking there, compelling them to go into the line and do their duty. He never sheltered his own person once during the battle, and I do not see how he escaped being killed.

But bullets were not the only bane of the command as the hot sun beat down, water being the other problem, as Lieutenant Godfrey recalled:

> The excitement and heat made our thirst almost maddening. The men were forbidden to use tobacco. They put pebbles in their mouths to excite the glands; some ate grass roots, but did not find relief; some tried to eat hard bread, but after chewing it awhile would blow it out of their mouths like so much flour. A few potatoes were given out and afforded some relief.

The exchange of gunfire slackened off, and at about 11 a.m. volunteer water parties were organised to get down to the river and fill camp-kettles. They moved out from Benteen's lines and worked their way through depressions and small ravines until they were within a few yards of the enticing water. So near and yet so far, Indians occupying a copse of trees a little distance away. The men would madly rush out and submerge the kettles while bullets splashed about them, and thudded into the riverbank. Several carriers were wounded and had to be rescued by their comrades, but water was carried back and poured into canteens, to be gratefully gulped by the parched troopers.

By about 1 p.m. the Indians seemed to have drifted off except for those down by the riverbank. But the kettles bravely filled by the volunteers had put water in canteens, enough to quench the troopers' thirst for the time being at least. At 2 p.m. men scrambled back into the pits as the enemy, having returned, opened fire with renewed vigour, but after about an hour this too slackened off, then all fell silent.

Late in the afternoon a few mounted warriors were seen in the valley keeping Reno's position under surveillance, then suddenly a smoke haze drifted skywards as the Sioux set fire to the grass. Before long an immense, moving mass of braves, women and children, and their ponies, were seen moving behind the sheltering smokescreen across the plateau. The village had been struck, and the victors were heading towards the distant, dark shape of the Big Horn Mountains.

'Thank God,' was the immediate response. But then some began to have doubts. Was it merely a ruse to have them drop their guard? Were the warriors going to double back for one last, desperate charge to wipe out the bluecoats once they had left their defensive hill? But it would be advantageous to move the command in any case, the stench from dead men, horses and mules making the present position hard to bear. They moved to a defensible location nearer the river and began digging in once more; better to be safe than sorry.

Night fell and men were seen approaching their lines under the moonlight. But they were more survivors from the fight in the valley, having hidden amongst the trees till it was safe to venture out; Will Jackson, a scout, Private O'Neal, Frederick Gerard and Lieutenant DeRudio all arrived in one piece, returned from the dead.

The following morning, June 27th, as the trumpeter sounded reveille, there was no barrage of gunfire to greet the dawn, and the troops enjoyed their first proper meal for some time. But there were still badly wounded men groaning in the makeshift hospital. Since Reno had charged the village, he had lost 53 men killed, and many more wounded of those companies now under his command. He would be well aware that this defeat was already the worst suffered by the U. S. army at the hands of the western tribes excepting the Fetterman fight ten years earlier. And he still had no knowledge of the 200 odd corpses strewn about a few miles to the north.

But this fine morning there were no Indians in sight, only a few untended ponies grazing below. Major Reno, however, remained apprehensive, suspecting a 'trap.' He insisted all men be ready for action at a moment's notice.

Then at about 9.30 a.m. the trumpeter sounded assembly. Perhaps Reno was right? Men scrambled to secure horses, canteens were filled and the men readied for action. A big dust cloud had been seen approaching from along the Little Bighorn valley. All eyes watched with suspense, cartridge belts filled to the hilt, Springfields in hand and ready to fire. But as time ticked by, the slow advance caused a sigh of relief. The Indians had disappeared to the south, and Terry's column, and Custer of course, were known to be in the north. This big haze of dust could only mean one thing; relief was on the way at long last.

***

The mission near Rorke's Drift, about 10 miles from Isandlwana, was a former farm homestead and separate store purchased by Otto Witt in 1878. The Buffalo River flowed a short distance away with Zululand on the opposite bank. The house was built from handcrafted bricks and local stone, and had a thatched roof covering 11 rooms and a verandah. The store, converted into a chapel, was a smaller building of similar construction. Two stone kraals and a vegetable garden completed the picture. Witt named his mission station 'Oskarberg' after the king of his native Sweden.

The missionary offered Chelmsford the use of his property, so the homestead was prepared as a hospital, and the chapel made into a storehouse holding provisions for the central column. Commanding this post was Major Henry Spalding of the 104th Regiment, the officer of Chelmsford's staff in charge of communications and supplies. The Reverend George Smith, the central column's chaplain, was also in residence. Having helped Durnford bury the Carbineers who lost their lives at Bushman's River Pass, Smith may have had a healthier respect for native prowess than did Lord Chelmsford, and tended most of his flock from this safe distance.

Company B of the 2nd Battalion, 24th Regiment provided the post's garrison, their tents neatly pitched near the hospital and store. The company commander was Lieutenant Gonville Bromhead, the 33 year-old son of a general and baronet who had fought Napoleon at Waterloo. The general's son was not highly regarded by his senior officers, because of his 'unconquerable indolence' and was only in command because the company's captain had been shot by accident. But he was popular with the men, and a sportsman of note. 'A great favourite in his regiment,' said one officer, 'and a capital fellow at everything except soldiering.' Better to keep such an officer away from the action, which was possibly why his company was placed on docile guard duty at Rorke's Drift. The men under Bromhead's command consisted of English and Irish from the city slums and country villages, and a few Welsh from the border regions; a cocktail typical of the enlisted men in Queen Victoria's army.

The senior NCO, from Sussex, was young at only 23, being known as 'the kid.' But Color Sergeant Frank Bourne had risen quickly through the ranks, having a natural aptitude for military life. He was intelligent, responsible, and could read and write, assisting the men with letters to and from home. Regarding Company B as 'a very happy family,' he was much at home with his position.

Lieutenant John Chard, 31, and a small detachment of Royal Engineers were also present, responsible for maintaining the two pontoon bridges spanning the Buffalo. Chard had come to South Africa after constructing forts in Bermuda and Malta, but had seen no combat. Like Bromhead, he was not held in high esteem by senior officers, being described by one as 'most useless.' His was short, bearded and quiet in manner, thus not one from the idealised mould of a heroic British officer. Maintaining ponts, no doubt, was seen as the role for one of his station.

Chard had been annoyed when most of his men had received orders to join the column in Zululand, under an NCO, while he was left behind with routine duties; his chance of seeing combat a forlorn hope. With Major Spalding's consent, he rode to Isandlwana on the morning of January 22nd to query the order. The order was confirmed, to Chard's irritation, but through binoculars he could see massed Zulus on the hills, many moving towards the rear of Isandlwana, thus posing a risk to Rorke's Drift. He rode back, encountering Durnford's approaching column on the way, and told Major Spalding of his concerns. The major listened to what Chard had to say, then decided to ride in person to Helpmekaar to check the progress of an additional infantry company expected to arrive. He could, of course, have sent a courier, but why do that when your command may be attacked by thousands of Zulus; much better to go yourself. He checked the seniority list to see who should be in command during his absence, then said to Chard, 'You will be in charge, although, of course, nothing will happen, and I shall be back again this evening, early.'

Spalding and the reinforcements would never arrive, and as he spoke these words, at about 2 p.m., the camp at Isandlwana was being overrun by the Zulu impi. But even Chard could not have been too concerned about the post's safety, for instead of making preparations to repel an attack he retired to his tent by the drift, about half a mile away, to enjoy a light lunch and write a letter. He was interrupted, however, by a sentry who reported riders approaching. He walked out to see a cloud of dust kicked up by two galloping horseman, the distant shape of Isandlwana behind them. They were shouting something, and when they crossed the river one rider, Lieutenant Adendorff of the NNC, blurted out that the camp had been attacked and overrun. Almost no one had escaped, he said, and Chelmsford's force had probably been wiped out too. And the Zulus were marching rapidly towards Rorke's Drift. The second horseman, a Natal Carbineer, corroborated Adendorff's story in panic stricken babble. Then a message arrived from Lieutenant Bromhead requesting Chard's presence at the mission station without delay.

Chard mounted up and galloped off to find the mission bustling as mealie sacks and wagons were put in place, forming a breastwork between the hospital and the store. Loopholes were being punched in the stone walls of the two buildings, and the tents had been struck, creating a clear line of fire. Bromhead unfolded a paper message and showed it to Chard. The scribbled pencil words from a staff officer said that the camp at Isandlwana had fallen, and the mission was to be fortified and held 'at all costs,' presumably to prevent an invasion of Natal across Rorke's Drift. They briefly discussed the feasibility of holding the post, then gave the order to pull out. Two wagons were being loaded up when Acting Assistant Commissary James Dalton intervened. He pointed out that if they fled, they would be overtaken in the open by the fleet-footed Zulus and wiped out. Better to stay and fight from behind barricades where they at least had some sort of chance.

Chard rescinded the evacuation order and instructed the men to resume fortifying the post. Chard recalled, omitting any mention of the order to move out, that:

> Several fugitives from the camp arrived and tried to impress upon us the madness of an attempt to defend the place...They proved the truth of their belief in what they said by leaving us to our fate, and in the state of mind they were in, I think our little garrison was as well without them.

Eighty native horsemen under Lieutenant Alfred Henderson arrived. They had been under Durnford's command when the battle began and fought alongside him in the Nyokana Donga. Henderson offered to help defend the mission and Chard gratefully deployed his men as scouts, and to delay the Zulu advance in any way possible.

Knowing the British soldier's fondness for a drink, he placed a guard in the former chapel with orders to shoot anyone who attempted to get the kegs of rum stored there, a drunken redcoat being of little use on the firing line.

Otto Witt, the Reverend Smith and Surgeon James Reynolds had climbed a height and came panting into the mission with news of the Zulu advance. They were surprised to see the place being fortified, expecting a withdrawal, and told Chard the Zulus would arrive in five minutes. The Reverend Smith wished to further distance himself from the action, but as his groom had galloped off on his horse, felt compelled to stay.

'Mein Gott, mein wife and mein children at Umsinga,' said Otto Witt, and quickly disappeared.

Also stationed at Rorke's Drift was a detachment of 100 NNC who had helped construct the barricade. Shots were heard in the distance and Lieutenant Henderson came galloping back with news of thousands of Zulus approaching. His men would not obey his orders, he said, and they had headed for Helpmekaar, and he was going off to rally them. He galloped off amidst a cloud of dust not to be seen by Chard again. News of this desertion quickly spread to the NNC who promptly scrambled over the barricade along with their commanding officer, Captain William Stephenson, and their two white NCOs. The outraged redcoats left behind sent a volley after the fleeing deserters and Corporal Anderson dropped to die in the dust where he fell. Captain Stephenson's performance was later rewarded with arrest and a dishonorable discharge

This left Chard with 104 men to defend the mission, plus any of the 35 soldiers in the hospital capable of bearing arms. Realising that the defence perimeter may now be over-extended, he ordered a second barricade of timber biscuit boxes be built to form a redoubt behind the first; a fall-back position.

Men sweated under the hot afternoon sun as the boxes were moved into place, then Private Hitch, on the storehouse roof, yelled he could see a huge Zulu column over the crest of a hill. Bromhead looked up. 'How many,' he asked. 'Four to six thousand,' was the reply.

Prince Dabulamanzi, 40, Cetshwayo's younger brother, was commander of the Zulus approaching the mission. He was intelligent, sophisticated, fond of wearing European clothes, and an expert marksman. But he was inexperienced in battle and had ordered the attack on Rorke's Drift without Cetshwayo's approval. The reserve Zulus under his command had missed the glory and plunder of Isandlwana, and he had seen a border raid one way of striking a balance.

'Here they come,' cried Sergeant Henry Gallagher on the south wall, 'as thick as grass and as black as thunder.' The Zulus lines advanced steadily forward, then, as they reached the 500-yard mark, the order to fire rang out. The south wall exploded in fire and smoke. Zulus dropped as the bullets smashed through their ranks, but the warriors kept moving forward using earth banks, trees and the cook house ovens at the rear for cover. 'Our firing was very quick,' recalled one ill artilleryman who had left the hospital to join the firing line, 'and, when struck by the bullets, the niggers would give a spring in the air and fall flat down.' At about 50 yards the Zulus fell back under the withering fire while another force struck the hospital wall and the northwest breastwork of mealie bags in front of the verandah where Bromhead, revolver in hand, fought alongside men of his company. The fighting was hand-to-hand as the Zulus attempted to force the four-foot barricade and Commissary James Dalton saved one corporal's life by shooting the Zulu who had grasped the man's rifle and was about to run him through. Inside the hospital Private Henry Hook fired through a loophole punched in the stone wall. 'The Zulus were swarming around us,' he recalled, 'and there was an extraordinary rattle as the bullets struck the biscuit boxes, and queer thumps as they plumped into the bags of mealies.' The Zulus forced the defenders back and clambered over the mealie bag wall where assegai and bayonet clashed. 'they seemed to have a great dread of the bayonet,' recalled Private Hitch, 'which stood us from beginning to end.' Hitch described how he killed one 'fine big Zulu' who grasped his rifle and bayonet with both hands, having seen Hitch shoot 'his mate' down. Under fire from the hospital and bayonets thrust by redcoats to their front, the warriors were forced back behind a five-foot stone wall between the hospital and the vegetable patch.

Hundreds of Zulus lined the heights to the mission's south and others took shelter behind the stone kraal to the mission's north. Along with those behind the garden wall, they launched a number of uncoordinated assaults against the north barricade and a weak link in the defence, the hospital. Warriors at a distance kept up a steady fire, the bullets whining overhead or thudding into the mealie bags. Then, at a given signal, the mass would rise up and rush furiously forward. Some would drop as the defenders' rifles cracked, then the Zulus would attempt scaling the wall while grasping at barrels and bayonets, stabbing furiously with their assegais. Rifles belched smoke and bayonets thrust, then the Zulus would retreat, leaving dead and wounded, to disappear into the bush once more, the gunfire from a distance resumed.

The Reverend Smith was affectionately renamed 'Ammunition Smith' as he walked the firing line handing out bullets. But the battle was distressing to him for more than one reason, as he felt obliged to ask the soldiers to cut back on the swearing. 'But the men continued to swear,' recalled Private Hitch, 'and fight the harder.'

Daylight was beginning to fade at around 6 p.m. when Prince Dabulamanzi ordered coordinated attacks on both the north and south walls. Again the warriors rushed with furious defiance into the blazing muzzles of the defenders, men dropping in pain amidst a confusion of smoke and curses. Commissary James Dalton moved along the firing line dangerously exposed as he fired into the attackers with his Martini-Henry, inspiring those about him to fight all the harder. Chard recalled that Dalton 'had been using his rifle with deadly effect, and by his quickness and coolness had been the means of saving many men's lives.' Storekeeper Louise Byrne also acted with great gallantry, but died with a bullet through the head while giving a wounded corporal water.

As defenders were either killed or wounded, Chard felt the firing line was too sparse and in danger of being overrun. He gave the order to pull back to their second line of defence, the biscuit box redoubt outside the storehouse, reducing the firing line by about two-thirds. The defenders scrambled back to their new position and the gleeful Zulus occupied the mealie bag barricade, using it for cover as they fired through the grey smoke haze. This retreat isolated the hospital from the main command, Zulus being able to shoot across the space inbetween. Inside were just six soldiers and 24 patients. The building's designer had little use for inside doors and passages, five of the eleven rooms having doors to the outside only, and five were without windows. The Zulus thrust flaming assegais onto the roof to burn the inmates out, and despite being damp the thatch soon caught fire on the western end. Surgeon Reynolds repeatedly braved Zulu fire to run across supplying ammunition to those trapped inside, his helmet being hit by rifle fire during one mad dash.

As the flames spread, Private Henry Hook was forced from his room by choking smoke, having to leave an NNC patient with a broken leg to fend for himself. He went through the inner door just to find nine sick and wounded in the next room, and resolved to stay put and fight. The Zulus broke into the room he had just left and killed the patient, but found the door to the next room shut tight. Hook fired through the door to keep them back, and then with a spatter and crumbling of dried mud, an inner wall opening appeared, punched through from the other side. 'The Zulus are swarming all over the place,' said Private John Williams through the gap, 'They've dragged

Joseph Williams out and killed him.' The two privates had been defending a room with four patients inside when they ran out of ammunition and the Zulus broke in. As Joseph Williams and two patients were dragged out to their deaths, John Williams and the remaining two patients managed to hold them off long enough to escape through a hole they had slashed with bayonet thrusts into the next unoccupied room. This was repeated, finding Hook, then they clambered through the opening to join him and the nine patients in his charge. The only escape route was to hack another hole into the next room. Williams swung furiously with a pickaxe while Hook shot and bayoneted Zulus who attempted to get through the doorway. An assegai flew through and struck Hook's white sun helmet, tipping it back and causing a slight wound to the scalp. Then another warrior managed to get through, grasping Hook's rifle, but the soldier struggled desperately, breaking free, slipped another round into the breech and fired. The brave Zulu died as he fell. Williams, meanwhile, was getting sick and wounded through the new opening, all except Private John Connolly, immobile with a broken leg. Hook got through the opening, dragging the patient after him. Hook recalled, 'His leg got broken again, but there was no help for it. As soon as we left the room the Zulus burst in with furious cries of disappointment and rage.' In the next room the mini-saga was repeated, Hook holding the Zulus at bay while Williams swung the pickaxe. What they did not know was that Private Waters, wounded, was hiding in a cupboard in the same room. Waters remained hidden when they retreated to the next room, soon to be driven out by heat and smoke from the burning roof. Covered by a dark cloak he escaped from the hospital to the cookhouse at the rear. Here he blackened his face with chimney soot and remained hidden. Hook, Williams and the patients, meanwhile, made it to the end room. Here were six more patients being guarded by Privates William Jones and Robert Jones. They held the Zulus at bay with fixed bayonets while Hook and Williams lowered the patients through a window beneath the spreading flames. The biscuit box redoubt was 40 yards away where Corporal Allen and Private Hitch exposed themselves providing covering fire as the escapees attempted to make it across. Hitch recalled 'One by one the poor fellows scrambled out of the burning building and ran the gauntlet.' Trooper Hunter of the Natal Mounted Police, dazed by the blazing roof and smoke, hesitated. A Zulu dashed out and stabbed him, only to die himself moments later under a hail of bullets. The two Jones's held the doorway filling it with dead and wounded warriors, Robert suffering from three assegai wounds. He made an attempt to save Sergeant Maxfield, delirious and bedridden, who refused to be moved and was killed, but the flames, heat and smoke forced the Zulus back, giving the two soldiers a chance to scramble out the window. Moments later the flaming roof came crashing down, sending smoke and cinders spiralling skyward, and the two survivors dodged bullets as they dashed to the relative safety of the redoubt, Hook and Williams having already made it safely across.

Gunner Arthur Howard and Private Robert Adams, meanwhile, had been defending another room beneath the flaming thatch. When it began to collapse, Howard dashed outside to take refuge amidst long grass, fallen horses and dead Zulus. Adams stayed behind to die, one of seven men killed in the hospital fight.

The flaming wreckage of the building cast an eerie light into the darkening sky and the spreading glow allowed the beleaguered garrison to see the Zulus as they renewed their attacks. Private Hitch recalled three warriors rushing at him:

The first fellow I shot; the second man I bayoneted; the third man got right inside the laager, but he declined to stand up against me. With a leap he jumped over the barricade and made off. A few yards from the barricade lay a wounded Zulu. We knew he was there...(but) were far too busy with the active members to find time to put him right out. Presently I saw him, rifle in hand, taking aim at one of my comrades. It was too late to stop him; he fired, and poor Nicholls fell dead, shot through the head.

As the fighting progressed, shoulders became bruised and swollen from the rifle recoil and men were forced to fire from either shoulder to spread the pain, or even fire with the weapon held at arm's length. Fingers were burned from grasping hot barrels, and some suffered powder burns to their faces. Sticking cartridges also caused problems. Private Hook recalled that the rifles became hot 'and the cartridge chamber jammed. My own rifle jammed several times, and I had to work away with a ramrod till I cleared it.'

With each repulse a Zulu war dance would follow, the warriors working themselves up to a fever pitch before facing the Martini-Henrys once again. One warrior crept forward and was shot while attempting to set fire to the thatch of the storehouse roof.

Major Reno's men, it will be recalled, had seen phantom troops coming to their aid when surrounded on the bluffs. Some redcoats at Rorke's Drift also claim they saw 'redcoats coming along the Helpmekaar road.' A cheer went up causing a hesitation on the Zulu's part, but seeing the hospital in flames, the relief column 'came to the conclusion that we had all been annihilated,' claimed Private Hitch, 'and with drooping spirits we saw our comrades turn back and retire.'

But were these troops phantoms or real? Major Spalding, the commanding officer at Rorke's Drift, it will be recalled, had left his post and headed towards Helpmekaar for reinforcements. He encountered two companies of the 24th Regiment under Major Upcher, and eventually led them back towards his post. Assured by refugees on the road that Rorke's Drift had fallen, he left the infantry behind and rode with two others to a height where they saw the hospital in flames. Convinced the garrison had been slaughtered, he told Major Upcher his two companies would 'share the same fate' if they marched on. The troops were ordered to about face, then trudged back the way they had come. But Chard later cast doubt on his men actually having seen this, saying the troops 'did come down to the foot of the hill, but not, I believe, in sight of us.'

Not only did the reinforcements retire, but the redcoats were driven from the stone kraal at the eastern end of the enclosure. Things were desperate, their defence line shrinking as the Zulus closed in. It was decided to construct yet another inner redoubt outside the storehouse verandah; a circular pile of mealie bags 20 feet high and 12 across. Commissary James Dalton was the first to be placed inside, having received a severe shoulder wound while helping defend an eight-yard gap in the biscuit box wall alongside Lieutenant Bromhead and others. Corporal Scheiss had made a particularly daring foray when he stole along the abandoned mealie bag barricade in an attempt to shoot a Zulu sniper who had come close to killing several men. He raised his head to take aim just to have his helmet shot off by a warrior on the other side. He jumped the wall and thrust his bayonet into the Zulu, then shot another, and bayoneted one more before scrambling back behind the boxes. Despite a later wound he stayed on the firing line until the relief column arrived.

Private Hitch saved Bromhead from an assegai thrust by bluffing a Zulu off with an empty rifle, and Bromhead later killed a warrior who had just shot Hitch in the rear of his shoulder blade. Hitch recalled:

> I got up again and attempted to use my rifle, but it was no use; my right arm wouldn't work, so I strapped it into my waist belt to keep it out of the way. Then Bromhead gave me his revolver to use, and with this I think I did as much execution as I had done before.

Four hours after receiving his wound, Hitch collapsed from loss of blood. His comrades pulled him inside the 20-foot mealie bag redoubt.

Twilight cast an eerie light over the dead Zulus sprawled around the mission, then night set in. The Zulus, despite vast numbers, had been unable to overwhelm the small garrison and their losses had been staggering. The Zulu warrior did not like fighting after dark and made no more serious attacks on the perimeter after 9.30 p.m. They did, however, kept up a constant fire from the abandoned mealie bag walls until midnight. After that the firing tapered off to the odd angry shot from both sides and a few false alarms. By 4.30 a.m. all was quiet, but the garrison remained on the alert, with bayonets fixed to meet the expected dawn assault. Being down to their last box and a half of ammunition, the defenders knew a repetition of the previous day's fighting would see them overwhelmed, their bayonets the last line of defence.

But the first rays of sunlight brought exclamations of delight. The main Zulu force was seen disappearing in defeat as it moved back towards the Buffalo River and Zululand. No doubt the same feeling of relief ran through the garrison that Reno's command experienced when the Sioux and Cheyenne were seen moving away towards the Big Horn Mountains. But, like Reno, Chard ordered the barricades repaired, believing the attack could be renewed, especially as some Zulus 'remained on the hill'. And, like Reno, when a relief column approached it was thought they were the enemy returning to the attack. Chard recalled 'There were a great number of our Native Levies in the Column, and the number of red-coats seemed so few that at first we had grave doubts that the force approaching was the enemy.' But a flag was improvised and run up, signals exchanged, and two mounted officers left the column and rode up through the Zulu dead, scattered and heaped around the barricades. Men waved their helmets and received their arrival with a hearty cheer, the siege of Rorke's Drift finally at an end.

Given the vicious, close fighting, the garrison was fortunate to count only 15 dead and 12 wounded, two of whom would later die of their wounds. But the mounds of dead around the perimeter walls showed the Zulus had not fared so well.

9
FINDING THE DEAD; AND THE LIVING

On June 22nd, having seen the dust cloud of Custer's command fade on the horizon as it headed down the Rosebud, General Terry and Colonel Gibbon steamed up the Yellowstone on board the *Far West*. They met the Montana column at the mouth of the Big Horn River early on a fine morning two days later. The mouth of the Little Bighorn was only 30 miles distant and easily reached by marching over relatively level ground along the Big Horn's west bank. But smoke had been seen above Tullock's Fork to the east a week earlier. Terry determined to march southeast checking its banks for any sign of hostiles.

Bugles blew and troops assembled on the morning of the 24th, Terry having no time to waste, wanting to be at the mouth of the Little Bighorn no later than the afternoon of the 26th. That afternoon the *Far West* belched smoke into the big Montana sky as she ferried Brisbin's cavalry, five companies of the 7th infantry and the Gatling guns to the south bank of the Yellowstone. Lieutenant Bradley's scouting detachment of 18 Crows and 11 mounted infantrymen were already across, and 12 of the Crows scouted in advance up Tullock's Fork.

The command set off down the Big Horn and then four miles up Tullock's Fork before calling a halt for the day and setting up camp. The Crow scouts sent in advance caused a stir when they thundered excitedly into camp shortly before nightfall. It seemed they must have spotted a hostile village. But no, all they had to report was a buffalo wounded with several arrows in its hide. Lieutenant Bradley was not happy 'after wasting eight hours in advancing ten miles, they return with this paltry bit of news,' he recalled.

The command pulled out at 5.30 the following fine, sunny morning, June 25th, then proceeded up Tullock's Fork in search of hostiles. But then, three miles later, Terry had a sudden change of heart. It was almost as though some sixth sense told him that Custer was then on the Crow's Nest peering towards the Little Bighorn, his scouts assuring him the village was there. The hostiles were not on Tullock's Fork, Terry decided, and ordered the command to strike overland, southwest, back towards the Big Horn. This led the troops over rugged terrain scarred by gullies, sharp ridges and ravines. The canteens emptied as the command straggled and separated, horses and men parched and wilting under a hot, beating sun. The troops could have been picked off from ambush with the greatest of ease, the scouts still moving up Tullock's Fork until they received word that they were scouting in advance of a command no longer to their rear. Perplexed, they moved cross-country to rejoin the command.

Eventually the thirsty and exhausted troops straggled along a dry watercourse into a fine, timbered camping place alongside the refreshing waters of the Big Horn. Then six of the Crow scouts who had been up Tullock's Fork arrived with news of far more interest than one wounded buffalo, having spotted a smoke cloud hanging above the lower Little Bighorn. This was a combination, no doubt, of smoke from burning valley grass, dust, and gunsmoke from hundreds of belching barrels as Custer fought his last stand.

There was to be no rest for the scouts, cavalry and Gatling gun battery, as Terry immediately ordered them to move out once more. Only the infantry and pack train men could sigh with relief, being allowed to rest in camp for the night.

Rain fell as the column marched, the gullies they crossed turning to slippery mud. Once night fell, the various units lost contact, one cavalry troop getting lost as it wandered from the trail, and the Gatling battery falling far to the rear. Baulked by a steep bluff, Lieutenant Bradley sent a Crow scout, Little Face, forward. He soon returned, having found a path around the slope. They set out once more following the guide and after marching a few miles came to a site, at midnight, which would do for a bivouac alongside the Big Horn. The troops were soaked and got what sleep they could 'in a slough of mud and disgust.'

Bradley's brief sleep was broken when he was ordered to scout ahead once more. He sent six Crows out at 3.30 a.m., and rode with the others shortly afterwards. Three miles down the track a heavy pall of smoke was spotted 20 miles to their front, and fresh tracks of Indian ponies were seen. He and his Crow allies followed the tracks for two miles before arriving at the banks of the Big Horn. Here objects were found which revealed Bradley had been tracking Crow scouts who had ridden out with Custer on the 22nd. Then three Indians were seen about two miles away on the opposite side of the river, watching their every move. Bradley told his scouts to signal that they were friendly, which they did with blankets, but there was no response. Then the distant braves built a fire and puffs of smoke wafted into the sky. Signals were exchanged, and the three warriors rode down and spoke across the water with the Crows. Little Face listened to what they had to say, then walked up to Bradley, tears streaming from his eyes. The

Indians on the opposite bank were White-Man-Runs-Him, Goes Ahead, and Hairy Moccasin. They had been singing death songs, mourning for the loss of White Swan and Half-Yellow-Face, believed to have been killed by the Sioux, and Curly, not realising he had survived. And all the dead soldiers of Custer's command. Bradley could scarcely believe his ears as the story unfolded, but could see from the anguish all round that the Crows knew this unbelievable tale to be true. He later recalled 'there were none in this whole horrified nation of forty millions of people to whom the tidings brought greater grief.' He could only hope their abysmal tale was a gross exaggeration.

He galloped back to the command and repeated the story to Terry, Gibbon and other officers mounted around them. The first reaction of shock was quickly replaced with one of scepticism. The story was ridiculed as an invention by Crow scouts who were using it as an excuse for their desertion from Custer's command. But Bradley recalled 'General Terry took no part in these criticisms, but sat on his horse, silent and thoughtful, biting his lower lip, and looking to me as though he by no means shared in the wholesale scepticism of the flippant members of his staff.'

Terry gave the order to advance, but pondering what he had heard, only marched a short distance before calling a halt. The infantry and pack train were allowed to catch up. The army was learning all too late the folly of a divided command against a wily enemy of unknown strength. The shocking rumours had reached the infantry officers by the time they caught up, and most scoffed at any chance of the impossible being true. The united command marched once more before midday. When passing the ford on the Big Horn Bradley asked his Crow scouts to bring back the three tribesmen who had delivered the bad news. They splashed across the ford to reunite, but they all turned and rode off, melting into the bluffs as though they'd never been. Perhaps they felt Terry was about to share Custer's fate? It was time for these warriors to go home.

Bradley led his remaining scouts, 11 mounted infantrymen, into the valley of the Little Bighorn where the smoke haze could be clearly seen. But there was still a chance the story was not true, the smoke resulting from Custer having burned the hostiles' village. If that had happened, however, one would expect to see some sign of fugitive Indians fleeing north. None came.

Terry's column, following Bradley, marched four miles up the west bank of the Little Bighorn before calling a halt. He had arrived on time, but had received no news from Custer's command, scout George Herendeen not having been sent by Custer as planned.

Terry wrote a despatch to Custer saying that he had been told he had been whipped and his men nearly all killed, he did not believe the story, but was coming with medical aid. Scouts Henry Bostwick and Muggins Taylor were each offered $200 to take a copy to Custer's command. Bostwick rode off up the west bank and Taylor forded the stream to ride through the bluffs to the east of the river valley.

Late in the afternoon Terry's column resumed its march up the west bank, Bradley in advance. It was not long before Bostwick galloped back from his foray to the front, reporting the valley ahead swarming with hostiles. There was no way he could get through. Terry immediately ordered his men to prepare for action. The troops were redeployed, then advanced in battle formation. Groups of Indians were seen riding across the hills to their front, and Lieutenant Roe, edging into the hills on the command's far right, saw what he thought was a column of cavalry in the twilight, complete with guidon fluttering in the breeze. A sergeant and two others approached with a white flag of truce only to draw fire from Indians dressed in the uniforms of Custer's dead. Muggins Taylor came galloping back also not having found Custer, and he too had seen what he took for cavalry, only to have one 'soldier' conceal himself in a ravine and open fire. As the command advanced Roe again saw what he thought were about 300 cavalrymen in the distance, but Dr. Paulding said 'they represented the exact appearance of an Indian camp on the march.'

Terry called a halt to bivouac for the night, much to Dr. Paulding's chagrin. He felt the command should have pursued the Indians they had seen rather than 'lay on their arms all night.' Had Terry proceeded he would have discovered the corpses of Custer's dead four miles up the valley, and Reno's injured command another four beyond that.

Lieutenant Bradley recalled:

> Before retiring, the officers assembled in groups and talked over the events of the day. I found that a majority of the infantry officers placed confidence in the report brought by the Crows of Custer's overthrow, and were prepared for unpleasant disclosures upon the morrow. Some of the cavalry officers shared in this conviction, but the majority of them, and about all the staff were wholly sceptical...to argue with them was worse than useless.

At dawn the next morning the command rose to see no feathered horsemen on the hills as they had the day before. The order to march was given and the troops moved warily forward with still no Indians to be seen. After an advance of four miles they came across cold ashes and debris; the northern end of the vast campsite where hundreds of tepees had been pitched along the banks of the Little Bighorn. The Indians seemed to have moved with some haste, leaving lodge poles and camp kettles, rugs, and other apparel scattered about. Then it was seen that two lodges were still standing. In one was found the bodies of three dead braves, and five in the other. Dead ponies for use in the afterlife lay outside. But then other items were found that sent a chill up more than one spine. Underclothing belonging to Lieutenant James Sturgis, 7th Cavalry, the son of Regimental Colonel Samuel Sturgis; bits of discarded cavalry uniform, a pair of gloves labelled 'Yates, 7th Cavalry,' army saddles and a bloody buckskin shirt belonging to Lieutenant Porter with a bullet hole through it. The sceptics were well shaken by the time an ashen-faced Lieutenant Bradley rode in with grim tidings. 'I have a very sad report to make,' he said. 'I have counted 197 bodies lying in the hills.' Having confirmed that the bodies were white, he went on to say he had never seen General Custer, but from pictures previously seen believed he was amongst the fallen. He had discovered them, stripped and mutilated, lying amidst the bluffs on the opposite side of the river. The horrible truth spread through the command like wildfire. Terry ordered the apprehensive troops to continue their advance. 197 bodies! Was that all, or did more horrors await them upstream? Yes, they realised, as dead, bloated horses and objects bristling with arrows came into view. Closer inspection revealed the scalped and hacked bodies of soldiers killed during Reno's retreat. The bodies of Lieutenant McIntosh and Isaiah Dorman were recognised, and that of Charlie Reynolds, who had not died 'lonesome', but fighting for his life with the 7th Cavalry.

Across the river, meanwhile, Muggins Taylor was the first to find Reno's beleaguered command. At least someone was still alive, and he belatedly delivered Terry's despatch promising medical aid.

Lieutenant Godfrey recalled:

Very soon after this, Lieutenant Bradley, 7th Infantry, came into our lines, and asked where I was. Greeting most cordially my old friend, I immediately asked, 'Where is Custer?' He replied, 'I don't know, but I suppose he was killed as we counted 197 dead bodies. I don't suppose any escaped.' We were simply dumfounded. This was the first intimation we had of his fate. It was hard to realize; it did not seem possible.

General Terry and his staff soon rode up the slope to be greeted with prolonged, hearty cheers. But he did not smile in reply, his grave countenance awing the rescued men to silence. There was little for him to be cheerful about this day. Godfrey continued 'There was scarcely a dry eye; hardly a word was spoken, but quivering lips and hearty grasping of hands gave token of thankfulness for the relief and grief of the misfortune.'

Benteen asked Terry where Custer was. 'To the best of my knowledge and belief he lies on this ridge about four miles below here with all of his command killed.'

'I can hardly believe it,' Benteen said, 'I think he is somewhere down the Big Horn grazing his horses. At the battle of the Washita he went off and left part of his command, and I think he would do it again.'

Terry replied that he was mistaken, and suggested he see for himself. Benteen mounted up and rode to the scene of carnage with some others. They found Custer's naked body lying amongst the fallen. 'There he is, God damn him,' Benteen said, 'he will never fight anymore.' When Benteen returned, he said to Lieutenant Maguire of the Engineers 'By the Lord, Harry, old man, 'twas a ghastly sight; but what a big winner the U.S. Govt. would have been if only Custer and his gang could have been taken!'

There were more than 50 wounded in the overworked Dr. Porter's care and he was quickly supported by Drs. Williams and Paulding from Terry's command. Those patients unable to walk were carried in blanket stretchers down the slope to the campsite located in the valley floor. Trooper Madden, given a battlefield promotion to sergeant for gallantry, had one leg amputated without anaesthetic. But he enjoyed the dram of brandy given afterwards so much that he jokingly suggested his other leg be removed as well. Terry offered $100 to those who would carry instructions to the *Far West*, at the mouth of the Little Bighorn, to prepare for the wounded. Two men, Bostwick and Goodwin, set out at midnight to claim the reward.

Terry questioned the survivors, piecing together the jigsaw puzzle of events that had taken place since the 7th rode out on June 22nd. Benteen and his troop were sent to the Custer battlefield to identify the dead where possible, and get a picture of what exactly had taken place; something no one has been able to do with certainty to the present day. Those soldiers still on Reno's hill went to work collecting their gear and other accoutrements, and destroying any animals too badly wounded to go on.

Whenever possible the Indians had taken their dead away, but the brave who had counted coup and then been shot while trying to escape lay where he fell close to the bluecoat lines, as Trooper Taylor recalled:

> In a little depression there lay outstretched a stalwart warrior, stark naked with the exception of a breech clout and moccasins. He lay with his head up the hill, his

right arm extended in the direction the fatal shot had come, a look of grim defiance on his face, which was not disfigured with the streaks of yellow, green, and crimson, so common to many. Perhaps in his hurry to get into the fight he could not stop to don his war paint. He had been scalped by some soldier, the greatest misfortune that could happen, for thereby his soul was annihilated; such was the belief of his people, and for him now there was no Happy Hunting Ground. Never had I seen a more perfect specimen of physical manhood, he must have been about thirty years old, nearly if not quite six feet in height and of splendid proportions. He looked like a bronze statue that had been thrown to the ground.

The campsite that night was not a happy place, the men weighed down with the loss of so many comrades, the malignant odour of unburied dead men and horses, and the resulting swarms of flies. Captain Walter Clifford of Gibbon's Infantry recalled:

> As the sun sinks from sight the listless breeze that has been lazily stirring dies away. The great round moon, bright as burnished silver, rolls slowly over our sorrowing heads. By its uncertain light a motionless black object can be seen at no great distance, which upon a nearer approach, proves to be a dead cavalry horse, and besides it the body of the rider, naked. Both are swollen almost to bursting. The legs of the horse are sticking straight out from the body, while the skin of the sleeping rider gleams in the moonlight like polished white marble...Half fearfully I hasten to the river bank and listen to the sobbing gurgle of its waters as they hasten towards the busy east with their heart-breaking story. Even this mournful music is better than the stillness out yonder. But the polluted air

is here also and one is forced to lie with face close to the water to be rid of the deadly poison that is permeating the clothing and filling the lungs with every respiration. A little delay on this death-stricken ground and we will remain forever. Let us hide our slain comrades from sight and resume, with quickened footsteps, our pursuit of their butchers...

Next morning, however, no real pursuit of the butchers took place, one company of Brisbin's cavalry following the Indian trail while the survivors of the 7th set out for the Custer battlefield to locate, identify and bury the dead. Lieutenant Godfrey recalled 'We saw a large number of objects that looked like white boulders scattered over the field. Glasses were brought into requisition, and it was announced that these objects were the dead bodies. Captain Weir exclaimed, "Oh, how white they look!"'

It was a sombre task under a bright blue sky as soldiers searched for a lost friend who could possibly never be identified. The squaws thought no more of carving up a dead soldier than they did a dead buffalo, and they were well practised in the art. But the soldiers had come to kill after the whites had broken the treaty; the Sioux and Cheyenne were angry. Trooper Taylor recalled:

> Heads crushed to an unrecognisable mass by stone war clubs, arms and legs slit with keen knives, parts of the bodies dismembered, and trunks cut open, and many with arrows left sticking in them. Nothing whatever of the belongings of man or horse was left on the field that I could see, the squaws had swept it clean. The sagebrush, broken and trampled by the horses and ponies of the contending forces, gave forth a strong odour which,

mingled with that of the swollen and fast decomposing remains of horses and men, was sickening in the extreme, and yet so hardened or indifferent were some that I saw men sitting down close by a mangled body and calmly munching their hardtack and bacon.

Many faces betrayed the ordeal of their death, having a 'pained, almost terrified expression.' The bodies of three officers; Sturgis, Porter and Harrington were never identified, nor was that of Dr. Lord. Tom Custer could only be recognised because of the initials T. W. C. being tattooed on one arm. Brother George lay nearby, shot through the body and head, amidst a cluster of bodies behind a barricade of dead horses on the slope of Last Stand Hill. He was stripped but not mutilated apart from a fingertip being removed, a slashed thigh, an arrow shot into his genitalia and his eardrums punctured.

Lieutenant Bradley recalled:

> Probably never did a hero who had fallen upon the field of battle appear so much to have died a natural death. His expression was that of a man who had fallen asleep and enjoyed peaceful dreams, than of one who had met his death amid such fearful scenes as that field had witnessed, the features being wholly without ghastliness or any impress of fear, horror or despair...

There is contradictory evidence regarding the precise nature of Custer's fatal wounds. Godfrey viewed the body and stated that 'he had been shot in the temple and the left side.' But First-Sergeant John Ryan of the burial detail claimed he had been shot in the head and body on the right side. They dug a wide grave about 18 inches deep where the bodies of Custer and brother Tom were laid to rest covered with blankets, canvas and soil. An Indian travois was brought up from the village and, having been turned face down, placed over the grave, pegged down and covered with rocks. The others had more rudimentary internments. The body of Sergeant Robert Hughes of Troop K was found near that of Custer. It was his task to carry Custer's personal guidon, which according to the Cheyenne was captured by one of their braves named Yellowstone before Hughes died. The Indians believed this flag to be 'big medicine' as the soldiers did their utmost to keep it aloft.

Indian testimony sometimes claims that Custer's men died bravely, others that they were easily cut down like sheep. Both probably occurred at different times on different parts of the field, as at Isandlwana, and soldiers of the 7th on Reno Hill had displayed both courage and cowardice. A soldier fighting bravely in the early stages of the Custer battle may well have attempted to flee once his comrades and officers had been cut down around him. The five British officers who escaped death at Isandlwana by galloping for their lives, while foot soldiers were cut down, were not condemned for their flight.

At the later Reno Court of Inquiry, various officers gave their first hand impressions of what had taken place:

Lieutenant Edgerly; 'There were a good many soldiers killed around Gen. Custer. There was no evidence of company organisations there—it seemed to have been a rallying point for all of them. I think that was where Gen. Custer planted the guidon.'

Captain Moylan; 'There was no evidence of organized and sustained resistance on the Custer field except around Calhoun, and in the circle where Gen. Custer lay.'

Lieutenant Hare; 'The evidence on the Custer field indicated very heavy fighting, especially where he fell,'

Lieutenant Godfrey; 'I think they had attempted to make a stand; there were fifteen or twenty bodies buried in one place by my company. All the troops I found appeared to have made a stand, though they were scattered. I supposed they had been dismounted and fought there.'

Lieutenant Wallace; 'The men around him were piled in a heap beside a horse, and the body of Custer was lying across one of them. They had struggled but not for long; they had apparently tried to lead the horses in a circle on the point of the ridge and killed them there and made an effort for a final stand.'

Captain Moylan; 'Calhoun's company was killed in regular position of skirmishers. I counted 28 cartridge shells around one man, and between the intervals shells were scattered.'

Benteen said it looked like a rout, the bodies scattered 'like a handful of corn,' but added 'Only where Gen. Custer was found were there any evidence of a stand...The officers' bodies, including Gen. Custer's, were in a position which indicated that they had not died in a charge; there was an arc of a circle of dead horses around them.'

The celebrated poet Walt Whitman would have no doubts regarding the circumstances of Custer's death. His piece in the New York *Herald* titled *A Death-Sonnet for Custer* would contain these words:

> The battle-bulletin,
> The Indian ambuscade, the craft, the fatal environment,
> The cavalry companies fighting to the last in sternest heroism,
> In the midst of their little circle, with their slaughter'd horses for breastworks
> The fall of Custer and all his officers and men.

23 Congressional Medals of Honor would be awarded to Reno's command as time moved on. Perhaps, if there had been survivors from Custer's battalion to tell their tale, more would have been awarded.

'The harrowing sight of the dead bodies crowning the height on which Custer fell,' recalled Reno, 'and which will remain vividly in my memory until death, is too recent for me not to ask the good people of this country whether a policy that sets opposing parties in the field, armed, clothed, and equipped by one and the same Government should not be abolished.'

The graves were rudimentary, sometimes only stones piled over a mutilated corpse. The remains of the enlisted men would later be disinterred and properly reburied on the field, and a granite monument erected in 1881. Custer's body would be laid to rest at West Point, and most other officers at various places in the east.

During the afternoon of the 27th the despondent command crossed the river to bury the dead of Reno's command, those who had fallen during the opening valley fight. They counted 259 bodies buried and, with the missing, the total dead was 265. Captain Myles Keogh's horse, Comanche, was found with several wounds but still alive, the other mounts either killed or captured by the victors. Comanche recovered, eventually dying in 1891, his remains preserved, mounted and put on display at the University of Kansas, thus the sole survivor still stands, viewed by thousands each year.

While the 7th buried its dead, Captain Ball followed the Indian village trail with Company H of the 2nd Cavalry. The hostiles had soon divided into two parties, one heading for the Big Horn Mountains and the other further east. He also discovered another large trail coming into the river valley; not that followed by Custer from the Rosebud. This was no more than five days old, indicating two large bands, unifying with perfect timing, as fate would have it, for Custer's annihilation. It seems probable that 2000 warriors or less took part in the fight, their number of killed not known. An estimate of between 50 and 100 has been bandied about, but with those who died afterwards because of their wounds it could have been more.

Couriers Goodwin and Bostwick had trouble locating the *Far West* as her crew had not identified the mouth of the Little Bighorn, steaming further upstream before a rapid return in a fast current. Without news that she was ready to receive the wounded, Terry decided only to march far enough to locate a healthier camping ground to the north. A site was chosen four miles downstream from the loathsome village site. The hand litters used to carry the wounded proved less than satisfactory so, on the 29th, travois and mule litters were fabricated to move those wounded unable to walk. Colonel Gibbon made an inspection of the battlefield, finding and burying two more bodies, including that of newspaperman Mark Kellogg.

Late that afternoon the march was resumed, the new litters proving to be worth their weight in gold, then the couriers rode into camp from the *Far West*. They carried a despatch from Captain Baker and the welcome news that she was being prepared to receive the casualties. Due to the steamer missing the river junction, Muggins Taylor, on his way to Fort Ellis, had actually located her first, and delivered the bad news. Curly the Crow scout had arrived earlier but due to his lack of English was unable to tell those on board what had actually happened.

Terry and the wounded boarded the *Far West* on the afternoon of June 30th. The general told Captain Marsh 'Every soldier here who is suffering with wounds is the victim of a terrible blunder; a sad and terrible blunder.' Terry received the following despatch, dated June 6th, from General Sheridan:

> Couriers from the Red Cloud Agency reported at Laramie yesterday that Yellow Robe arrived at the agency, six days from the hostile camp. He said that 1800 lodges were on the Rosebud and about to leave for Powder River below the point of 'Crazy Horse's fight' and says they will fight and have about 3000 warriors. This is sent for your information.

Too little news too late? But indications had been there all along that a lot more than 800 warriors could well be in the fight. Only a little over a decade earlier, the Little Bighorn casualties would have been accepted with a shrug in a civil war where thousands died. But it was a different world now. The campaign against savages who knew little of the modern, sophisticated world had been a bleak failure. A famous general; a Civil War hero, and a battalion of U. S. Cavalry had been wiped out to a man. Both public and politicians, having just celebrated the nation's 100th year, were outraged at the news—So who was to blame?

***

During the early afternoon of January 22nd 1879, a lone horseman approached the British campsite at Isandlwana. Commandant Rupert Lonsdale was dazed, suffering from both sunstroke and fatigue. He was returning to procure rations for his men of the Natal Native Contingent who had eaten little during the past few days. As he blearily trotted into camp on his jaded pony, Dot, he noted nothing amiss, just the usual bustle of redcoats, but then something caught his eye. A man moved from a tent wielding an assegai, the weapon moist with fresh blood. Instantly alert, he noticed the scruffy redcoats about him were not on the backs of British soldiers, but Zulu warriors. No one seemed to notice his presence, busy as they were with plundering the camp and, with supreme self-control, he gently turned his horse's head and gave a subtle nudge with his heels. The animal, however, exhausted from days on the march, would not move faster than a walk. Then there was a sudden shout. The Zulus looked around to see the British officer and bolted towards him. Lonsdale's forbearance ended with a sudden thrust of his spurs, and Dot managed to work up to a canter. Assegais whizzed past and bullets zapped by. 'I shall never close my eyes in sleep again without seeing that yelling horde of Zulus rushing after me, brandishing their bloody spears and wondering whether my poor horse had steam enough left in him to carry me out of their reach.' Dot raised steam, and Lonsdale was soon moving through the countryside. He glanced back over his shoulder to see no mounted warriors in pursuit. They had had their share of killing that day, but plundering the camp and the dead was another matter.

Chelmsford, meanwhile, had joined the "Indian fighter' Commandant Hamilton-Browne and his NNC, only to be informed that the camp had fallen. The Commandant was told 'How dare you tell me such a falsehood. Get your men into line at once and advance.'

But soon Lonsdale arrived. He was taken to headquarters by a sergeant where, at about 4 p.m., he saw Chelmsford, Crealock and other staff officers. 'The Zulus have the camp,' he said.

'How do you know?' asked the Wasp, astonished as the truth finally sank in.

'Because I have been into it.'

Chelmsford was aghast. 'But I left 1,000 men to guard the camp,' he said.

Major Gosset immediately rode out with orders for Colonel Glyn to lead the infantry and guns back to Isandlwana. He rode into Glyn's camp with apparent calm, the British stiff upper lip, his facade creating the impression that all was well. When told they were moving out for action, many soldiers cheered, unaware there was little to cheer about.

The Natal Native Contingent, meanwhile, advanced under Chelmsford back towards Isandlwana. The troops were deployed in three ranks, the first with whites and natives bearing firearms, those with assegais falling in behind. The Mounted Infantry and volunteers advanced on the flanks. Chelmsford peered at the camp through binoculars when a few miles away, then sent Colonel Russell forward to reconnoitre. Soon he rode back with the inevitable news 'as bad as it could be,' an estimated 7000 Zulus pillaging the camp.

Chelmsford's force held its ground awaiting Glyn's redcoats and artillery. The army was learning all too late the folly of a divided command. The sun had set and night approached by the time Glyn's tired column arrived, bristling with rumours of their comrades' fate.

Chelmsford addressed the troops. 'Twenty-fourth, whilst we have been out yonder the enemy has outflanked us and taken our camp. They are probably holding it now. At any cost we must take it back tonight and cut our way back to Rorke's Drift tomorrow. This means fighting, but I know I can rely on you.'

A resounding cheer went up, then the troops marched out. As they approached, Zulus in profusion could be seen moving away from the camp to the right driving cattle and carrying plunder. About half a mile from Isandlwana the column halted and redeployed in battle order; artillery in centre front, flanked by three companies of redcoats, a battalion of NNC and cavalry on each side, and the Natal Mounted Police behind. The guns roared and shells exploded on the neck illuminating the base of Isandlwana, and the 24th unleashed a few rifle volleys, evoking no response. Then Major Wilsone Black advanced with three companies of redcoats, bayonets to the fore. They charged over rocks, camp debris and a few bodies to occupy the stony koppie, to be known afterwards as Black's Koppie. A cheer went up as a signal for Chelmsford's force to advance. The gloom of night was falling over a grisly scene when the troops marched in over grass trampled quite flat by the Zulu horde. By the neck, Captain Hartford of the NNC recalled 'where the 24th and others made their stand, the dead lay thick, and it was a ghastly sight.' His native troops were not happy with what they saw; naked, mutilated and bloody bodies, many disembowelled. 'Nothing on earth could make those who were armed with rifles keep their place in the front rank, and all the curses showered on them by their officers could not prevent them from closing in and making up in clumps.'

Colonel Henry Degacher of the 24th Regiment discovered the body of his slain brother, Captain William Degacher. As he looked down, he recalled thinking 'Old boy, I shall be with you in half an hour.' Expecting another Zulu attack, he considered their lives not 'worth two minutes purchase.'

Captain Hartford sought out his tent amidst the litter, bodies and shambles:

> Everything had gone, and the same with Lonsdale's tent, which was next to it. Between our two tents lay the bodies of two artillery men, disembowelled and terribly mutilated. Within a few yards of where our wagon had been drawn up I found the dead bodies of our two drivers, with their faces blackened, and it struck me at the time

that they must have done this themselves in the hope of being able to escape.

An 'abominable stench' came from the looted hospital wagons, the medicine bottles having been smashed, and there Hartford discovered the body of Surgeon-Major Shepherd. 'He was lying face downwards, and had been stabbed in the neck.'

While Black's men maintained their position on the stonie koppie, the main force formed a defensive square on the saddle, the guns and horses in the centre. The night was long, nervous and icy cold, the Zulu enemy warming themselves by hundreds of campfires on the surrounding hills. The distant rattle of gunfire and the odd flash of light from the direction of Rorke's Drift heightened the state of tension. Was it possible for such a small garrison to hold out against a Zulu horde who had overrun a camp guarded by over 1000 troops? Many wished to march to their relief, and Chelmsford decided to move out as early as possible, leaving the dead where they lay. Their current campsite was as depressing as General Terry's that first awful night after relieving the besieged on Reno's hill. And at Isandlwana darkness cloaked the magnitude of the disaster which surrounded them.

An observer wrote in the Natal *Mercury*:

> Oh! How dreadful were those fearful hours which followed when all of us had to wait with what patience we could for daybreak, knowing that we were standing and living among the bodies of our own comrades, though how many we little knew then. Many and deep were the sobs which came from the breasts of those who, may be, never sobbed before, at discovering, even in the dim morning light the bodies of dear friends brutally massacred, stripped of all clothing, disembowelled, and in some cases with their

heads cut off. How that night passed, I fancy few of us knew...

Chelmsford explained his decision to move without burying the dead.

> The troops had no spare ammunition and only a few biscuits, a large portion of it had had no other food for 48 hours; all had marched at least 30 miles the day before, and had passed an almost sleepless night on the stony ground. No one was fit for any prolonged exertion, and it was certain that daylight would reveal a sight which could not but have a demoralizing effect upon the whole force. I determined therefore to reach our supply depot at Rorke's Drift as quickly as possible.

The troops pulled out next morning amidst an early fog, mercifully softening many gruesome sights. But what they did see was bad enough, as one artillery sergeant recalled 'There were bullocks, horses, and mules lying dead all over the place, waggons thrown down very steep precipices, and smashed all to bits; ammunition and medicines of all descriptions lying about, our tents burnt and torn to ribbons.' Captain Penn Symons saw 'One little Band Boy of the 2/24th Regiment, a mere child, was hung up by his heels to the tail of an ox wagon, and his throat cut. Even the dogs and goats about the camp, and the horses and mules tied to the picket ropes, were butchered. Further details would be too sickening.'

A Zulu boy who visited the sight shortly after the battle recalled 'Dead was the horse, dead too, the mule, dead was the dog, dead was the monkey, dead were the wagons, dead were the tents, dead were the boxes, dead was everything, even to the very metals.'

Chelmsford's force moved towards Rorke's Drift and it would be three months before a burial party returned to Isandlwana when Major General Sir Frederick Marshall, recently arrived in South Africa with reinforcements, would lead a force of cavalry, infantry and two guns from Rorke's Drift to the battlefield. Two newspaper correspondents, Archibald Forbes and Melton Prior, reported what they saw. Forbes wrote in the *Daily News*:

> No Zulus were seen. Flanking parties covered the hill on each side of the track, along which the column pressed on the trot, with small detachments of Natal Carbineers in front of the Dragoon Guards. Now we were down in the last dip, had crossed the rocky bed of the little stream, and were cantering up the slope that stretched up to the crest on which were the waggons. Already tokens of the combat and bootless flight were apparent. The line of retreat towards Fugitive's Drift…lay athwart a rocky slope to our right front, with a precipitous ravine at its base. In the ravine dead men lay thick—mere bones with toughened, discolored skin like leather covering them, and clinging tight to them, the flesh all wasted away. Some were almost wholly dismembered, heaps of clammy yellow bones. I forbear to describe the faces, with their blackened features and beards blanched by rain and sun. Every man had been disembowelled. Some were scalped, and others subjected to yet ghastlier mutilation. The clothes had lasted better than the poor bodies they covered, and helped to keep the skeletons together.
>
> All the way up the slope, I traced, by the ghastly token of dead men, the fitful line of flight. Most of the men hereabouts were infantry of the 24th. It was like a long string with knots in it, the string formed of single corpses, the knots of clusters of the dead, where, as it

seemed, little groups might have gathered to make a hopeless, gallant stand and die. I came on a gully with a gun limber jammed on its edge, and the horses, their hides scored with assegai stabs, hanging in their harness down the steep face of the ravine. A little further on was a broken and battered ambulance waggon, with its team of mules mouldering in their harness, and around lay the corpses of soldiers, poor helpless wretches, dragged out of an intercepted vehicle, and done to death without a chance of life.

Melton Prior wrote in the *Illustrated London News*:

Scattered over the field of carnage were letters from wives or parents at home to their husbands or sons in the field, & portraits of babies and children sent by mothers to loving fathers—one was signed 'dear darling Dadda'. I could not help the tears coming to my eyes.

Forbes described the Discovery of Durnford's body on the saddle near the base of the stony koppie, 'his long moustache still clinging to the withered skin of his face.' One can't help but compare the situation of Durnford's body with that of Custer on Last Stand Hill:

Durnford had died hard—a central figure of a knot of brave men who had fought it out around their chief to the bitter end. A stalwart Zulu, covered by his shield, lay at the Colonel's feet. Around him, almost in a ring, lay about a dozen dead men, half being Natal Carbineers, riddled by assegai stabs. These gallant fellows were easily identified by their comrades who accompanied the column. Poor Lieutenant Scott was hardly at all decayed. Clearly they had rallied round Durnford in a last desperate attempt to cover the flank of the camp, and had stood fast from choice when they might have essayed to fly for their horses.

Durnford, lying on his back, was covered with assegai wounds, but unlike most others, not stripped and, like Custer, not mutilated. His body was wrapped in canvas by the burial party, then laid to rest beneath a cairn of stones. It would eventually be exhumed to be reburied with full military honor at Pietermaritzburg. Other bodies were also buried, but not those of the 24th. Colonel Glyn had requested that they be left as they fell, so men of their own regiment could bury them later. This did not happen until June 1879, six months after their final battle, and three years after men of the 7th Cavalry buried Custer's dead.

Forbes continued his description of the carnage:

> Close beside the dead, at the picquet line, a gully traverses the ground in front of the camp. About 400 paces beyond this was the ground of the battle before the troops broke from their formation, and on both sides of this gully the dead lie very thickly. In one place nearly fifty of the 24th lie almost touching, as if they had fallen in rallying square. The line of straggling rush back to camp is clearly marked by skeletons all along the front.

Chelmsford fully expected a repeat of the ghastly scene at Isandlwana as his column approached Rorke's Drift. It was scarcely possible such a small garrison could withstand a full Zulu onslaught. The sight of the charred ruins of the hospital building confirmed his worst fears. But then there was something fluttering in the breeze; that improvised flag that Lieutenant Chard had run up! Major Russell and Lieutenant Walsh were despatched to the front, to be received with cheers from the garrison. Chard recalled 'Lord Chelmsford, with his Staff, shortly after rode up and thanked us all with much emotion for the defence we had made.'

Which was hardly surprising. One gleam of sunlight on a very dark day for the lieutenant general. He dismounted and spoke at length with Chard and Bromhead about the fight, then asked to see Private Hook who was busily making tea for the wounded. When informed that Bromhead wanted to see him, Hook said 'Wait till I put my coat on.'

'Come as you are, straight away,' replied the sergeant.

'With my braces hanging about me,' Hook recalled, 'I went into the midst of the officers. Lord Chelmsford asked me all about my defence of the hospital, as I was the last to leave the building. An officer took our names and wrote down what we had done.'

The wounded Frederick Hitch had the honor of receiving a visit from Chelmsford who said he would do his best to get him a Victoria Cross. Chelmsford would wish to focus the public's attention on Rorke's Drift rather than the not-so-glorious slaughter ten miles to the east.

Lieutenant Banister arrived with the 2nd Battalion to find Bromhead 'as cheery as ever and not a scratch about him.' He noted that the post 'was a scene of awful confusion' with 'dead niggers everywhere.' Lieutenant Mainwaring was taken around the post as Bromhead described the battle. Outside the hospital verandah they saw dead Zulu warriors laying three deep. A young induna lay there, amidst the carnage, adorned with a plumed headdress. Bromhead pointed to him, saying that he had gallantly led charges three times, 'But we got him in the end,' he said.

Redcoats falling into Zulu hands received the same treatment as those at Isandlwana. One of those who died in the hospital, Private Hayden, had been stabbed sixteen times, his stomach cut open, his face mutilated. One Zulu never finished the grisly work, being shot dead in the act of mutilating a 'poor fellow,' the knife still in his hand. The heavy .45 calibre bullets fired by the troops, however, did some mutilation of their own. One warrior had been shot in the face, the bullet passing neatly through, but blowing away the 'whole of the back of his head.' Another warrior's head was shattered 'as if done by an axe.'

Picks and shovels were put to work over the next few days, the native troops digging large grave pits for 351 dead Zulus. But they refused to actually touch the bodies, the British soldiers having to drag them through the grass and throw them in. Timber and scrub were thrown in on top, then set alight. But many others were found dead, having died from wounds, in caves and among the rocks, and scores of wounded were hunted down and killed. 'as deliberate a bit of butchery as I ever saw,' said Inspector George Mansel of the Natal Mounted Police, and ordered his men to have no part in it. Others who had witnessed the mutilation carried out by the Zulus were not so charitable. Commandant Hamilton-Browne recalled what happened when his men discovered a large number of fatigued and wounded Zulus in mealie fields near Rorke's Drift.

> My two companies of Zulus with some of my non-coms and a few of the 24th quickly drew these fields and killed them with the bayonet, butt and assegai. It was beastly but there was nothing else to do. War is war and savage war is the worst of the lot. Moreover our men were worked up to a pitch of fury by the sights they had seen in the morning and the mutilated bodies of the poor fellows laying in front of the burned hospital.

Some wounded Zulus died still resisting. They had given no quarter to fleeing troops and civilians at Isandlwana and along the fugitives' trail, and they expected none now.

But regardless of how many Zulus had died, and the gallant defence at Rorke's Drift, it was a black day for the British Army. 'The General, poor fellow,' wrote Lieutenant Curling to home on February 2nd, 'seemed quite off his head and so nothing is being done, nor it would seem has he recovered himself yet.'

It was an embarrassment of international proportions that the world's pre-eminent power could suffer such a defeat. Public and politicians alike would be outraged that mere savages could shatter their modern, sophisticated army—So who was to blame?

10
SO WHO WAS TO BLAME?

General Alfred H. Terry's funeral took place on December 29th 1890. The Reverend Dr. T. T. Munger took his place behind the lectern and, looking out across the assembly of Terry's family, friends and army comrades, delivered his sermon. He used the opportunity to clarify who, he believed, was responsible for the Little Bighorn:

> Custer's fatal movement was in direct violation of both verbal and written orders. When his rashness and disobedience ended in the total destruction of his command, General Terry withheld the fact of the disobeyed orders and suffered an imputation hurtful to his military reputation to rest upon himself, rather than subject a brave but indiscreet subordinate to a charge of disobedience.

Some Custer exponents took exception to the reverend's words and later asked him on what authority they were made. Dr. Munger quoted General Terry's brother-in-law, Colonel Robert Hughes, his former aide-de-camp and present on the 1876 campaign, as the source. While Hughes admitted having told Munger the details, he denied having given permission for him to repeat the allegations. When challenged to provide proof that Custer had disobeyed Terry's orders, Hughes was conspicuous by his silence.

But it is, nevertheless, a common view held by many to the present day, and can be traced back to the first days following Custer's defeat. The story quickly circulated that the location of the hostile village was known at the planning stage and both columns were to arrive on the 26th for a coordinated attack. But Custer recklessly disobeyed his orders, driving the command to arrive first and achieve an individual victory for himself. There can be no doubt that Custer cherished an individual victory, and one must question his judgement in a variety of ways, including not taking the battalion of 2nd Cavalry. But Terry could have ordered Custer to take the additional troops if he thought it necessary, or even rode with that wing in command. Grasshopper Jim Brisbin had asked Terry to do just that, but the general had declined, saying that Custer needed a chance to vindicate himself with his own regiment, having been removed from command of the Dakota expedition. And besides, said Terry, Custer had more experience fighting Indians and seemed positive he could whip anything he met.

'General,' replied Brisbin, 'you have more sense in your little finger than Custer has in his whole body. You underrate your ability and overrate Custer's.'

Brisbin approached Custer with the offer to take the 2nd Cavalry troops, which he declined. Brisbin also claimed to have warned Custer that scouts estimated a force of 3000 warriors. If true, perhaps Custer did not believe him, or just counted on 'Custer's luck' to see him through.

On June 27th, just two days after the defeat, Terry wrote his first report in which there was no hint of Custer having disobeyed orders. It is claimed that members of his staff were not happy with this report, and influenced Terry to reconsider his position, to cover both him and them. On July 2nd a second report appeared, which made mention of a definite plan which

Custer had not followed. 'I think I owe it to myself to put you more fully in possession of the facts of the late operations,' he wrote to General Sheridan, and followed with an account of a plan for the two columns to converge on the hostile camp on June 26th. When news of Custer's death hit the headlines on July 6th, the Bismarck *Tribune* stated:

> He was instructed to strike the trail of the Indians, to follow it until he discovered their position, and report by courier to Gen. Terry who would reach the mouth of the Little Horn by the evening of the 26th, when he would act in concert with Custer in the final wiping out.

There was no mention of 'impossible to give you any definite instructions' or no 'wish to impose on you precise orders' as Terry had written, and no mention that Custer's regiment would 'strike the blow' the Montana column not being 'present at the capture of the great village' as stated in Brisbin's newspaper despatch written before the battle. Thus the rot was already in.

Terry reiterated the story in his annual report for 1876, which stated that Custer was to find the Indian trail discovered by Reno and:

> if it led to the Little Big Horn, it should not be followed, but that Custer should keep still further to the south before turning to the river, in order to intercept the Indians should they attempt to pass around his left, and in order by a longer march, to give time for Gibbon's column to come up...This plan was founded on the belief that the two columns might be brought into cooperating distance of each other, so either of them which should be first engaged might, by a 'waiting fight' give time for the other to come up.

In order for this plan to be formulated in detail, the location of the village would have to be known. But Terry himself was still looking for it on the lower Tullock's Fork as Custer's scouts viewed it on the Little Bighorn from the Crow's Nest. In any case, Terry had given Custer a free hand, and when he discovered a fresh trail over the old originally found by Reno, he exercised the latitude given in his orders, following it directly to the village. And, of course, a 'waiting fight' of sorts did occur, Reno still being engaged with the Indians until they sighted Terry's advance, when the hostiles simply slipped away to the south.

Despite the room for manoeuvre given, the perception of Custer having disobeyed orders was easy to plant, largely because it fitted the image Custer had created for himself. At West Point he had displayed an early disregard for orders with the huge number of demerits accumulated, then allowed two cadets to indulge in a fist fight while he, as officer of the guard, was obliged to break it up and put them on charge. He liked being seen as the bold cavalier riding to the sound of the guns, and at Culpepper during the Civil War he abandoned his command to take part in an attack on a rebel train. He liked playing centre stage with his ornate gold-braided uniforms during the war, then donning buckskin frontier apparel when serving out west. He kept himself in the public eye by writing of his exploits in *Galaxy* magazine, amongst others. During the Black Hills expedition he was under orders from Phil Sheridan not to go off hunting, abandoning his command, as he had done in the past.

Regimental Colonel Sturgis, his own son one of the Little Bighorn victims, described Custer as brave but exceedingly selfish, and 'insanely ambitious for glory and the phrase "Custer's luck" a good clue to his ruling passion.'

Custer's court-martial and suspension for leaving his command to chase across the plains after his wife also reinforced the image of one with a lax attitude towards his own discipline. The Board of Revue concluded that Custer's anxiety regarding his wife had overcome 'his appreciation of the paramount necessity to obey orders.' When Grant had removed Custer from command, some newspapers had supported the president, the St. Paul *Pioneer Press* calling Custer 'an extra-ordinary compound of presumptuous egotism and presumptuous mendacity which makes him the reckless and lawless being he is.'

If someone was going to disobey orders, Custer was just the man who was going to do it. A few months after the battle, Terry showed a copy of Custer's orders to a Chicago *Times* reporter and said that had Custer survived, he would have been court-martialled for disobedience. But did Terry admit Custer had been following a fresh trail? Had a victory been the result, obviously there would have been no court-martial as he had, in fact, been operating within the perimeters given. But Custer was, of course, no longer alive to explain why he sent one quarter of his regiment on a mission which could have been done by a few sharp-eyed scouts, or why he did not send the 'Be quick' message at the time of Reno's attack. It must have had military heads shaking in wonder. President Grant told a correspondent for the New York *Herald* 'I regard Custer's massacre as sacrifice of troops, brought on by Custer himself, that was wholly unnecessary—wholly unnecessary.'

And Captain Benteen was only to happy to sink the boot in, stating in a letter to his wife 'Custer disobeyed orders from the fact of not wanting any other command—or body to have a finger in the pie—and thereby lost his life.' Was the 'body' Benteen referred to his own? Did he suspect Custer's motives? His comments at the Court of Inquiry emphasising the futility of his detour to the left could indicate his perception of what had taken place.

Friends of Custer's wife wrote to her with sympathy, saying that he had, in fact, fulfilled his destiny by dying such a hero's death. Would Custer have been so glorified or vilified if he had been a soldier with a supine image, possibly more in the mould of General Terry? But would the disaster have occurred had Terry been in command? Elizabeth Custer would become a vehement defender of her husband's reputation. Shortly after the bad news arrived, she requested that friends collect all newspaper stories praising her husband. She outlived Custer by nearly 57 years and during that time devoted her life to his memory, attempting to keep an untarnished image alive, attacking anyone who cast any slurs. In 1885 her book *Boots and Saddles* was published, a sympathetic portrayal of her life with Custer on the plains. She refers to his part in the battle as leading 'that final charge.' She includes letters sent by Custer and concludes with his instructions from Terry regarding his 'confidence in your zeal, energy and ability' and not wishing to 'hamper your action when nearly in contact with the enemy.'— a reminder to critics of what Custer's actual orders were. The book was a success, followed by *Tenting on the Plains* and *Following the Guidon*, also tributes to her husband's memory, which fuelled rather than quelled debate about Custer's last fight. She had the satisfaction of outliving his contemporary critics and others withheld their censure until after her death in 1933, a few days short of 91. The only officer who served at the Little Bighorn to outlive her was Colonel Charles A. Varnum, the young Lieutenant alongside Custer on the Crow's Nest on the morning of June 25th. He died In February of 1936.

Custer's defenders found their own counter-scapegoat in the form of Major Marcus Reno, accusing him of having sat on his hands while Custer was being wiped out. While the news was still headlines, Custer's West Point roommate, ex-Confederate General Thomas Rosser, wrote to the St. Paul *Pioneer Press*:

> I feel that Custer would have succeeded had Reno, with all the reserve of seven companies, passed through and joined Custer after the first repulse...As a soldier I would sooner today lie in the grave of Gen. Custer and his gallant comrades alone in that distant wilderness, that when the 'last trumpet' sounds I could rise to judgement from my post of duty, than to live in the place of the survivors of the siege on the hills.

Lieutenant DeRudio is reputed to have said, 'If we had not been commanded by a coward we would have all been killed,' which could have been a sarcastic way of saying Reno had, I fact, done the right thing, but condemned as a coward because of it. In 1879 a veteran of the 3rd Cavalry who had served under Custer during the Civil War wrote to the *National Republican*:

> My estimate of Reno and Custer is this: The former was brave but not rash and Custer was both. Through rashness Custer and the 3rd Cavalry Division got surrounded at Trevillian Station in 1864, and it was a brave but not rash man who cut him out. I mean Wesley Merritt, who commanded the 1st Cavalry, of which Marcus Reno's Regiment...formed a part. It was Custer's rashness that got him into the scrape at the Little Big Horn in 1876, and it would require a larger force than Reno had at his command to cut him out.

General Sherman's official report for 1876 commended 'the brave and prudent conduct of Major Reno.' The innuendo continued, however, including suggestions that Reno had become drunk, swigging from a hip flask both before and after the halted valley charge. Trooper Thompson of Troop C claimed that Reno's performance had been 'cowardly in the extreme' and that he had avoided his responsibilities on the hill, crouching in a dip, and 'he would have pulled the hole in after him if he could.' Others testified differently, however, Benteen saying that he had been with Reno most of the night of the 25th and his conduct had been cool and collected. Lieutenant Wallace stated that Reno spent most of the 26th on that part of the defence line where the heaviest attacks were expected.

Late in 1876 Frederick Whittaker, with Libby's collaboration, published a biography praising Custer and denouncing Reno and Benteen for having failed in their duty, and then demanded a government investigation. As a result, Reno also requested a Court of Inquiry into his own conduct during the battle in an attempt to clear his name. The President of the United States sanctioned his request and the inquiry examined Reno's performance, and the fight in general, sitting early in 1879. It found that 'the conduct of the officers throughout was excellent, and while subordinates in some instances did more for the safety of the command by brilliant displays of courage than did Major Reno, there was nothing in his conduct which requires animadversion from this court.' This was a qualified vindication for Reno and he would live in the shadow of the Little Bighorn for the rest of his life— and beyond. In 1926, the battle's 50th anniversary, there was a suggestion to erect a separate memorial to Reno's command where it had been besieged. Mrs Custer wrote an indignant response requesting that no memorial 'to so great a coward as Major Reno' be placed upon the battlefield. 'I feel almost my husband's hand taking the pen away from me,' she continued,

'I long for a memorial to our heroes on the battlefield of the Little Big Horn but not to single out for honor, the one coward of the regiment.' She had been informed of the plan by General Godfrey, retired, commander of Company K during the battle, one of those who disparaged Reno's conduct. Another three years would pass before a granite memorial to Reno's command would be erected, but conspicuous by its absence was Reno's name.

Perhaps both Chelmsford's and Reno's failure to ride to the sound of the guns was due to the fact that neither they, nor those officers about them, had any doubt that the beleaguered party was strong enough to hold its own.

***

'I cannot tell you what a relief it is for me to hear this,' said Chelmsford at Rorke's Drift on the morning of January 23rd. He had just been told by Major Clery that either Colonel Pulleine or Colonel Durnford, or both, had disobeyed the written orders he had left, having taken troops out of camp to attack the Zulus rather than holding a defensive line. Chelmsford could now see light at the end of a dismal tunnel, having seen his own career in tatters, his recall to Britain a certainty. But now there was someone else to blame, a couple of scapegoats just in the nick of time. And then Colonel Crealock, Chelmsford's 'evil genius', came to his aid, narrowing the field to one scapegoat only, stating that he had issued orders for Durnford to 'take command' of the camp. This would have obliged him to inherit Pulleine's orders to hold a defensive line. The Wasp was wrong, having only instructed Durnford to march his command to the camp, but dead men tell no tales. As in the case of Terry's staff officers after the Little Bighorn, Crealock did not want the tarnish of Isandlwana to rub off on him, his career being on the line along with that of Chelmsford. So, as Custer had disobeyed his orders in attacking the hostile village too early, Durnford had disobeyed his orders by taking troops out of camp to attack the Zulus. Or so their senior officers claimed.

'Lord C's staff did every thing in their power to shelter him as it was in their own interest to do, 'recalled Inspector Mansel of the Natal Mounted Police. 'I really believe, if justice had been done, the whole lot should have been tried for cowardice and shot.' As with General Terry, Chelmsford's first account, written on January 23rd, laid no blame but, as with Terry, the tone quickly changed. Only four days later he wrote an account to Secretary of State for War Colonel Stanley which said that Pulleine was left in charge of the camp, and received strict instructions that he was left there to defend it. Then information was received that Zulus had been seen in force on the left flank. Durnford had arrived with 'his 450 natives' and asked Pulleine for two companies of British infantry so that he might attack. Pulleine at once stated that his orders were to defend the camp and he could not allow the companies to move without positive orders. Chelmsford continued:

> Durnford then took his 450 natives up the heights and went so far as I can learn 5 miles from the camp, when he found himself in front of a very large army of Zulus…Had the force in question but taken up a defensive position in the camp itself, and utilized there the material for a hasty entrenchment which lay near at hand, I feel absolutely confident that the whole Zulu army would not have been able to dislodge them.

Chelmsford spoke to a bemused Sir Bartle Frere on January 26th. The Cape governor was, no doubt, all too aware that this tragedy would come back to haunt him—those letters from

Hicks Beach saying 'no war,' yet Frere had done all he could to bring it on. Yes, some specific person to blame would have seemed like a good idea. He wrote to the Duke of Cambridge, the queen's cousin, and commander-in-chief of British forces regarding Chelmsford:

> He feels the calamity the more because he is naturally averse, pending the result of the inquiry he has ordered, to express any opinion as to who, of the poor fellows who are gone, was to be blamed for the undoubted neglect of orders which led to the disaster. It will probably never be known how such a large body of the enemy got so close, without being seen & their force earlier reported. Nor why the main column with the general were not apprised & recalled earlier in the day. But from all I can learn there was ample time after the enemy were discovered to park the wagons & the detaching of the companies of the 24th more than a mile from the camp instead of concentrating them at the camp, was objected to by Lt. Col. Pulleine, when Lt. Colonel Durnford took command.

The late 1870s seem to have been an unhealthy time for lieutenant colonels fighting savages far from home. In Custer's case it was easy to convince people he had disobeyed orders because of his track record and image, and perhaps Durnford's 'brigand' costume did not help either. This, coupled with his previously having disobeyed Chelmsford's orders, and lingering doubts about his leadership at Bushman's River Pass, made it easy to believe he had disobeyed at Isandlwana. Bushman's River Pass had been bad enough, but Durnford had lost over a thousand lives this time, so some said. And why would anyone doubt Crealock when he claimed he had instructed Durnford to take command of the camp, especially as his order book was genuinely missing in action.

Chelmsford's Court of Inquiry, mentioned in Frere's letter, consisted of the president, Colonel Fairfax Hassard, and Lieutenant Colonels Francis Law and Arthur Harness. Chelmsford was judicious in selecting Harness for this role, as it was he who had attempted to take his command to the camp's relief when under attack, just to be ordered back. As a member of the court he could not give evidence, and such evidence would be damaging to Chelmsford. The Court was merely to hear testimony. It was not to form an opinion, or reach any conclusion. Various officers made statements with no cross-examination, and Crealock repeated his claim to have ordered Durnford to take command at Isandlwana.

A transcript of the proceedings was despatched to the secretary of state for war on February 8th with no conclusions or opinions offered by either the Court or Chelmsford. Included, however, was a memorandum from Colonel Bellairs, Chelmsford's deputy adjutant-general who was, apparently, permitted to reach a conclusion:

> From the statements made before the Court of Inquiry it may be clearly gathered that the cause of the reverse at Isandhlwana was that Lt. Colonel Durnford, as senior officer, overruled the orders which Lt. Colonel Pulleine had received to defend the camp and directed that the troops should be moved into the open, in support of a portion of the Native Contingent which he had brought up and was engaging with the enemy. Had Lt. Colonel Pulleine not been interfered with and been allowed to carry out his distinct orders given him to defend the camp, it cannot be doubted that a different result would have been obtained.

Possibly, but this made no mention of Chelmsford's own orders regarding the deployment of troops when under attack, closely followed by Pulleine.

In yet another twist of fate, only three days after the inquiry's deliberations were forwarded to London, another investigation wound up its proceedings in Chicago, Illinois. The Reno Court of Inquiry regarding the Battle of the Little Bighorn had taken over two years to be convened, whereas Chelmsford's Court of Inquiry had sat within one week of Isandlwana. Testimony regarding each disaster had been heard in chorus at the same time on different sides of the world.

News of the Isandlwana debacle reached London early on February 11th 1879, to be greeted with shock and astonishment by government, the army and the general public alike. Less than two weeks had passed since the masses had learned that they were at war with Zululand. Now this! The British people were used to easy victories over savages, and there had not been such a reverse since the early days of the Indian Mutiny in 1857.

Queen Victoria was residing at Balmoral Castle when she received the ill tidings. So bad was the news to her, she suffered from a headache for the remainder of the day. Little wonder, Chelmsford being a favorite, and once having been her aide-de-camp. She wrote in her journal 'How this could happen we cannot imagine, but fear Colonel Durnford was enticed away.' Already Chelmsford's plan to shift the blame was having its effect. Her private secretary, General Ponsonby, wrote to his wife 'I think it will turn out that Col. Durnford was left in charge of the camp and ought never to have left it. Why he was enticed out we will never know, but I think the blame is his—and not the fault of Chelmsford or the others.' Secretary for War Colonel Stanley received instructions from the queen to send a message of support to Chelmsford. She wanted him to know that she 'sympathises most sincerely with him in the dreadful loss which deprived her of so many gallant officers and men,' and she 'places entire confidence in him and in her troops to maintain our honour and our good name.'

She also sent a similar message of support to Sir Bartle Frere via Colonial Secretary Hicks Beach. Both he and Stanley sent her messages without consulting the Cabinet, and the queen would later be criticised in both press and Parliament for pre-judging the events prior to an impartial inquiry. And others were not so easily convinced. An Intelligence Department report of February 11th signed by three generals was critical of Chelmsford's role:

> He does not seem to have fortified the camp at Isandlana. He did not keep up proper communication with his Camp. He was led away by the Zulus who decoyed him from the Camp. In the meantime the Zulus collected in thousands under the hills near the Camp…Why were not scouts sent to explore?

'Did not keep up proper communication…' had both Custer and Chelmsford paid more attention to this vital role, both disasters may have been avoided. Little wonder Colonel Buller was to say some time afterwards 'I hope I may often meet Chelmsford as a friend but I trust I may never serve under him again as a general.'

Chelmsford did receive criticism from both press and opposition MPs for his role, but he and others did all they could to lay the blame at Durnford's feet. Queen Victoria felt Chelmsford was being treated unfairly and could not *'bear'* injustice or want of generosity towards those who have unbounded difficulties to contend with,' she informed Prime Minister Disraeli, who was enraged with the embarrassing affair. The Russians were difficult enough without the army being made to look ridiculous, cut to shreds by a mob of spear-wielding savages in some far-flung colonial war. Isandlwana would help bring down his government at the next election.

But the queen new nothing of machinations behind the scenes. When Durnford's body was discovered on May 21st, Captain 'Offy' Shepstone was seen to take papers from his coat. As Elizabeth Custer had become a vocal defender of her man's reputation, so now did Frances Colenso become a vocal defender of Durnford. She got wind of the papers' removal and approached Shepstone for an explanation. It made sense that the actual orders the Wasp had issued to Durnford would be on his body. Shepstone denied having removed any papers from Durnford, saying that he had taken some from his dead brother, George, causing the confusion, and in any case, Durnford was not wearing a coat, a fact refuted by several other witnesses.

Chelmsford engineered a cover-up of his own ineptitude following Isandlwana, and it seems that Shepstone became part of the scheme. Chelmsford was still commander-in-chief of British forces in South Africa, someone who could look after those who assisted him.

Frances met Offy Shepstone, an officer of the Natal Carbineers, in person and commented on his false words regarding Durnford:

> I was rather struck by the warm manner in which he spoke of Col. Durnford and his own extreme satisfaction at having been the man to find, & show respect to, the body of such a hero. For I was well aware that Mr. Shepstone had never felt warmly towards Col. Durnford during the latter's life time, since the volunteers were condemned

and Colonel Durnford highly commended by the Court of Inquiry upon the Bushman's Pass Affair in 1873.

Durnford's brother Edward, a British colonel stationed in England, got wind of a letter written by Veterinary Surgeon Longhurst to his family describing Durnford's burial. It stated that papers had been removed from the body. Edward contacted Frances Colenso asking her to look into the matter, and Longhurst reiterated his story, stating that he saw Captain Shepstone 'distinctly take' a packet of letters from his coat pocket. She approached Shepstone for an explanation, who replied 'Captain Longhurst's statements regards papers is a *deliberate untruth*. I took no papers of any kind from Col. Durnford's body, nor were any taken from him in my presence.'

In 1880 the book *My Chief and I* appeared. As Libby Custer published *Boots and Saddles* in 1885, Frances had already written a defence of her man, but under the nom de plume 'Atherton Wylde.' Her book was a romantic vindication of Durnford in which Atherton Wylde observes Durnford during his time in Natal including the Bushman's River Pass skirmish. 'I longed to have been at his side, fighting with and for him upon that day,' writes the hero-worshipping Atherton. Despite the Isandlwana battle still being fresh and controversial in the public mind, the book was not a success. In 1884 she released a revised edition revealing the writer to be a woman, but it did no better. She was saved from financial embarrassment when Durnford's chivalrous brother Edward loosened his purse strings to save the day.

Chelmsford probably took comfort from the British 66th Regiment and their Indian allies being routed at the Battle of Maiwand by the Afghanis in July of 1880, proving he was not the only British general capable of being beaten in a colonial war, but on August 19th of the same year he made a speech in the House of Lords regarding the camp's fall. 'In the final analysis,' he stated, 'it was Durnford's disregard of orders that had brought about its destruction.' Chelmsford repeated this charge to his fellow lordships the following month.

In response, Edward Durnford published a pamphlet *Isandhlwana: Lord Chelmsford's Statements compared with the Evidence*, and followed this two years later with a book about his brother, *A Soldier's Life and Work in South Africa*.

On May 18th 1882, the Wasp finally divulged the true wording of Durnford's orders. Colonel Black had returned to Isandlwana during June of 1879 to bury the dead of the 24th Regiment. Amidst the debris still scattered about he had discovered Colonel Crealock's order book which, of course, contained the proof that Durnford had only been ordered to the camp, not take command. Despite Crealock finally admitting that Durnford had not received orders to take charge of the camp, the perception continued in both public and military minds that Durnford was to blame, the official published account by the Intelligence Department conveying that impression.

The *Natal Witness*, on May 27th 1879, had printed a story stating that papers had been taken from Durnford's body, and Shepstone approached the editor to borrow the paper's file late in 1882, explaining 'that he wished to look up some points connected with the Zulu War.' Frances Colenso was told of the borrowing, and checked the file herself to find that the incriminating issue of May 27th and a Supplement of June 7th, had been removed.

She found a sympathetic ear in the form of Colonel Charles Luard, commander of the Royal Engineers in Natal, who agreed to help clear Durnford's name, and force Shepstone to admit having taken papers from his body. Luard wrote to the head of the Royal Engineers, Sir Andrew Clark, requesting permission to convene a Court of Inquiry. Regarding Durnford taking charge of the camp, he wrote:

> It must be apparent to any Military man that it never could have been intended that he should have assumed that charge, being at the time in independent command of another column of the army, more especially as not a word appears to have been said, either to Colonel Glyn whose camp it was, or to Colonel Pulleine who was left in temporary charge of it, that such a change of command was contemplated!

Shepstone agreed to appear before the inquiry, held during 1886. But Commander of British forces in South Africa, General Henry Torrens, wrote to Luard 'I have taken measures to limit proceedings and to prevent, I trust, the possibility of other names, distinguished or otherwise, being dragged into it.' Luard was unable to prove that Shepstone had taken papers from Durnford's body, many of his witnesses being unable to get leave from the civil service or army to attend. The inquiry found in Shepstone's favor, and Torrens instructed Luard to write the captain a letter of apology. Torrens wrote to Chelmsford, saying he had been informed 'that you are gratified at the action I have taken in this wretched charge against Theophilus Shepstone, in which an attempt has been made to involve you.'

Frances Colenso did not accept the findings, and wrote to the *Times of Natal* on December 10th 1886 that 'Durnford's last orders were on him when he fell' and the following January Edward Durnford wrote to the same paper saying the inquiry was 'eminently unsatisfactory.'

Her attempts to clear Durnford's name came to an unfortunate end with her death from tuberculosis on April 26th 1887. Ultimately, however, nothing changed the fact that Durnford's last orders regarding combat were those of January 19th from Chelmsford stating 'I shall want you to operate against the Matyanas' which he was doing when he led his troops from the camp. Whether or not he was judicious in the prosecution of those orders will be forever open to debate, as has proven to be the case with Custer at the Little Bighorn.

11
THE FADING COMET

The huge village on the Little Bighorn had come together just long enough to kill the man who had invaded the Black Hills two years before, declaring 'gold in the grassroots.' How ironic. In doing so, Long Hair had sown the golden roots of his own destruction at the hands of Sitting Bull, a mere savage, as Longfellow portrayed him in *The Revenge of Rain-in-the-face:*

> In his war paint and his beads
> Like a bison among the reeds
> In ambush the Sitting Bull
> Lay with three thousand braves
> Crouched in the clefts and caves,
> Savage, unmerciful!

But the battles with both Crook and Custer took their unmerciful toll on the victors also. Ammunition was now a problem and large villages were hard to maintain, quickly hunting out the local wildlife. The hostiles split up, and separate bands with fewer warriors made life easier for the army once they could track them down. On July 17th General Wesley Merritt surprised a party of Cheyennes and forced them back to their reservation with the death of one warrior. During the same month Lieutenant F. W. Sibley exchanged gunfire with a war party under White Antelope. The chief was killed and the rest retreated. But most troops hunted with no result, the hostiles easily eluding their blueclad pursuers.

American Horse, a trusted friend and lieutenant of Crazy Horse, camped on Rabbit Creek, not far from Slim Buttes. On the morning of September 8th they were surprised by troops under Captain Anson Mills. His command had discovered the village accidentally while escorting a wagon train to Deadwood, in the Black Hills, to pick up supplies for General Crook. The Indians fled as the soldiers charged, but American Horse and four warriors along with a group of women and children were trapped in a cave at the end of a ravine. Twice the soldiers charged, and twice they were driven back. One trooper and 'Buffalo Chips' Charley, a scout, were killed and nine others wounded. Lieutenant Von Luettwitz's leg received such a severe wound it had to be amputated later in the day. Then General Crook arrived with the main force and took command.

'Come and get us!' was American Horse's mocking reply when scout Frank Grouard called on him to surrender. Crook took the chief at his word and positioned 200 men around the ravine. The air was split by a crescendo of rifle fire, the troops pouring bullets into the mouth of the cave. A truce was called and again the Sioux were given a chance to surrender. Soon about thirteen women and children emerged from the dark, but American Horse remained defiant. 'Crazy Horse will rub you out,' he yelled.

Again Crook gave the order to open fire, and for two hours a hail of bullets rained into the cave. The five rifles cracking in reply dwindled, then became silent.

Grouard crept forward once more and yelled out for the trapped warriors to give up the fight. A young Sioux took a few tentative steps into daylight, and the scout repeated the offer. 'Weshte helo,' (Very good) the brave replied, then turned and retreated into the darkness. Soon American Horse appeared, supported by the young warrior and another brave. The chief was biting on a flat chunk of wood to avoid grinding his teeth in agony, having received a critical body wound with a piece of intestine protruding. But he still had an air of dignity as he surrendered his rifle to Crook. Inside the cave were the dead bodies of the other two warriors, a squaw and a child.

Then more Indians appeared. Crazy Horse and a few hundred braves had arrived from their camp several miles away and opened fire. Crook's full force of 2000 men had their hands full as the Sioux skipped from vantage point to vantage point until, vastly outnumbered, the attackers retired under cover of dark.

American Horse died from his wound that night, stoic and defiant till the very end. For an old warrior it was probably a better way to go than fading to oblivion on a white mans' reservation. In the camp were found various items of 7th Cavalry equipment including a company guidon. In all, it was a thin victory for the bluecoats following the humiliation of the Little Bighorn.

The winter of 1876-77 was severe. Not only did the hostiles have to contend with temperatures plunging to 60 degrees Fahrenheit below zero, but a new, resolute army commander in the person of Colonel Nelson A. Miles, 37, another Civil War hero. Involved in Boston mercantile pursuits before the war, he joined up with the rank of lieutenant when hostilities broke out. He was severely wounded at the Battle of Chancellorsville, but received a Congressional Medal of Honor for his trouble and, rising through the ranks, was promoted to brigadier general of volunteers in 1864.

Having been ordered to tackle the Sioux and Cheyenne in late 1876, he set about planning a winter campaign despite the advice of locals who thought the idea unfeasible so far north. 'I equipped my command as if they were going to the artic regions,' he recalled. The troops were supplied with thick garments of wool and fur, and masks to protect the face.

The prime target for Miles' campaign was the chief troublemaker himself, Sitting Bull, camped in the valley of the Big Dry. To spread the hunting grounds, he had separated from Crazy Horse who, with his band, was on the headwaters of the Rosebud and the Tongue.

Miles marched against the hostiles but it was not long before vigilant Sioux scouts discovered his approach on Sitting Bull's camp. On the night of October 17th a war party swooped in an attempt to stampede the command's horses. The attempt failed, however, but the braves fired into the rows of tents before riding off into the night. They almost killed their new antagonist, a few bullets passing mere inches above his camp stretcher.

The troops marched out next morning and again the braves rode to the attack, this time concentrating on the strung-out supply train. Colonel Otis ordered the train to keep moving as he deployed his men as a guard flanking each side. The Indians kept their distance, riding to and fro, firing at the lumbering wagons, then one brave rode far to the front, leaving an object on the brow of a hill. It was picked up to reveal a note from the great chief himself:

> I want to know what you are doing travelling on this road. You scare all the buffalo away. I want to hunt in this place. I want you to turn back from here. If you don't I will fight you again. I want you to leave what you have got here and turn back from here.

I am your friend,
Sitting Bull
I mean all the rations you have got and some powder.
Wish you would write me as soon as you can.

'Big Leggins' Brughiere, a half-breed living with the Sioux, wrote the note for Sitting Bull as dictated. But Otis sent a reply back to the chief saying he would go where he wished and if Sitting Bull wanted a fight he would have no trouble finding it. The Sioux kept up a long-range fire, but the relentless supply wagons kept rolling.

A white flag was seen fluttering in the distance on the morning of October 21st. A group of Indians on horseback approached, then stopped some distance away. Sitting Bull sent the flag bearer, Long Feather, forward to give a message to the troops. It requested a conference, and Colonel Miles invited the chief to meet him within the army lines. Trusting the word of no white man, Sitting Bull sent three envoys forward instead. They parleyed with the general, but returned in frustration when no compromise could be reached.

Realising he would have to do the talking himself, Sitting Bull requested another conference, to be held in no-man's-land between the lines the following day. Miles agreed, and went forward accompanied by one officer and six soldiers. Sitting Bull had with him seven braves, including White Bull. The red and white lines looked on from a distance. What was actually said varies with those who took part. The Indians later accused Miles of verbally attacking Sitting Bull for being the enemy of the white man. The chief calmly replied, they said, that he would not be the whites' enemy if they simply left him alone. The parley went nowhere, and the two groups returned to the safety of their own lines, but agreeing to continue the talk next day.

They met in the same place, escorted as before. 'Sitting Bull looked like a conqueror and spoke like one,' Miles later recalled. The chief said that he had not fought a war of aggression, and was willing to abandon hostilities if the troops withdrew from his hunting grounds and abandoned their forts. But Miles was in no position to accede to Sitting Bull's demands even if he wished. He shook his head and replied that unconditional surrender was the only terms he would accept. Then, according to Miles, the chief flew into a rage, looking more like a 'wild beast' than a human 'and you could see his eyes glistening with the fire of savage hatred.'

'Almighty God made me an Indian,' Sitting Bull shouted, 'but not an agency Indian!'

There was nothing more to be said. The two parties turned their horse's heads and trotted back to their own lines. Miles ordered his men to prepare for action, the bugles blared and the cavalry leapt forward with a charge. The Indians had fired the prairie grass to cover their retreat, but the blades were short and the charging troops galloped right through the flames and clouds of white smoke. The Sioux escaped, breaking into different bands, but Miles kept on in pursuit after the largest group who fled back to the Yellowstone. A large number of Sioux, realising the bluecoats would give them no rest, surrendered at the mouth of Cabin Creek on October 27th. They gave up hostages to guarantee their voluntary return to their agencies, but conditions at these places were so bad that only a few actually stayed.

Sitting Bull remained on the loose, doubling back towards Fort Peck with his band of devoted followers. Miles refitted his infantry, then marched into the area around Fort Peck. He split his men into three commands so every report and rumour could be followed up, and on December 8th Lieutenant

Frank Baldwin's detachment struck Sitting Bull's village on Red Water Creek. But the Indians scattered and again the wily chief escaped.

On December 8th, Miles struck another Sioux village during a snowstorm near the mouth of Hanging Woman's Fork. The Indians scattered, starving, barely able to survive in the frozen wilderness.

While Miles relentlessly pursued the Sioux, General Ranald S. McKenzie received word of the hostiles at his base, Fort Reno in Northern Wyoming, regarrisoned since the Custer fight. His Arapahoe scouts had captured a young Cheyenne, Beaver Dam, who said Crazy Horse was camped on the Rosebud, and his own Cheyenne village, under Dull Knife and Little Wolf, was on the Upper Powder. On November 24th McKenzie marched his 1100 troops and scouts out across the chilly landscape, and soon a fresh fall of snow revealed an Indian trail leading to the Cheyenne camp. The Arapahoe scouts went ahead, then galloped back to report a big village in a canyon to their front. During that night the soldiers made their cautious way forward alongside the splashing waters of an icy mountain stream. Across the frigid night sky the sounds of an Indian celebration were heard; the beating of tom-toms, singing and chanting. The Cheyenne were celebrating a recent victory over the Shoshones who had scouted for Crook before his defeat at the Battle of the Rosebud.

Then the village became silent as the revellers tired and returned to their tepees, not knowing McKenzie's troops were closing in. As the sun's frosty glow brightened the eastern sky on November 25th, the Cheyenne were startled by the dreaded call of a bugle. They rushed from their slumber into the icy, fresh air. Scouts Frank and Luther North led the Pawnee scouts in first, followed by the galloping hooves of the troops.

Indians dropped in the snow as guns cracked, but most bolted with their weapons for the sides of the canyon, naked except for breechclouts. They turned at the head of the gorge and, working the levers on their Henrys and Winchesters, sent a fusillade of bullets back towards their attackers. Some braves got hold of their mounts and, with wild war whoops, dashed headlong back at the advancing troops in a delaying action to allow fleeing squaws and children from the lower end of the village time to escape. The troops stalled, and the Cheyenne fired back as they retreated on foot. Yellow Nose, prominent at the Custer fight, led some warriors to a squat, rocky hillock which overlooked the village. McKenzie saw the danger and ordered Lieutenant McKinney forward with his troop to drive them off. The young Lieutenant led the charge but he dropped from his saddle amidst a fusillade of bullets. His men took refuge in a deep gulch while three braves dashed forward and counted coup on McKinney's dead body.

Chief Little Wolf had several braves killed around him as he shepherded women and children to safety up a canyon pathway. Bullets ricocheted about him but he held his position, resolute and calm, until the last of the defenceless were out of harm's way. An attempt by two troops of cavalry to pursue was cut short when a trooper fell from his saddle, shot down by warriors fighting a rear-guard action. The soldiers drew back, dismounted, and bullets flew up the gorge as they opened fire. More shots were exchanged, then the few remaining braves of the rear guard dashed to the safety of another gully. Nine dead warriors were later found here, having sold their lives while the women and children made their way to temporary safety, cold and hunger their next threat to survival.

Most of the Indians had made their way from the valley, but five braves had been trapped on a knoll. They lay flat on the stony ground returning fire as the troops closed in, but all attempts at rescue by the Cheyenne were driven off. Then Yellow Nose appeared with about 25 mounted braves. They were all skilled warriors adorned in eagle-feather war bonnets. With a whoop, Yellow Nose led the charge towards the besieged men on the knoll. The braves made a spectacular sight as they galloped through the haze of gunsmoke, shooting and uttering wild war cries. The startled troopers turned their guns on this new threat, and a volley crashed out. Suddenly Yellow Nose pulled back on his horse's reigns and threw one arm in the air. At this signal the whole war party swept round to one side and disappeared into the rocky terrain. The troops stared after them, then returned their attention to the knoll. But where were those braves now? They quickly realised they had been taken in by a ploy. The charge had been a distraction allowing the trapped Cheyennes to escape.

Then warriors appeared along the upper heights, firing down into the village. Soldiers were hit, but soon the Indians' ammunition ran out and they were forced to withdraw. The troops destroyed the Cheyennes' remaining ammunition and supplies, along with 173 lodges, and shot 150 ponies. They had lost five killed and 25 wounded. They found 25 dead braves on the field, and the Cheyenne later said 40 or more died from gunshot wounds.

It was a horrid night for the survivors. Yellow Nose and others had been severely wounded. The Indians were used to harsh conditions, but that night they huddled about six miles from the destroyed village without shelter, food, and many had little clothing. As the temperature plunged, more Cheyenne died, the elderly and the very young. It was later claimed that about 14 froze to death that bitter night. Some ponies were killed and disembowelled, babies saved by being placed in the protective warmth of the cavity. Some elderly avoided frostbite by placing their hands and feet alongside.

Next day the desperate band struck out to find the village of their Sioux ally, Crazy Horse. It was not hard for army scouts to discover their trail, being red with the blood of the wounded, and small bleeding feet. Three days later the refugees were warmly welcomed into the lodges of Crazy Horse's band who shared what little they had. Some of the embittered Cheyenne stayed to continue the fight with the Sioux, but others, crushed by the frigid weather and the white mans' bullets, soon surrendered at the despised Indian agencies.

Crazy Horse found his situation increasingly desperate. Colonel Miles kept doggedly after him, and on January 7th made contact near the snow covered slopes of Wolf Mountain where Crow scouts captured a party of Cheyenne women and children. That night Crazy Horse attacked, but failed to rescue the prisoners. Next morning, the troops' breakfast ended abruptly with the rattle of gunfire from the surrounding heights. The Sioux were in force and they yelled insults at the invaders between firing shots. But Miles had an unpleasant surprise in store. Very quickly shells were hurled into the Indian positions, canvas having been pulled back to reveal the black muzzles of two big guns disguised as ordinary wagons. The Sioux warriors dropped from sight, exploding shells something they could not easily combat, but Crazy Horse rallied them and the rifle fire was kept up.

Miles ordered Major Casey to take a strategic height occupied by about 50 warriors, and the troops made their way up into the rocks, fighting as they went. They could see a brave warrior adorned with a war bonnet dangerously expose himself as he urged the braves to fight. This was Big Crow, a leading warrior, but the Sioux pulled back when he finally fell victim to a soldier's bullet. The troops moved forward and occupied the bluff. The percussions of the shells continued to echo along the valley, then a snowstorm struck. With their ammunition low, Crazy Horse gave the order to retire and the Sioux melted into the snow-bound wilderness.

About one month later, February 4th, Miles sent a summons to Crazy Horse to surrender. The message was carried by Big Leggins Brughiere, who had written Sitting Bull's trail message to Colonel Otis the previous October. Crazy Horse's snow-bound village was found, the Indians suffering from hunger and cold, most of their ponies dead. But even then they held out for a few more months.

The agencies sent out 'peace-talkers,' friendly Indians who told the hostiles that they were fighting for a lost cause; the troops would harass them till they surrendered. The only hope for the safety of their women and children was to return to the reservations,

Finally, on April 22nd, Two Moons and Little Chief surrendered with a few hundred Cheyennes, and a few days later the Sioux under Crazy Horse, two thousand in number, came into the Red Cloud Agency. Throughout the spring various bands turned themselves in, but Sitting Bull still refused to yield. Harassed by Miles' troops, he moved north with about 1000 followers and crossed the border into Canada where, on May 7th, he came into contact with Major James M. Walsh of the North-West Mounted Police. He showed Walsh medals his grandfather had been given for helping the British during the War of 1812 and claimed the protection of Queen Victoria, whose own troops, ironically, would repeat the unjust war and the Little Bighorn in South Africa only thirty-one months later.

As Sitting Bull parleyed with Walsh, Colonel Miles struck

the final blow south of the border. Chief Lame Deer had been determined not to flee to Canada or surrender. He was going to stay in his own country, free, till the bitter end. May 2nd saw Colonel Miles on the trail once more, his Indian scouts in the advance. Five days later Lame Deer's village was attacked and several Indians killed before the chief waved a white flag, requesting a truce. He ordered his braves to lay down their arms. But Lame Deer's own son, Big Ankle, refused. His grandmother had been killed during the attack and, furious with grief, he cried, 'I am a soldier on my own land.' His gun discharged when an officer and a scout attempted to take it from him. Lame Deer snatched up his own rifle and fired at Miles who saved himself by rearing his horse, but his orderly dropped from his saddle, killed. Moments later the soldiers opened fire. When the smoke cleared both Lame Deer and his son were amongst several more dead Sioux. A total of 14 Indians died that day, along with four soldiers.

By the end of May 1877, it was all over. All organised resistance had ceased. As the bluecoat army had vanquished the Confederate army with a war of attrition rather than brilliance and daring, so too had it vanquished the Sioux and Cheyenne.

***

Only Noggs had been on hand to cover the invasion of Zululand, but Isandlwana changed all that. Public interest in the Afghanistan campaign quickly shifted to South Africa, and numerous newspapermen travelled with the reinforcements who were to teach the Zulus a lesson only the British Empire could inflict. As painters had taken up brushes to depict the last stand of the heroic 7th, painters took up brushes to depict the last stand of the heroic 24th, and poets like Robert Buchanan also painted vivid pictures with patriotic words:

Still as stone, our soldiers face the savage crew—
'Fix your bayonets! Die as English soldiers do!'
It is done—all stand at bay—
But their strength is cast away;
And the black swarms shriek anew
As they slay!
Ah God! The battle-throes!
With their dead as shields, they close, -
Where the slaughter ebbs and flows, in Isandula!

Revenge was demanded. But the next sorry saga to hit the street was not what was expected, a repeat of Isandlwana in miniature; more bad news for the beleaguered Lord Chelmsford. Captain David Moriarty, leading a supply train of 18 wagons carrying supplies and ammunition for Chelmsford's second thrust into Zululand, reached Myer's Drift on the Ntombe River in northern Zululand on March 7th. After two days of toil in torrential rain the river was swollen, preventing the wagons crossing, and a raft was constructed. As the problems persisted, Moriarty's force was split, 70 men protected by laagered wagons on one riverbank, and 35 bivouacked on the other. Early on March 12th several thousand Zulus appeared, marching on the laagered camp. The crack of a sentry's rifle brought men scrambling from beneath sheltering wagons and out of tents. The advancing Zulus paused just long enough to fire a volley, then threw down their guns and charged with assegai and shield. Before any proper defence could be organised, the Zulus were slashing their way through the wagon defence. Captain Moriarty shot three warriors with his revolver before feeling the thrust of an assegai between his shoulder blades. As he slumped to his knees a Zulu bullet also hit home. 'I am done,' he cried, 'fire away, boys!' But most men fell beneath the warriors' stabbing thrusts before they had a chance. Color Sergeant Anthony Booth, on the opposite bank, later reported:

> I saw the kaffirs on the opposite side of the river, they were then crowding on the tents and wagons. We at once opened fire, and kept the fire up for about ten minutes or ¼ of an hour; the kaffirs were then in the river, in great numbers coming towards us, and at the same time assegaing the men from the other side who were attempting to cross; about 200 Zulus came to our side of the river, and as we saw no more of our men crossing the river, we commenced firing and retiring, having received the order from Mr. Harward.

That order was Lieutenant Henry Harward's only good work for the day. He mounted the first horse he could lay his hands on and galloped off saying he was going for help, like Major Spalding at Rorke's Drift, abandoning his command to the tender mercies of the Zulu horde. Color Sergeant Booth formed his men and a few survivors from the opposite bank into a tight, defensive knot who fought their way towards Luneberg, about four miles distant. Harward galloped into this post, then fainted while blurting out that his men had all been slaughtered. Mounted soldiers soon rode to the rescue, and arrived at the campsite to find the mutilated dead, a scene reminiscent of the carnage at Isandlwana. One white soldier, however, and two African drivers were found to have survived when they emerged from hiding.

Sergeant Booth received the Victoria Cross for his valor, and Lieutenant Harward received a court-martial for his desertion. He was, however, acquitted. But General Wolseley publicly repudiated the verdict. 'The more helpless the position in which an officer finds his men,' he wrote, 'the more it is his bounden duty to stay and share their fortune, whether for good or ill.' Although Harward was allowed to return to his regiment, he had no future in the army, and resigned his commission in May of 1880.

And more bad news was to come. On March 28th Colonel Wood launched a two-prong attack against Hlobane Mountain, the seat of a Zulu stronghold, with little knowledge of either the strength of his enemy or the terrain at the top. The mountain was not very high, but was protected by huge boulders, scrub, steep paths and rocky outcrops. It was topped by a plateau about two miles long and a mile and a half wide, a rock-strewn grassland. Colonel Redvers Buller led one force from the east while Lieutenant Colonel Cecil Russell set out up the western slope. Unluckily for the British, Cetshwayo had remobilised the impi which had attacked Isandlwana, his overtures for peace having been ignored. They arrived at Hlobane Mountain the day of the assault, but the British had moved to attack the stronghold believing the Zulu reinforcements' to be a few days off. Russell's force never made it to the top, baulked by the rugged terrain and a lack of determination. Buller's unsupported force was soundly defeated and chased from the mountain. Russell was removed from active service and given command of a remount depot after the battle, Buller and other officers refusing to serve with him again. 'My metier is not South African fighting,' Russell admitted.

But the tide was about to turn. The fight at Hlobane Mountain had at least delayed the Zulu advance, giving Colonel Wood time to finalise his formidable defences at nearby Kambula Hill. His camp was protected by an earthwork redoubt, laagered wagons with earth filling the gaps, a wooden palisade, and a mealie-bag wall with firing embrasures. Along with half a dozen 7-pounders, a garrison of 2,086 men, and range markers set up at varying distances, the structure was virtually impregnable. Some doubted the strength of the palisade, saying it would be pushed over by sheer weight of numbers, but Wood replied 'it would cause a delay of several minutes, during which 300 or 400 rifles, at 250 yards range, ought to make an additional barricade of human bodies.'

At 11 a.m. on March 29th word was received that the Zulus were advancing but Wood was not fussed, confident with the strength of his defences. Later in the day he was asked if the men should hurry their dinners. 'No,' he replied, 'there's plenty of time.' His men had been drilled to strike their tents and be on the firing line within 70 seconds of the bugler sounding the Alert.

The Zulus advanced, only intending to harass the garrison from a distance, but the British wanted them to make a suicidal charge into the muzzles of their weapons. As an enticement, Buller galloped out with a force of Mounted Infantry and fired into their flank. The Zulus took the bait and rushed to the attack, warriors dropping at 300 yards as the British line spat fire and smoke. Then the 7-pounders opened up, the shrapnel carving large gaps in the Zulu lines. The warriors, having expected yet another easy victory, fell back in disarray leaving many dead and wounded scattered behind.

Thirty minutes later the Zulus attacked once more only to be repulsed by rapid rifle fire, then fell back again. They then resorted to more subtle tactics, firing from vantage points into the defenders' positions before closing in once more with great determination.

Lieutenant Frederick Slade recalled:

I never expected to leave the neck alive. In less time than it takes me to write this, my No. 2...was shot right through the body. My dear old horse Saracen was shot... But my men stood at their guns like bricks...On came the Zulus in 1000s and by 3.30 p.m. they had actually driven our infantry out of and occupied the cattle laager which was only 40 yards from my guns. I fired round after round of case into them, hitting oxen and Zulu alike, & a merry hail of bullets were pouring into us. Gardner was shot through the thigh...I shot the man who wounded Gardner with my revolver, so you can imagine how close they were.

The redcoats counter-attacked with bayonet charges against the Zulu left horn, driving it back, and soon the warriors in the cattle kraal were driven out. As night fell the Zulus were falling back right across the field, leaving a carpet of dead and wounded behind. Then the fearsome British horsemen were unleashed. Galloping from behind the defences, they pursued the Zulus across the terrain, cutting them down, showing as little mercy as the Zulus had at Isandlwana.

Mass graves accommodated 785 dead Zulus found around the camp perimeter next day, and more had been killed while fleeing by the avenging horsemen. 'I cannot think that the killed & wounded in the pursuit was less than 300 at the least,' recalled Buller. It was a one-sided battle, British losses being 28 killed, and 55 wounded.

About 70 miles to the south, Chelmsford was leading a column marching to the relief of Eshowe. With most of Cetshwayo's warriors in the north, his force of 3,390 white and 2,280 black troops would only have to face odds of three to one, unfavorable to the Zulus considering British firepower.

On April 1st John Dunn, Cetshwayo's former European ally, informed Chelmsford of an impending attack. The command camped on a knoll alongside the Gingindlovu Stream and made their preparations, strongly fortifying their position with a wagon laager redoubt behind a shelter trench where the redcoats took position.

A warning shout was heard the following morning as the long black lines of the Zulu impi were seen advancing. The rattle of Gatling guns and the fiery whoosh of rockets from the north side broke the morning stillness. Then the infantry opened fire from the shelter trench. Captain Hart was impressed by the Zulu advance, 'as brave as it was possible for any men to be, they bounded towards us from all sides, rushing from cover to cover, gliding like snakes through the grass…and firing upon us, always from concealment.'

Some of the raw British recruits were less impressive, as one officer recalled 'Our men were awfully frightened and nervous at first, could not even speak and shivered from funk, so we—the officers—had enough to do to keep the men cool.'

But British firepower won the day, the Zulu attack faltering, withering, then fading away as the dispirited warriors fell back over their fallen comrades. As at Kambula a few days before, the horsemen then galloped from behind the British lines to counter-attack. The Zulus fled to be cut and shot down as they ran. Fleet-footed warriors of the Natal Native Contingent followed up, completing the bloody work.

Chelmsford estimated Zulu losses at about 1000, while his own command lost a mere 13 killed and 48 wounded.

Cetshwayo could see the writing on the wall, his chances of driving the British juggernaut from his homeland fading to nothing. Since Isandlwana, he had lost almost 3000 warriors killed and many times that wounded. While his men retired to heal their wounds and enact post-combat purification rituals, he attempted to re-establish negotiations with the white invaders.

But Chelmsford was not in a mood for talking. Despite the recent victories, the Zulu capital of Ulundi remained intact and unscathed. His military career was a under a dark Isandlwana cloud and would remain so until he achieved a decisive victory that would bring Zululand under British control. Reinforcements had been marching into Durban, and his second invasion would be much stronger than the first. Two main columns would thrust into Zululand this time, each campsite taking stringent precautions; wagons laagered with scrupulous reconnaissance of the surrounding terrain. Their supply line to Natal would be protected by a string of fortified posts.

The First Division would use reinforcements along with Pearson's troops from the original invasion. It would move northwards up the coast. The Wasp's older brother, Major General Henry Crealock, recently arrived with reinforcements, would be in command. On receiving news of Isandlwana, the British government had sent an additional six infantry battalions, two cavalry regiments, a company of engineers and two artillery batteries.

Marching from the west would be the Second Division under Major General Edward Newdigate following a similar path to that of the previous central column, but bypassing Isandlwana where many decayed corpses still lay unburied. Chelmsford would accompany these fresh troops, and Newdigate, like Colonel Glynn before him, would find his role somewhat superfluous. Colonel Wood would move from the northwest once more with what was now called the Flying

Column, to join the Second Division and march with it towards Cetshwayo's capital.

The first division, or 'Crealock's Crawlers,' as they became known, did not move fast. A lack of adequate transport vehicles combined with outbreaks of typhoid and dysentery slowed his march. But two of his targets, Zulu kraals totalling over 900 huts, went up in flames, this substantial loss with no resistance revealing the weakened state of the Zulu defence.

Chelmsford's Second Division set out on May 31st 1879. Prince Louis Napoleon, the exiled heir to the French throne, was riding with the column. The Zulus had numerous parties watching the white advance, skirmishing with British patrols. On June 1st 1879 Louis accompanied a small patrol to reconnoitre a suitable campsite for the main army. Despite being warned to avoid a deserted homestead, they stopped there for a break and were attacked by a small force of Zulus who had observed their approach from concealment. Lieutenant Jaheel Carey and others galloped off leaving the prince to his fate. Unable to mount his moving horse, the prince opened fire with his revolver only to be cut down.

The story of the heir's death hit the British newspapers with the weight of Isandlwana, causing outrage. The end of a royal dynasty, even French, at the hands of savages, was an abuse not to be tolerated.

Much to the relief of many, Sir Garnet Wolseley arrived in South Africa on June 23rd to take charge of military operations. He quickly sent word to Chelmsford to halt his advance. But Chelmsford, so indignant with Durnford's disobedience, having threatened to relieve him of his command, felt no need for Wolseley's orders to apply to him. He was going to quash any doubts about his military abilities, come hell or high water. He simply ignored the order and continued his march. His troops burned any Zulu homestead they came across regardless of military value, and drove off any cattle they could round up, while Cetshwayo sent repeated overtures for peace.

By June 30th Chelmsford had arrived at the White Mfolozi River where, at last, he had the capital of Ulundi in his grasp. The smart troops who had marched out in pristine uniforms now looked more like scarecrows than the queen's soldiers, their red coats in tatters, hair and beards unkempt. But they were ready to avenge Isandlwana yet again.

On July 3rd Zulu snipers opened fire on water parties and on the camp itself. A mounted counter-attack was organised under Colonel Buller. Commandant Baker led 100 men across the wagon drift and attacked the riflemen on the heights head-on, while Buller's force of 400 splashed across the river lower down to hit them in the flank. This was the same basic tactic attempted by Custer at the Little Bighorn, and came close to achieving the same result. Initially the ploy appeared to surprise the Zulus and they beat a hasty retreat. Buller followed, lured on by a small party of mounted warriors. But then his well-honed instincts told him all was not well. Chelmsford had issued instructions before Isandlwana 'A common ruse with the natives is to hide a large force in the bush and then show a few solitary individuals to invite an attack. When the troops enter the bush in pursuit of the latter the hidden men rise and attack them.' Buller called a halt, and 4000 Zulus warriors rose from concealment in the long grass ahead. They fired a volley, killing three men and wounding others, then charged. Buller saved his command from Custer's fate by beating a hasty retreat, one man being saved from beneath his shot horse as the Zulus closed in.

At dawn the following morning Chelmsford ordered his command across the river. They were going to take the offensive, and many were nervous as to the outcome of meeting the fearsome Zulus in open battle without protective breastworks. They formed a massive, hollow square, about 5,000 men, four ranks deep, and advanced on Ulundi, screened by cavalry on all flanks. 12 cannon and two Gatling guns moved in the centre. A cavalry unit rode out and put flaming torches to a kraal, which seemed to trigger the battle. Thousands of Zulus moved in for the attack, the cavalry falling back within the square. 'The fire opened from the artillery at a long range,' recalled Corporal Roe, 'and did fearful execution as we could see their heads, legs and arms flying in the air.' Then the redcoats opened a withering fire with their Martini-Henrys. Lieutenant Slade recalled 'Our fire was so hot and well directed that no troops in the world could have stood up to it & it was marvellous the way in which the Zulus came on, not seeming to care in the least for gun, Gatling or rifle.' But many felt the Zulu attack was not as spirited as in the past. 'Our hearts were broken at Kambula,' admitted one induna after his surrender. Despite the heroism displayed by the Zulus, many coming within 30 yards of the British lines, others hung back out of range, and within 30 minutes it was all over, the black defenders of Ulundi falling back in retreat. Once again the awesome British horsemen were unleashed, many fugitives to be chased, brought down with gun, lance and sabre.

The triumphant troops moved on to Cetshwayo's capital. Corporal Roe recalled ' In a very short time the whole of the King's city, Ulundi, was in flames. This was a fearful sight to see. You would think the whole world was on fire when there was a dense mass of flames seven miles in length.'

Cetshwayo had removed himself to a safe distance from Ulundi the night before the battle, but was captured by a patrol on August 28th. Their work done, the victorious troops marched from the land they had ravaged, most boarding steamers for home. They were given a boisterous welcome from general public and newspapers alike, and Queen Victoria appeared after years of mourning for her lost Prince Albert to pin decorations on the uniforms of the heroes, some of whom, like John Chard, became household names.

12
AFTERMATH

Very few hostile Sioux were still at large by the close of May 1877. A fortunate few hundred had given themselves up to Colonel Miles at the recently established Fort Keogh at the mouth of the Tongue River where he set up an unofficial agency. For five years they remained there, exceptionally well treated in contrast with those at the regular agencies, now under military jurisdiction. These unfortunate Sioux were marched from their homelands to the despised Missouri River agencies, causing many to flee northwards and join Sitting Bull in Canada. The northern Cheyenne were marched to Indian Territory to join their southern kinfolk where, starved and dying of fever, more trouble eventually broke out, Chiefs Little Wolf and Dull Knife leading a desperate band of followers back north

Crazy Horse did not live long after his surrender, dying by a soldier's bayonet while resisting being locked in a cell at the Spotted Tail Agency. One who had campaigned against him, Captain John G. Bourke, recalled 'Crazy Horse was one of the great soldiers of his day and generation. As the grave of Custer marked the high-water mark of Sioux supremacy in the trans-Mississippi region, so the grave of Crazy Horse marked the ebb.'

Sitting Bull, the leading spirit of resistance, was eventually forced to lead his hungry people from Canada, the buffalo herds having been annihilated by white hunters. The Canadian government had allowed his band to live within their borders, but would not provide a formal reservation or provisions. Sitting Bull surrendered at Fort Buford in 1881, and kept as a virtual prisoner at Fort Randall for two years before being allowed to rejoin his people at the Standing Rock Agency. By this time the Black Hills being Indian land was just a memory, the great Sioux reservation having been broken up and the Treaty of 1868 discarded.

In a book about Custer published in 1881, Judson E. Walker stated:

> Instead of hearing the oft-heard war whoop and murderous yells of the hideous savages on the battlefield and the retort by our Gatling guns and musketry, and the loud cheering of our brave boys in blue, you will hear the persuasive eloquence of the kind-hearted theologian and the knightly young schoolmaster, pleading the cause of Christianity and education; and where Sitting Bull ofttimes held his medicine lodges and war dances on the banks of the Little Missouri and the Little Big Horn Rivers, for no other purpose only to strengthen and bolster up the heart of hundreds of Gall-hearted warriors, and urge them on to cold-blooded, heart-rending and blood-thirsty murders, you will see stately court-houses, with their benches occupied by the ablest jurists in the land to mete out justice, and members of the bar ably defending the cause of peace and good order.

In 1885 Sitting Bull travelled with Buffalo Bill's Wild West Show, crowds flocking to see Custer's nemesis take part in a re-enactment of the Little Bighorn, and circle the arena on horseback. He signed autographs and met President Grover

Cleveland, shaking him by the hand in a gesture of peace. Once back on the reservation, however, the authorities attempted to strip Sitting Bull of his power, and at one negotiation refused to let him speak. With a wave of his hand, the entire Sioux delegation stood up and walked out. Sitting Bull was heard by the white delegates with great respect next time round.

The year 1890 saw more trouble erupt between white man and red as the Ghost Dance rebellion broke out. The desperate Sioux believed they were on the verge of deliverance, the white man to be swept away, the buffalo herds and the dignity of the Indian restored.

On the wintry morning of December 15th the door of Sitting Bull's cabin was thrown open by Indian Police who placed him under arrest. A hostile crowd of the chief's supporters quickly converged and shooting broke out as he was lead to his horse. When the smoke cleared Sitting Bull lay dead, shot in head and chest, along with seven of his family and friends. Five Indian policemen, including Little Bighorn veteran Bull Head, also died. Sitting Bull's body was carted off to an obscure grave, but his fame lived on, his cabin being shipped to the 1893 World's Fair in Chicago.

Major Walsh of the Mounties, who had formed a somewhat tempestuous friendship with the chief during his Canadian retreat, wrote of him:

> He was not the bloodthirsty man reports made him out to be. He asked for nothing but justice. He was not a cruel man. He was kind at heart. He was not dishonest, he was truthful. He loved his people and was glad to give his hand in friendship to any man who was honest with him.

But it was the 7th Cavalry who had the last word. In December of 1890 they were sent out to bring in a dissident village of Ghost Dancers under Chief Big Foot. They surrounded the camp and set up a stove for the ailing chief, and distributed food. But next morning's attempt to disarm the tribe saw a single shot fired by one Indian, a fight broke out, and the troops opened up with Hotchkiss guns from the surrounding knolls. As men, women and children fled they were pursued and cut down by the avenging troopers up to three miles from the village. Dr. Charles Eastman visited the scene:

> It was a terrible and horrible sight to see the women and children lying in groups, dead. Some of the young girls wrapped their heads in their shawls and buried their faces in their hands. I suppose they did that so they would not see the soldiers come up to shoot them. At one place there were two little children, one about a year old, the other about three, lying on their faces, dead, and about thirty yards away from them a woman lay on her face, dead. These were away from the camp about an eighth of a mile. In front of the tents, which were in a semi-circle, lay dead most of the men...this was where the Indians were ordered to hold a council with the soldiers.

This 'battle' was the last significant action between the US military and the redman, the culmination of over two centuries of conflict since the arrival of the first permanent settlers at Jamestown in 1607.

In 1926, fifty years after the Little Bighorn, two old adversaries met on Last Stand Hill. Chief White Bull, 76, led a procession of 80 Indian veterans of the battle, with hundreds of others following, to meet retired General Edward Godfrey, 82, who, as a young lieutenant, had fought alongside Reno on the bluffs in 1876. He had just led a detachment of the 7th Cavalry, with seven surviving veterans, over Custer's trail to the monument, and now he sheathed his sword as White Bull raised his palm in a gesture of peace. Having shaken hands, White Bull handed Godfrey a fine Sioux blanket, and the general responded with a large American flag.

The Custer National Monument became the Little Bighorn National Monument in 1991 in deference to the fact it was, in many ways, the red mans' last stand against wanton aggression, and memorials to fallen warriors have appeared.

Little Phil Sheridan summed it up 'we took away their country and their means of support, broke up their mode of living, their habits of life, introduced disease and decay among them, and it was for this and against this that they made war. Could anyone expect less?'

***

Following the Zulu war's conclusion, many travelled to the scene of tragedy at Isandlwana. They discovered a disturbing scene, the carnage still evident—overturned wagons, ammunition and personal effects scattered about, along with rotting shreds of uniform and the bleached bones of humans and animals alike. Despite the 1880 clearing, rains exposed the aftermath of battle. Bertram Mitford noted in 1882 'In spite of a luxuriant growth of herbage the circles where stood the rows of tents are plainly discernable, while strewn about are tent pegs, cartridge cases, broken glass, bits of rope, meat tins and sardine boxes pierced with assegai stabs, shrivelled up pieces of shoe-leather, and rubbish of every description, bones of horses and oxen gleam white and ghastly, and here and there in the grass one stumbles upon a half-buried skeleton.'

The Natal authorities organised a party to restore the site to some semblance of order. The task was completed on March 9th 1883 after one month's hard work, including 298 graves, each containing at least four bodies. It was at this time that Durnford's remains were exhumed by his family and reburied at Pietermaritzburg.

Time passed, fresh news replaced the old and sober minds sifting through hard facts saw the Zulu Campaign in a different light. One Parliamentarian described Cetshwayo as 'a gallant monarch defending his country and his people against one of the most wanton and wicked invasions that ever could be made upon an independent people.' The instigator of the wicked invasion, Sir Bartle Frere, was recalled from his post under a cloud of disapproval in 1880, and died four years later at the age of 69. He always insisted he had acted correctly, and on his deathbed said 'Oh, if only they would read "The Further Correspondence" they would understand.' Frere saw himself as carrying out British policy, and there is much truth in that. But by choosing his own timing rather than that of his superiors, he had left himself open to censure. Lord Chelmsford weathered the storm to have more honors bestowed upon him by an admiring Queen Victoria, but was never entrusted with another command. He died of a heart attack in April of 1905, at the age of 78, while playing billiards at his London Club.

Following his capture, Cetshwayo was exiled and detained in Cape Town where he could cause no trouble, sending petitions to the queen to grant him an audience. Sitting Bull met President Grover Cleveland during his travels, and in 1882 Cetshwayo finally got his wish, sailing to Britain where he met Queen Victoria at Osborne House on the Isle of Wight. The meeting had positive results for Cetshwayo, being returned to his homeland and reinstated as King of the Zulus. But it was not the same Zululand he had once ruled, having been divided by Sir Garnet Wolseley into 13 chiefdoms, the rulers of which had no desire for Cetshwayo's return. In 1883 he was forced to take flight when rival Zulus attacked his kraal. He received protection from the British Resident at Eshowe, but died on February 8th 1884. As Sioux police killed Sitting Bull, it is believed Cetshwayo also died at the hands of his own people, but by poison rather than the bullet, not living to see Zululand formally declared British territory in 1887, and annexed by Natal ten years later.

The Isandlwana battlefield has become one of the most visited sights in South Africa. A section was declared a national monument in 1972 and, in 1989, a larger area became a protected historic reserve. A long overdue memorial to fallen Zulus was erected in 1999, in close proximity to the burial site of the many warriors who fell in victory there, defending their country against an unwarranted invasion.

The name of Lieutenant Colonel Anthony W. Durnford is not well known outside the realms of Zulu War scholars, unlike that of George A. Custer, which has lived conspicuously on through the years since his famous last stand. At the Reno Court of Inquiry, Recorder Lieutenant Jesse M. Lee stated:

> Custer and his comrades died a death so heroic that it has but few parallels in history. Fighting to the last and against overwhelming odds, they fell on the field of glory. Let no stigma of panic or rout and panic tarnish their blood-bought fame. Their deeds of heroism will ever live in the hearts of American people, and the painter and the poet will vie with each other in commemorating the world-wide fame of Custer and his men.

Lee forgot to mention sculptors fashioning statues, and today the filmmaker and novelist join the painter and poet. But Custer's image has hardly remained untarnished as the American treatment of native peoples has been reappraised. Custer, however, has emerged as one of the best-known men in American history with many still defending his name, and even his detractors probably harboring secret strains of jealousy. What red-blooded man would not wish to be a remembered as a dashing cavalier going out in such a manner, fighting valiantly for flag and country against savage hordes, rather than in the bed of an old folks' home? Durnford died an identical death, his heroism established by both survivors and those Zulu warriors who fought him. He was portrayed in the film *Zulu Dawn*, his part played by Burt Lancaster. St. Vincent's church erected at Isandlwana has both a stained glass window and tablet dedicated to his memory, and there is a memorial in St. Peter's Cathedral, Pietermaritzburg, where Bishop Colenso delivered his sermons. And he was not forgotten in the old country where the Durnford Window graces Rochester Cathedral, dedicated to him by the Corps of Royal Engineers for 'bravely fighting to the last...endeavouring to cover the retreat on the fateful day at Isandhlwana.'

Despite this, very few remember the name Anthony Durnford, while most in the western world have at least heard of Custer and his Last Stand. Long Hair achieved in death far greater fame than he could have hoped for had he achieved victory at the Little Bighorn and lived to a ripe old age. Perhaps his one unaccomplished ambition was to become president of the United States? Legend has it that shortly before the regiment marched, Custer visited the camp of the Ree scouts. He presented Bloody Knife with gifts including a medal which Custer said he had received in Washington. He told the Rees of his visit to the capital, and said that this was to be the last big campaign against the western tribes. A victory over the Sioux would make him Great Father, or President. He said he would take Bloody Knife to Washington with him, then Bloody Knife would return to live in a fine house amongst his people. Those now acting as his scouts would be employed to work under Bloody Knife's supervision. As Great Father, Custer told them, he would always look after his children, the Arikaras.

If this story is true, it is easy to imagine Custer seeing himself in this role, a fresh political career launched by a resounding victory over the Sioux and Cheyenne, capping off his Civil War exploits and the Washita. He had been a Lieutenant Colonel for a decade; promotion in the small, post-Civil War army slow, the chances for glory in battle few, routine garrison duty being the lot of most troops on the frontier. Eight years separated the Washita and Little Bighorn. He was still young at only 36, and soldiers like George Washington, Andrew Jackson and Ulysses S. Grant had been elevated to the highest office in the land on the backs of their military victories. But they had beaten modern, white armies. Would beating primitive tribesmen do the job?

Yes, it would seem.

General William Henry Harrison, 'Old Tippecanoe' became president in 1841, his main claim to fame resting on his defeat of Tecumseh's warriors at the Battle of Tippecanoe in 1811. With vice presidential running mate, John Tyler, the campaign slogan had been 'Tippecanoe and Tyler too,' one of the most famous ever used in American politics.

Why wait long years for promotion to mere colonel when, as President of the United States, the many perks included being commander-in-chief of the armed forces? Perhaps

President Grant summarily dismissing Custer from command of the Dakota column gave birth to the idea, Long Hair having a few scores to settle of his own. But history, of course, tells us that George A. Custer never got to be President of the United States.

Or did he?

Custer did, in fact, become president of the United States in 1981!—Kind of.

Ronald Reagan, who played Custer in the 1940 Warner Brothers movie *Santa Fe Trail,* was elected president in that year. The Boy General elected by proxy, so to speak.

George Armstrong Custer died at the Little Bighorn, but perhaps his famed luck lived on.

APPENDIX A

REPORT ON THE BATTLE OF THE LITTLE BIG HORN MAJOR M. A. RENO
Camp on the Yellowstone River, 5 July 1876

The command of the regiment having developed upon me as the senior surviving officer from the battle of the 25th and 26th of June, between the Seventh Cavalry and Sitting Bull's band of hostile Sioux, on the _____ River, I have the honor to submit the following report of its operations from the time of leaving the main column until the command was united in the vicinity of the Indian village:

The regiment left the camp at the mouth of the Rosebud River, after passing in review before the department commander, under command of Bvt. Maj. Gen. G. A. Custer, lieutenant-colonel, on the afternoon of the 22nd day of June, and marched up the Rosebud 12 miles and encamped; 23rd, marched up the Rosebud, passing many old Indian camps, and following a very large pole-trail, but not fresh, making 33 miles; 24th, the march was continued up the Rosebud, the trail and signs freshening with every mile, until we had made 28 miles, and we then encamped and waited for information from the scouts. At 9:25 p.m. Custer called the officers together and informed us that beyond a doubt the village was in the valley of the Little Big Horn, and in order to reach it was necessary to cross the divide between the Rosebud and the Little Big Horn, and it would be impossible to do so in the day-time without discovering our march to the Indians; that we would prepare to march at 11 p.m. This was done, the line of march turning from the Rosebud to the right up one of its branches which headed near the summit of the divide. About 2 a.m. on the 25th the scouts told him that he could not cross the divide before daylight. We then made coffee and rested for three hours, at the expiration of which time the march was resumed, the divide crossed, and about 8 a.m. the command was in the valley of one of the branches of the Little Big Horn. By this time Indians had been seen and it was certain that we could not surprise them, and it was determined to move at once to the attack. Previous to this, no division of the regiment had been made since the order had been issued on the Yellowstone annulling wing and battalion organizations, but Custer informed me that he would assign commands on the march.

I was ordered by Lieut. W. W. Cooke, adjutant, to assume command of Companies M, A, and G; Captain Benteen of Companies H, D, and K. Custer retained C, E, F, I, and L under his immediate command, and Company B, Captain McDougall, in rear of the pack- train.

I assumed command of the companies assigned to me, and, without any definite orders, moved forward with the rest of the column, and well to its left.

I saw Benteen moving farther to the left, and, as they passed, he told me he had orders to move well to the left, and sweep everything before him. I did not see him again until about 2.30 p.m. The command moved down to the creek toward the Little Big Horn Valley, Custer with five companies on the right bank, myself and three companies on the left bank, and Benteen farther to the left, and out of sight.

As we approached a deserted village, and in which was standing one tepee, about 11 a.m., Custer motioned me to cross to him, which I did, and moved nearer to his column until about 12.30 a.m. when Lieutenant Cook, adjutant, came to me and said the village was only two miles above, and running away; to move forward at as rapid a gait as prudent, and to charge afterward, and that the whole outfit would support me. I think those were his exact words. I at once took a fast trot, and moved down about two miles, when I came to a ford of the river. I crossed immediately, and halted about ten minutes or less to gather the battalion, sending word to Custer that I had everything in front of me, and that they were strong. I deployed, and, with the Ree scouts on my left, charged down the valley, driving the Indians with great ease for about two and a half miles. I, however, soon saw that I was being drawn into some trap, as they would certainly fight harder, and especially as we were nearing their village, which was still standing; besides, I could not see Custer or any other support, and at the same time the very earth seemed to grow Indians, and they were running toward me in swarms, and from all directions. I saw I must defend myself and give up the attack mounted. This I did. Taking possession of a front of woods, and which furnished, near its edge, a shelter for the horses, dismounted and fought them on foot, making headway through the woods. I soon found myself in the near vicinity of the village, saw that I was fighting odds of at least five to one, and that my only hope was to get out of the woods, where I would soon have been surrounded, and gain some high ground. I accomplished this by mounting and charging the Indians between me and the bluffs on the opposite side of the river. In this charge, First Lieut. Donald McIntosh, Second Lieut. Benjamin H. Hodgson, Seventh Cavalry, and Acting Assistant Surgeon J. M. De Wolf, were killed.

I succeeded in reaching the top of the bluff, with a loss of three officers and twenty-nine enlisted men killed and seven wounded. Almost at the same time I reached the top, mounted men were seen to be coming toward us, and it proved to be Colonel Benteen's battalion, Companies H, D, and K. We joined forces, and in a short time the pack-train came up. As senior, my command was then A, B, D, G, H, K, and M, about three hundred and eighty men, and the following officers: Captains Benteen, Weir, French and McDougall, First Lieutenants Godfrey, Mathey, and Gibson, and Second Lieutenants Edgerly, Wallace, Varnum, and Hare, and Acting Assistant Surgeon Porter.

First Lieutenant DeRudio was in the dismounted fight in the woods, but, having some trouble with his horse, did not join the command in the charge out, and hiding himself in the woods, joined the command after night-fall on the 26th.

Still hearing nothing of Custer, and, with this re-enforcement, I moved down the river in the direction of the village, keeping on the bluffs.

We had heard firing in that direction and knew it could only be Custer. I moved to the summit of the highest bluff, but seeing and hearing nothing sent Captain Weir with his company to open communication with him. He soon sent word by Lieutenant Hare that he could go no farther, and that the Indians were getting around him. At this time he was keeping up a heavy fire from his skirmish line. I at once turned everything back to the first position I had taken on the bluffs, and which seemed to me the best. I dismounted the men and had the horses and mules of the pack-train driven together in a depression, put the men on the crests of the bluffs, and which seemed to me the best. I dismounted, the men and had the horses and mules of the pack-train driven together in a depression, put the men on the crests of the hills making the depression, and had hardly done so when I was furiously attacked. This was about 6 p.m. We held our ground, with a loss of eighteen enlisted men killed and forty-six wounded, until the attack ceased, about 9 p.m. As I knew by this their overwhelming numbers, and had given up any support from that portion of the regiment with Custer, I had the men dig rifle pits, barricade with dead horses and mules, and boxes of hard bread, the opening of the depression toward the Indians in which the animals were herded, and made every exertion to be ready for what I saw would be a terrific assault the next day. All this might night the men were busy, and the Indians holding a scalp-dance underneath us in the bottom and in our hearing. On the morning of the 26th I felt confident that I could hold my own, and was ready, as far as I could be, when at daylight, about 2.30 a.m., I heard the crack of two rifles. This was the signal for the beginning of a fire that I have never equalled. Every rifle was handled by an expert and skilled marksman, and with a range that exceeded our carbines, and it was simply impossible to show any part of the body before it was struck. We could see, as the day brightened, countless hordes of them pouring up the valley from the village and scampering over the high points toward the places designated for them by their chiefs, and which entirely surrounded our position. They had sufficient numbers to completely encircle us, and men were struck from opposite sides of the lines from where the shots were fired. I think we were fighting all the Sioux Nation, and also all the desperadoes, renegades, half-breeds, and squaw-men between the Missouri and the Arkansas and east of the Rocky Mountains, and they must have numbered at least twenty-five hundred warriors.

The fire did not slacken until about 9.30 a.m., and then we found they were making a last desperate effort and which was directed against the lines held by Companies H and M. In this charge they came close enough to use their bows and arrows, and one man lying dead within our lines was touched with the coup-stick of one of the foremost Indians. When I say the stick was only ten or twelve feet long, some idea of the desperate and reckless fighting of these people may be understood.

This charge of theirs was gallantly repulsed by the men on that line, lead by Colonel Benteen. They also came close enough to send their arrows into the line held by Companies D and K, but were driven away by a like charge of the line, which I accompanied. We now had many wounded, and the question of water was vital, as from 6 p.m. the previous evening until now, 10 a.m., about sixteen hours, we had been without.

A skirmish line was formed under Colonel Benteen to protect the descent of volunteers down the hill in front of his position to reach the water. We succeeded in getting some canteens, although many of the men were hit in doing so. The fury of the attack was now over, and to our astonishment the Indians were seen going in parties toward the village. But two solutions occurred to us for this movement; that they were going for something to eat, more ammunition, (as they had been throwing arrows,) or that Custer was coming. We took advantage of this lull to fill all vessels with water, and soon had it by camp-kettles full. But they continued to withdraw, and all firing ceased save occasional shots from sharp-shooters sent to annoy us about the water. About 2 p.m. the grass in the bottom was set on fire and followed up by Indians who encouraged its burning, and it was evident to me it was done for a purpose, and which purpose I discovered later on to be the creation of a dense cloud of smoke behind which they were packing and preparing to move their village. It was between 6 and 7 p.m. that the village came out from behind the dense clouds of smoke and dust. We had a close and good view of them as they filed away in the direction of the Big Horn Mountains, moving in almost perfect military order. The length of the column was full equal to that of a large division of the cavalry corps of the Army of the Potomac as I have seen it in its march.

We now thought of Custer, of whom nothing had been seen and nothing heard since the firing in his direction about 6 p.m. on the eve of the 25th, and we concluded that the Indians had gotten between him and us and driven him toward the boat at the mouth of the Little Big Horn River. The awful fate that did befall him never occurred to any of us as within the limits of possibility.

During the night I changed my position in order to secure an unlimited supply of water, and was prepared for their return, feeling sure they would do so as they were in such numbers; but early in the morning of the 27th, and while we were on the *qui vire* for Indians, I saw with my glass a dust some distance down the valley. There was no certainty for some time what they were, but finally I satisfied myself they were cavalry, and, if so, could only be Custer, as it was ahead of the time that I understood that General Terry could be expected. Before this time, however, I had written a communication to General Terry, and three volunteers were to try and reach him. (I had no confidence in the Indians with me, and could not get them to do anything.) If this dust were Indians it was possible they would not expect any one to leave. The men started, and were told to go as near as it was safe to determine whether the approaching column was white men, and to return at once in case they found it so, but if they were Indians to push on to General Terry. In a short time, we saw them returning a note from Terry to Custer saying Crow scouts had come to camp saying he had been whipped, but that it was not believed. I think it was about 10.30 a.m. when General Terry rode into my lines, and the fate of Custer and his brave men was soon determined by Captain Benteen proceeding to the battle-ground, and where was recognized the following officers, who were surrounded by the dead bodies of many of their men; Gen G. A. Custer, Col. W. W. Cook, adjutant; Capts. M. W. Keogh, G. W. Yates, and T. W. Custer; First Lieuts. A. E. Smith, James Calhoun; Second Lieuts. W. V. Reily, of the Seventh Cavalry and J. J. Crittenden, of the Twelfth Infantry, temporarily attached to this regiment. The bodies of Lieut. J. E. Porter and Second Lieuts. H. M. Harrington and J. G. Sturgis, Seventh Cavalry, and Asst. Surg. G. W. Lord, U. S. A., were not recognized; but there is every reasonable probability they were killed. It was more certain that the column of five companies with Custer had been killed.

The wounded in my lines were, during the afternoon and evening of the 27th, moved to the camp of General Terry, and at 5 a.m. of the 28th I proceeded with the regiment to the battleground of Custer, and buried 204 bodies, including the following-named citizens: Mr. Boston Custer, Mr. Reed (a young nephew of General Custer,) and Mr. Kellogg, (a correspondent for the New York *Herald*.) The following-named citizens and Indians who were with my command were also killed: Charles Reynolds, guide and hunter; Isaiah Dorman, (colored,) interpreter; Bloody Knife, who fell from immediately by my side; Bobtail Bull, and Stab, of the Indian scouts.

After travelling over his trail, it was evident to me that Custer intended to support me by moving farther down the stream and attacking the village in flank; that he found the distance greater to ford than he anticipated; that he did charge, but his march had taken so long, although his trail shows that he had moved rapidly, that they were ready for him; that Companies C and I, and perhaps part of E, crossed to the village or attempted it; at the charge were met by a staggering fire, and that they fell back to find a position from which to defend themselves, but they were followed too closely by the Indians to permit time to form any kind of a line.

I think had the regiment gone in as a body, and from the woods from which I fought advanced upon the village, its destruction was certain. But he was fully confident they were running away, or he would not have turned from me. I think (after the great number of Indians that were in the village,) that the following reasons obtain for the misfortune; His rapid marching for two days and one night before the fight; attacking in the day-time at 12 m., and when they were on the qui vire, instead of early morning; and lastly, his unfortunate division of the regiment into three commands.

During my fight with Indians, I had the heartiest support from officers and men, but the conspicuous services of Bvt. Col. F. W. Benteen I desire to call attention to especially, for if ever a soldier deserved recognition by his Government for distinguished services he certainly does. I inclose herewith his report of the operations of his battalion from the time of leaving the regiment until we joined commands on the hill. I also inclose an accurate list of casualties, as far as it can be made at the present time, separating them into two lists: A, those killed in General Custer's command; B, those killed and wounded in the command I had.

The number of Indians killed can only be approximated until we hear through the agencies. I saw the bodies of eighteen, and Captain Ball, Second Cavalry, who made a scout of thirteen miles over their trail, says that their graves were many along their line of march. It is simply impossible that numbers of them should not be hit in the several charges they made so close to my lines. They made their approaches through the deep gulches that led from the hill-top to the river, and, when the jealous care with which the Indian guards the bodies of killed and wounded is considered, it is not astonishing that their bodies were not found. It is probable that the stores left by them and destroyed the next two days was to make room for many of these on their travois. The harrowing sight of the dead bodies crowning the height on which Custer fell, and which will remain vividly in my memory until death, is too recent for me not to ask the good people of this country whether a policy that sets opposing parties in the field, armed, clothed, and equipped by one and the same Government should not be abolished.

Annual Report of the Secretary of War, 1876, 44th Congress, 1st Session, pp. 476-480.

REPORT OF CAPT. F. W. BENTEEN.

Camp Seventh Cavalry, July 4, 1876

Sir,

In obedience to verbal instructions received from you, I have the honor to report the operations of my battalion, consisting of Companies D, H, and K, on the 25th ultimo.

The directions I received from Lieutenant-Colonel Custer were, to move with my command to the left, to send well-mounted officers with about six men who should ride rapidly to a line of bluffs about five miles to our left and front, with instructions to report at once to me if anything of Indians could be seen from that point. I was to follow the movement of this detachment as rapidly as possible. Lieutenant Gibson was the officer selected, and I followed closely with the battalion at times getting in advance of the detachment. The bluffs designated were gained, but nothing seen but other bluffs quite as large and precipitous as were before me. I kept on to those and the country was the same, there being no valley of any kind that I could see on any side, I had then gone about fully ten miles; the ground was terribly hard on horses, so I determined to carry out the other instructions, which were, that if in my judgment there was nothing to be seen of Indians, valleys, &c., in the direction I was going, to return with the battalion to the trail the command was following.

I accordingly did so, reaching the trail just in advance of the pack-train. I pushed rapidly on, soon getting out of sight of the advance of the train, until reaching a morass, I halted to water the animals, who had been without water since about 8 p.m. of the day before. This watering did not occasion the loss of fifteen minutes, and when I was moving out the advance of the train commenced watering from that morass. I went at a slow trot until I came to a burning lodge with the dead body of an Indian in it on a scaffold. We did not halt. About a mile farther on I met a sergeant of the regiment with orders from Lieutenant-Colonel Custer to the officer in charge of the rear—guard and train to bring it to the front with as great rapidity as was possible. Another mile on I met Trumpeter Morton, of my own company, with a written order from First Lieut. W. W. Cook to me which read:

"Benteen, Come on,
Big village, Be quick, bring packs.
W. W. Cooke
P. S. bring pacs."

I could then see no movement of any kind in any direction; a horse on the hill, riderless, being the only living thing I could see in my front. I inquired of the trumpeter what had been done, and he informed that the Indians had "skedaddled," abandoning the village. Another mile and a half brought me in sight of the stream and plain in which were some of our dismounted men fighting, and Indians charging and recharging them in great numbers. The plain seemed to be alive with them. I then noticed our men in large numbers running for the bluffs on right bank of stream. I concluded at once that those had been repulsed, and was of the opinion that if I crossed the ford with my battalion, that I should have had it treated in like manner; for from long experience with cavalry, I judge there were 900 veteran Indians right there at that time, against which the large element of recruits in my battalion would stand no earthly chance as mounted men. I then moved up to the bluffs and reported my command to Maj. M. A. Reno. I did not return for the pack-train because I deemed it perfectly safe where it was, and we could defend it, had it been threatened, from our position on the bluff; and another thing, it savored too much of coffee-cooling to return when I was sure a fight was progressing in the front, and deeming the train as safe without me.

Very respectfully,

F. W. BENTEEN,
Captain Seventh Cavalry

Lieut. Geo. D. Wallace,
Adjutant Seventh Cavalry

APPENDIX B

THE COURT OF INQUIRY—ISANDLWANA

Adjutant-General, camp, Helpmekaar, Natal January 29, 1879.

Herewith proceedings of court of inquiry, assembled by order of the Lieutenant General Commanding. The court has examined and recorded the statements of the chief witnesses.

The copy of the proceedings forwarded was made by a confidential clerk of the Royal Engineers.

The court has refrained from giving an opinion, as instructions on this point were not given it.

F. C. Hassard, CB,
Colonel Royal Engineers, President.

Proceedings of a Court of Inquiry, assembled at Helpmekaar, Natal, on the 27th January 1879, by order of His Excellency the Lieutenant-General Commanding the Troops in South Africa, dated 24th January 1879.
President—Colonel F. C. Hassard, CB, Royal Engineers.
Members—Lieutenant-Colonel Law, Royal Artillery.
Lieutenant-Colonel Harness, Royal Artillery.

The court, having assembled pursuant to order, proceeded to take the following evidence:

1st **Witness**—

Major Clery states: I am senior staff officer to the 3rd column, commanded by Colonel Glyn, CB, operating against the Zulus. The General Commanding accompanied this column from the time it crossed the border into Zululand.

On the 20th January 1879 at the camp, Isandula, Zululand, the Lieutenant General Commanding gave orders to Commandant Lonsdale and Major Dartnell to go out the following morning in a certain direction from camp with their men, i.e., the Native Contingent, and the police and volunteers, part of the 3rd column. On the evening of the following day (the 21st) a message arrived from Major Dartnell that the enemy was in considerable force in his neighbourhood, and that he and Commandant Lonsdale would bivouac out that night. About 1.30 a.m., on the 22nd, a messenger brought me a note from Major Dartnell to say that the enemy was in greater numbers than when he last reported, and that he did not think it prudent to attack them unless reinforced by two or three companies of the 24th Regiment. I took this note to Colonel Glyn, CB, at once; he ordered me to take it to the General. The general ordered the 2nd Battalion 24th Regiment, the Mounted Infantry, and four guns, to be under arms at once to march. This force marched out from camp as soon as there was light enough to see the road. The Natal Pioneers accompanied this column to clear the road. The General first ordered me to write to Colonel Durnford at Rorke's Drift, to bring his force to strengthen the camp, but almost immediately afterwards he told Colonel Crealock that he (Colonel Crealock) was to write to

Colonel Durnford these instructions, and not I. Before leaving the camp I sent written instructions to Colonel Pulleine, 24th Regiment, to the following effect: 'You will be in command of the camp during the absence of Colonel Glyn; draw in (I speak from memory) your camp, or your line of defence'—(I am not certain which)—'while the force is out; also draw in the line of your infantry outposts accordingly, but keep your cavalry vedettes still far advanced.' I told him to have a wagon ready loaded with ammunition ready to follow the force going out at a moment's notice, if required. I went to Colonel Pulleine's tent just before leaving camp to ascertain that he had got these instructions, and I again repeated them verbally to him. To the best of my memory, I mentioned in the written instructions to Colonel Pulleine that Colonel Durnford had been written to, to bring up his force to strengthen the camp. I saw the column out of camp and accompanied it.

2nd Evidence.—

Colonel Glyn, CB, states: From the time the column under my command crossed the border I was in the habit of receiving instructions from the Lieutenant-General Commanding as to the movements of the column, and I accompanied him on most of the patrols and reconnaissances carried out by him. I corroborate Major Clery's statement.

3rd Evidence.—

Captain Alan Gardner, 14th Hussars, states: I accompanied the main body of the third column as acting staff officer to officer commanding 3rd column when it left the camp at Isandula on the 22nd January 1879. I was sent back with an order from the General between 10 and 11 a.m. that day into camp. Which order was addressed to Colonel Pulleine, and was that the camp of the force was to be struck and sent out immediately, also rations and forage for about seven days. On arriving in camp I met Captain George Shepstone, who was also seeking Colonel Pulleine, having a message from Colonel Durnford that his men were falling back, and asking for reinforcements. We both went to Colonel Pulleine, to whom I delivered the order. Colonel Pulleine at first hesitated about carrying out the order, and eventually decided that the enemy being already on the hill on our left in large numbers, it was impossible to do so.

The men of the 24th Regiment were all fallen in, and the artillery also, and Colonel Pulleine sent two companies to support Colonel Durnford to the hill on the left and formed up the remaining companies in line, the guns in action on the extreme left flank of the camp, facing the hill on our left. I remained with Colonel Pulleine by his order. Shortly after, I took the mounted men, by Colonel Pulleine's direction, about a quarter of a mile to the front of the camp, and left them there under the direction of Captain Bradstreet, with orders to hold the spruit. I went back to Colonel Pulleine, but soon after, observing the mounted men retiring, I went back to them, and, in reply to my question as to why they were retiring, was told they were ordered by Colonel Durnford to retire, as the position taken up was too extended. This same remark was made to me by Colonel Durnford himself immediately afterwards.

By this time the Zulus had surrounded the camp, the whole force engaged in hand-to-hand combat, the guns mobbed by Zulus, and there became a general massacre. From the time of the first infantry force leaving the camp to the end of the fight about one hour elapsed. I estimated the number of the enemy at about 12,000 men. I may mention that a few minutes after my arrival in camp I sent a message directed to the staff officer 3rd column, saying that our left was attacked by about 10,000 of the enemy; a message was also sent by Colonel Pulleine.

The Native Infantry Contingent fled as soon as the fighting began, and caused great confusion in our ranks. I sent messages to Rorke's Drift and Helpmekaar camp that the Zulus had sacked the camp, and telling them to fortify themselves.

4th Evidence.—

Captain Essex, 75th Regiment, states: I hand in a written statement of what occurred; I have nothing to add to that statement. [This statement is marked A].

5th Evidence.—

Lieutenant Cochrane, 32nd Regiment, states: I am employed as transport officer with No. 2 column, then under Colonel Durnford, RE, on the 22nd January 1879, the column marched on that morning from Rorke's Drift to Isandula in consequence of an order received from the Lieutenant-General. I do not know the particulars of the order received. I entered the Isandula camp with Colonel Durnford about 10 a.m., and remained with him as acting staff officer. On arrival he took over command from Colonel Pulleine, 24th Regiment. Colonel Pulleine gave over to Colonel Durnford a verbal slate of the troops in camp at the time, and stated the orders he had received, viz., to defend the camp; these words were repeated two or three times in the conversation. Several messages were delivered, the last one to the effect that the Zulus were retiring in all directions—the bearer of this was not dressed in any uniform. On this message Colonel Durnford sent two troops mounted natives to the top of the hills to the left, and took with him two troops of rocket battery, with escort of one company Native Contingent, on to the front of the camp about four or five miles off. Before leaving, he asked Colonel Pulleine to give him two companies 24th Regiment. Colonel Pulleine said that with the orders he had received he could not do it, but agreed with Colonel Durnford to send him help if he got into difficulties. Colonel Durnford, with two troops, went on ahead and met the enemy some four or five miles off in great force, and, as they showed also on our left, we retired in good order to the drift, about a quarter of a mile in front of the camp, where the mounted men reinforced us, about two miles from the camp. On our retreat we came upon the remains of the rocket battery, which had been destroyed.

6th Evidence.—

Lieutenant Smith-Dorrien, 95th Regiment, states: I am transport officer with No. 3 column. On the morning of the 22nd I was sent with a Dispatch from the General to Colonel Durnford at Rorke's Drift; the Dispatch was an order to join the camp at Isandula as soon as possible, as a large Zulu force was near it.

I have no particulars to mention besides.

7th Evidence. -

Captain Nourse, Natal Native Contingent, states: I was commanding the escort to the rocket battery when Colonel Durnford advanced in front of the camp, on the 22nd, to meet the enemy. Colonel Durnford had gone on with two troops mounted natives. They went too fast, and left us some two miles in the rear. On hearing heavy firing on our left, and learning that the enemy were in that direction, we changed our direction to the left. Before nearly reaching the crest of the hills on the left of the camp, we were attacked on all sides. One rocket was sent off, and the enemy was on us; the first volley dispersed the mules and the natives, and we retired on to the camp as well as we could. Before we reached the camp it was destroyed.

8th Evidence.—

Lieutenant Curling, RA, states: I was left in camp with two guns when the remaining four guns of the battery went out with the main body of the column on 22nd January 1879. Major Stuart Smith joined and took command of the guns about 12 noon.

I hand in a written statement [marked B]. I have nothing to add to that statement.

(Signed) F. C. Hassard,
Colonel, Royal Engineers, President.
F. T. A. Law, Lieutenant-Colonel, RA.
A. Harness, Major, RA and Lieutenant-Colonel.

A—CAPTAIN ESSEX'S EVIDENCE.

Sir,

I have the honour to forward for the information of the Lieutenant-General Commanding an account of an action which took place near the Isandula Hills on the 22nd instant.

After the departure of the main body of the column nothing unusual occurred in camp until about 8 a.m., when a report arrived from a picket stationed at a point about 1,500 yards distant, on a hill to the north of the camp, that a body of the enemy's troops could be seen approaching from the north-east. Lieutenant-Colonel Pulleine, 1st Battalion 24th Regiment, commanding in camp, thereupon caused the whole of the troops available to assemble near the eastern side of the camp, facing towards the reported direction of the enemy's approach. He also dispatched a mounted man with a report to the column, presumed to be about 12 or 15 miles distant. Shortly after 9 a.m., a small body of the enemy showed itself just over the crest of the hills, in the direction they were expected, but retired a few minutes afterwards, and disappeared. Soon afterwards, information arrived from the picket before alluded to that the enemy was in three columns, two of which were retiring, but were still in view; the third column had disappeared in a north-westerly direction.

At about 10 a.m. a party of about 250 mounted natives, followed by a rocket battery, arrived with Lieutenant-Colonel Durnford, RE, who now assumed command of the camp.

The main body of this mounted force, divided into two portions, and the rocket battery, were, about 10.30 a.m., sent out to ascertain the enemy's movements, and a company of 1st Battalion 24th Regiment, under command of Lieutenant Cavaye, was directed to take up a position as a picket on the hill to the north of the camp at about 1,200 yards distant; the remainder of the troops were ordered to march to their private parades, when the men were to be down in readiness; at this time, about 11 a.m., the impression in camp was that the enemy had no intention of advancing during the daytime, but might possibly be expected to attack during the night. No idea had been formed regarding the probable strength of the enemy's force.

At about 12 o'clock, hearing firing on the hill where the company 1st Battalion 24th Regiment was stationed, I proceeded in that direction. On my way I passed a company of the 1st Battalion 24th Regiment under command of Captain Mostyn, who requested me, being mounted, to direct Lieutenant Cavaye to take special care not to endanger the right of his company, and to inform that officer that he himself was moving up to the left. I also noticed a body of Lieutenant-Colonel Durnford's Mounted Natives retiring down the hill, but did not see the enemy. On arriving at the far side of the crest of the hill, I found the company in charge of Lieutenant Cavaye, a section being detached about 500 yards to the left, in charge of Lieutenant Dyson. The whole were in extended order engaging the enemy, who was moving in similar formation towards our left, keeping at about 800 yards from our line.

Captain Mostyn moved his company into the space between the portions of that already on the hill, and his men then extended and entered into action. This line was then prolonged on our right along the crest of the hill by a body of native infantry. I observed that the enemy made little progress as regards his advance, but appeared to be moving at a rapid pace towards our left. The right extremity of the enemy's line was very thin, but increased in depth towards and beyond our right as far as I could see, a hill interfering with an extended view. About five minutes after the arrival of Captain Mostyn's company, I was informed by Lieutenant Melville, Adjutant 1st Battalion 24th Regiment, that a fresh body of the enemy was appearing in force in our rear, and he requested me to direct the left of the line formed, as above described, to fall slowly back, keeping up the fire. This I did; then proceeded towards the centre of the line. I found, however, that it had already retired. I therefore followed in the same direction, but being mounted, had great difficulty in descending the hill, the ground being very rocky and precipitous. On arriving at the foot of the slope I found the two companies of 1st Battalion 24th Regiment drawn up at about 400 yards distant in extended order, and Captain Younghusband's company in a similar formation in echelon on the left. The enemy was descending the hill, having rushed forward as soon as our men disappeared below the crest, and beyond the right of the line with which I was present had even arrived near the foot of the hill. The enemy's fire had hitherto been very wild and ineffective, now, however, a few casualties began to occur in our line. The companies 1st Battalion 24th Regiment first engaged were now becoming short of ammunition, and at the request of the officer in charge I went to procure a fresh supply, with the assistance of Quartermaster 2nd Battalion 24th Regiment and some men of the Royal Artillery. I had some boxes placed on a mule cart and sent it off to the companies engaged, and sent more by hand, employing any men without arms. I then went back to the line, telling the men that plenty of ammunition was coming. I found that the companies 1st Battalion 24th Regiment before alluded to had retired to within 300 yards of that portion of the camp occupied by the Native Contingent. On my way I noticed a number of native infantry retreating in haste towards the camp, their officers endeavouring to prevent them, but without effect. On looking round to that portion of the field to our right and rear I saw that the enemy was surrounding us. I rode up to Lieutenant-Colonel Durnford, who was near the right, and pointed this out to him. He requested me to take men to that part of the field and endeavour to hold the enemy in check; but while he was speaking, those men of the

Native Contingent who had remained in action rushed past us in the utmost disorder, thus laying open the right and rear of the companies of 1st Battalion 24th Regiment on the left, and the enemy dashing forward in the most rapid manner poured in at this part of the line. In a moment all was disorder, and few of the men of 1st Battalion 24th Regiment had time to fix bayonets before the enemy was among them using their assegais with fearful effect. I heard officers calling to their men to be steady; but the retreat became in a few seconds general, and in a direction towards the road to Rorke's Drift. Before, however, we gained the neck near the Isandula Hill, the enemy had arrived on that portion of the field also, and the large circle he had now formed closed in on us. The only space which appeared open was down a deep gully running to the south of the road, into which we plunged in great confusion. The enemy followed us closely and kept up with us at first on both flanks, then on our right only, firing occasionally, but chiefly making use of the assegais. It was now about 1.30 p.m.; about this period two guns with which Major Smith and Lieutenant Curling, RA, were returning with great difficulty, owing to the nature of the ground, and I understood were just a few seconds late. Further on the ground passed over on our retreat would at any other time be looked upon as impracticable for horsemen to descend, and many losses occurred, owing to horses falling and the enemy coming up with the riders; about half a mile from the neck the retreat had to be carried on in nearly single file, and in this manner the Buffalo River was gained at a point about five miles below Rorke's Drift. In crossing this river many men and horses were carried away by the stream and lost their lives; after crossing, the fire of the enemy was discontinued; pursuit, however, was still kept up, but with little effect, and apparently with the view of cutting us off from Rorke's Drift. The number of white men who crossed the river at this point was, as far as I could see, about 40. In addition to these, there were a great number of natives on foot and on horseback. White men of about 25 or 30 arrived at Helpmekaar between 5 and 6 p.m., when, with the assistance of other men joined there, a laager was formed with wagons round the stores. I estimate the strength of the enemy to have been about 15,000. Their losses must have been considerable towards the end of the engagement.

I have, etc.
E. Essex,
Captain 75th Regiment,
Sub-Director of Transports.

B—FROM LIEUTENANT CURLING TO OFFICER COMMANDING No 8.

Sir, Helpmekaar, January 26, 1879

I have the honour to forward the following report of the circumstances attending the loss of two guns of N Brigade, 5th Battery Royal Artillery, at the action of Isandula on January 22. About 7.30 a.m. on that date a large body of Zulus being seen on the hills to the left front of the camp, we were ordered to turn out at once, and were formed up in front of the 2nd Battalion 24th Regiment camp, where we remained until 11 o'clock, when we returned to camp with orders to remain harnessed up and ready to turn out at a minute's notice. The Zulus did not come within range and we did not come into action. The infantry also remained in column of companies. Colonel Durnford arrived about 10 a.m. with Basutos and the rocket battery; he left about 11 o'clock with these troops in the direction of the hills where we had seen the enemy. About 12 o'clock we were turned out, as heavy firing was heard in the direction of Colonel Durnford's force. Major Smith arrived as we were turning out, and took command of the guns; we trotted up to a position about 400 yards beyond the left front of the Natal Contingent camp, and came into action at once on a large body of the enemy about 3,400 yards off. The 1st Battalion 24th Regiment now came up and extended in skirmishing order on both flanks and in line with us.

In about a quarter of an hour Major Smith took away one gun to the right, as the enemy were appearing in large numbers in the direction of the drift, in the stream in front of the camp.

The enemy advanced slowly, without halting; when they were 400 yards off the 1st Battalion 24th Regiment advanced about 30 yards. We remained in the same position. Major Smith returned at this time with his gun, and came into action beside mine. The enemy advancing still, we began firing case, but almost immediately the infantry were ordered to retire. Before we could get away the enemy were by the guns, and I saw one gunner stabbed as he was mounting on to an axle-tree box. The limber gunners did not mount, but ran after the guns. We went straight through the camp but found the enemy in possession. The gunners were all stabbed going through the camp, with the exception of one or two. One of the two sergeants was also killed at this time. When we got on to the road to Rorke's Drift it was completely blocked up by Zulus. I was with Major Smith at this time, he told me he had been wounded in the arm. We saw Lieutenant Coghill, the ADC, and asked him if we could not rally some men and make a stand, he said he did not think it could be done. We crossed the road with the crowd, principally consisting of natives, men left in camp, and civilians, and went down a steep ravine heading towards the river.

The Zulus were in the middle of the crowd, stabbing the men as they ran. When we had gone about 400 yards we came to a deep cut in which the guns stuck. There was, as far as I could see, only one gunner with them at this time, but they were covered with men of different corps clinging to them. The Zulus were on them almost at once, and the drivers pulled off their horses. I then left the guns. Shortly after this I again saw Lieutenant Coghill, who told me Colonel Pulleine had been killed.

Near the river I saw Lieutenant Melville, 1st Battalion 24th Regiment, with a colour, the staff being broken.

I also saw Lieutenant Smith-Dorrien assisting a wounded man. During the action cease fire was sounded twice.

I am, etc.
H. T. Curling, Lieutenant, RA

BIBLIOGRAPHY

Ambrose, Stephen E. *Crazy Horse and Custer, The Parallel Lives of Two American Warriors,* Doubleday & Company, New York, 1975

Beckett, Ian, *Isandlwana 1879,* Brassey's, London, 2003

Bengough, Harcourt, *Memories of a Soldier's Life,* Edward Arnold, London, 1913

Brady, Cyrus T. *Indian Fights and Fighters,* University of Nebraska Press, 1971

Brown, Dee, *Bury My Heart at Wounded Knee, An Indian History of the American West,* Holt, Rinehart & Winston, 1970

Carroll, John M. (Editor) *The Benteen-Goldin Letters on Custer and His Last Battle.* University of Nebraska Press, 1991

Cary, Lucian, *The Colt Gun Book,* Fawcett Publications, Greenwich, Conn. 1961

Clements, W. H. *The Glamour and Tragedy of the Zulu War,* Bodley Head, London, 1936

Coupeland, R. *Zulu Battle Piece: Isandlwana,* Collins, London, 1948

Coffeen, Herbert, *The Custer Battle Book,* Carlton Press, New York, 1964

Connell, Evan S. *Son of the Morning Star, General Custer and the Battle of the Little Bighorn,* Pan Books, London, 1986

Custer, Elizabeth B. *Boots and Saddles,* University of Nebraska Press, 1987

Custer, George A. *My Life on the Plains,* University of Nebraska Press, 1966

Darling, Roger, *General Custer's Final Hours: Correcting a Century of Misconceived History,* Vienna, VA, Potomac-Western Press, 1992

David, Saul, *Military Blunders, The How and Why of Military Failure,* Constable & Robinson Ltd. London, 1997

David, Saul, *Zulu, The Heroism and Tragedy of the Zulu War of 1879,* Penguin Books, London, 2005

Dowd, James Patrick, *Custer Lives!* Ye Galleon Press, Fairfield, WA, 1982

Droogleever, R. W. F. *The Road to Isandhlwana, Colonel Anthony Durnford in Natal and Zululand 1873—1879,* Greenhill Books, London, 1992

Durnford, Edward, *A Soldier's Work and Life in South Africa, 1872-79,* Sampson Low, Marston & Rivington, 1882

Emery, Frank (ed.) *The Red Soldier: Letters from the Zulu War, 1879,* Hodder & Stoughton, London, 1977

Furneaux, Rupert, *The Zulu War: Isandhlwana and Rorke's Drift,* Weidenfield & Nicholson, 1963

Frost, Lawrence A. *Custer Album,* Superior Publishing Co. Seattle, 1964

Godfrey, E. S. *Custer's Last Battle, 1876,* Outback Books, Olympic Valley, C.A. 1976

Gon, Philip, *The Road to Isandlwana: The Years of an Imperial Battalion,* Donker, Johannesburg, 1979

Graham, W. A. *The Reno Court of Inquiry, Abstracts from the Official Record of Proceedings,* Stackpole Books, Mechanicsburg, P. A. 1995

Gray, John S. *Centennial Campaign, The Sioux War of 1876,* University of Oklahoma Press, 1988

Gray, John S. *Custer's Last Campaign, Mitch Boyer and the Little Bighorn Reconstructed,* University of Nebraska Press, 1991

Greaves, Adrian, *Isandlwana,* Cassell & Co. London, 2001

Greene, Jerome A. *Evidence and the Custer Enigma,* Outbooks, Reno, N. V. 1979

Gump, James O. *The Dust Rose Like Smoke, The Subjugation of the Zulu and the Sioux,* University of Nebraska Press, 1994

Guy, Jeff, *The Destruction of the Zulu Kingdom,* Longmans, London, 1979

Holme, Norman, *The Silver Wreath: Being the 24th Regiment at Isandlwana and Rorke's Drift, 1879,* Samson Books, London, 1979

Knight, Ian, *Brave Men's Blood: The Epic of the Zulu War,* Greenhill Books, London, 1990

Laband, John, *Kingdom in Crisis: The Zulu Response to the British Invasion of 1879,* Manchester University Press, 1992

Liddic, Bruce R.—Harbaugh, Paul, (Editors) *Custer & Company,* University of Nebraska Press, 1998

Michno, Gregory F. *Lakota Noon, The Indian Narrative of Custer's Defeat,* Mountain Press Publishing Co. Missoula, M. A. 2004

Mitford, Bertram, *Through the Zulu Country,* Keagan Paul, Trench and Co. 1883

Molyneaux, W.C. F. *Campaigning in South Africa and Egypt,* Macmillan, 1896

Moodie, D.C. F. *Moodie's Zulu War,* N & S Press, Cape Town, 1988

Morris, Donald, *The Washing of the Spears,* Cape, London, 1966

Perret, Geoffrey, *Ulysses S. Grant, Soldier and President,* Random House, New York, 1997

Scott, Douglas D.—Fox, Richard A. *Archaeological Insights into The Custer Battle,* University of Oklahoma Press, 1989

Smith-Dorrien, Horace, *Memories of Forty-Eight Years' Service,* John Murray, London, 1925

Stewart, Edgar I. *Custer's Luck,* University of Oklahoma Press, 1955

Taylor, William O. *With Custer on the Little Bighorn,* Penguin Books, New York, N. Y. 1997

Vestal, Stanley, *The Man who Killed Custer,* American Heritage, Vol. V111, No.2, New York, February 1957
Wellman, Paul I. *Death on the Prairie,* W. Foulsham & Co. Ltd, London, 1962

INDEX

Adams, Arthur   79
Adams, Robert   265
Adendorff, Lt. G.   258
Albert, Prince   341
Allison, Capt.   12-3
American Horse   118, 320-1
Anderson, Cpl.   260
Anstey, Lt. Edgar   235
Avery, Lt.   140
Backnall, Henry   12
Bad Soup   214
Baker, Capt. Stephen   286
Baker, Commandant   339
Baldwin, Lt. Frank   325
Ball, Capt. Edward   285
Banister, Lt. George   362
Barker, Walwyn   178
Barry, Capt. A.J.   215
Barter, Capt. Charles   13-4
Barton, Capt. William   183-4, 220-2, 335
Bear Lice   213
Beaver Dam   325
Belknap, William   37, 40, 49, 52, 67-70
Bell, Alexander Graham   56
Bellairs, Col. William   310

Bemis, Joseph G.   80
Bengough, Maj. Harcourt   134-5, 142
Benteen, Capt. Frederick W.   150-3, 164-8, 170, 183-4, 194-207, 212, 214, 241, 244-5, 250-3, 278-9, 284, 303, 306, 354-6, 358, 360, 362-5
Big Ankle   330
Big Belly   163,164
Big Foot   346
Bighead, Kate   211
Biyela   228
Black, Maj. Wilsone   290-1
Bloody Knife   75, 148, 157, 160, 190, 350, 351, 361
Bloomfield, Quartermaster Edward   226
Bobtailed Bull   149
Booth, Col. Serg. Anthony   332
Bostwick, Henry   275, 279, 286
Bourke, Capt. John G.   59, 97, 343
Bourne, Col. Sgt. Frank   256-7
Boyer, Mitch   107, 110, 114-5, 153, 161, 271-8, 282
Bozeman, John M.   3
Bradley, Lt. James   103-4, 110, 114-5, 153, 161, 271-8, 282
Bradstreet, Capt. R.   224, 370
Brickhill, James   234
Brinkerhoff, Henry   157
Brisbin, Maj. James   53-4, 106, 114, 116, 147, 161, 206, 271, 281, 300-1
Bromhead, Lt. Gonville   256-8, 260-1, 267-8, 296
Browne, Lt. Edward   136
Brughiere, 'Big Leggins'   323, 329
Bull Head   345
Buller, Capt. Ernest   138
Buller, Lt. Col. Redvers   312, 334-5, 339

Bulwer, Sir Henry   27-30, 32, 40-3, 62, 82, 87, 92
Burkman, John   98, 248
Butler, Gen. Ben   109
Byrne, Louise   263
Calhoun, Lt. James   75, 208-9, 283-4, 360
Carey, Lt. Jaheel   338
Carnarvon, Lord   22, 26-8
Carrington, Col. Henry B.   3-4
Casey, Maj.   328
Cavaye, Lt. Charles   221-2, 374-5
Cetshwayo kaMpande   22-7, 30-1, 40-3, 48, 61-5, 81, 92, 121-2, 126-7, 130-4, 136-8, 145, 228, 239, 260, 333, 335-8, 340, 348-9
Chandler, Zachariah   36-7, 40, 49, 52
Chard, Lt. John   179-81, 257-60, 262-3, 267, 269, 295-6, 341
Chelmsford, Lord   30-2, 41, 44-6, 64-5, 81-2, 87-92, 98, 121-30, 32-6, 138-43, 157, 171-5, 176-8, 182, 199, 216-20, 256, 258, 289-93, 295-6, 307-317, 331, 335-9, 348
Chivington, Col. J.M.   6
Church, Capt. Hugh   175
Clark, Sir Andrew   316
Clery, Maj. Francis   121, 129, 138, 141, 143-4, 173, 177, 210, 307, 368-9
Cleveland, Grover   344-5
Clifford, Capt. Walter   280-1
Clymer, Heister   69
Cochrane, Lt. Francis   181-2, 239, 371
Coghill, Lt. Nevill   233-4, 236, 379-80
Coleman, James   108
Colenso, Bishop John   86-7
Colenso, Frances E.   87, 89-90, 240, 313-6, 350,

Comanche (Horse)   285
Connolly, John   264
Cooke, Lt. William W.   168-9, 184, 196, 199, 201, 205, 354, 364
Cooper, Maj.   120
Crazy Horse   4, 19, 55, 58, 77, 117-9, 209, 287, 320-2, 325, 328-9, 343
Crealock, Gen. Henry   337-8
Crealock, Lt. Col. John N.   89-90, 127, 130, 141, 175-6, 177, 180, 288, 307, 309-10, 313, 315, 337, 368
Crook, Gen. George   19, 37, 39, 50, 52, 55-8, 60, 66, 74, 77-8, 80, 97, 104, 108, 116-20, 167, 249, 319-21, 325
Crow Boy   213
Cunynghame, Sir Arthur   31, 99
Curling, Lt. Henry   93, 179, 218, 223, 228, 233, 236, 239, 298, 373, 377-80
Curly   201, 274, 286
Curtis, William T.   38-40
Custer, Boston   75, 79, 101, 201, 361
Custer, Capt. Thomas W.   75, 101, 164, 195, 208-9, 282
Custer, Elizabeth   53, 68, 79, 119, 304, 306-7, 313
Custer, Lt. Col. George A.   1-2, 5, 9-12, 15-6, 18-9, 33, 38, 53-4, 67-81, 83-6, 89, 97-117, 119, 124-5, 128, 147-171, 176, 180, 182-4, 189-214, 232, 243-5, 248-9, 255, 271-9, 281-6, 294-5, 299-309, 312, 317, 319, 326, 339, 343-347, 349-61, 363-4,
Dabulamanzi   260, 262
Dalton, James   258, 261-2, 267
Dartnell, Maj. John   135, 138-9, 141-45, 171-2, 216, 368
Davern, Bob   192
Davies, Harry   234
DeRudio, Lt. Charles C.   148, 205, 254, 305, 356

De Wolf, Dr.   193, 356
Degacher, Col. Henry   122, 290
Delano, Columbus   36, 70
Disraeli, Benjamin   43, 313
Dodge, Col. R.I.   18
Dorman, Isaiah   76, 277, 361
Dull Knife   325, 343
Dunbar, Maj. William   127
Dunn, John   64, 335
Durnford, Col. Edward   314-6
Durnford, Lt. Col. Anthony W.   12-15, 28, 30, 34, 83-90, 92, 99-100, 123-6, 128, 134-5, 141-2, 144, 148, 180-4, 202, 216-28, 231-2, 237-8, 240, 256-7, 259, 294-5, 307-17, 348-50, 368-72, 374-6, 378-9,
Dymes, Capt.   89, 125
Dyson, Lt. Edward   221-2, 375
Eastman, Dr. Charles   346
Edgerly, Lt. Winfield S.   167, 197, 200, 244, 246, 283, 356
Egan, Capt. James   58-9, 78
Elliot, Maj. Joel   85-6, 151, 248
Erskin, Robert   85
Essex, Capt. Edward   220-223, 226, 228, 239, 371, 373, 378
Far West (steamboat)   103, 105-6, 108, 110, 112, 269, 279, 286
Feihler, Sgt.   247
Fetterman, Capt. William F.   4-6, 55, 119, 255
Finerty, John   8
Flynn, Henry F.   126, 129, 130, 138, 144
Forbes, Archibald   293-5
Forsyth, Col. James W.   18
French, Capt. Thomas H.   205, 306

Frere, Sir Bartle   21-4, 26, 28-32, 40-46, 61-65, 81-2, 93, 123, 308-10, 312, 348
Fynney, F.B.   81
Gallagher, Sgt. Henry   261
Gallway, M.H.   28
Gamble, Sgt.   234
Gamdana   136, 138
Gardner, Capt. Alan   173, 218-9, 222, 232, 239, 335, 369
Gerard, Frederick   76, 145, 157, 160, 163, 167, 169-70, 182, 202, 254
Gibbon, Col. John   67, 77, 81, 100, 102-3, 104-15, 119, 145-148, 153-4, 271, 274, 280, 286, 301
Gibson, Lt. Francis M.   152, 166, 194, 251, 356, 363
Glyn, Col. Richard   92, 120-1, 139, 142, 172-3, 177, 289, 295, 316, 337, 368-9
Godfrey, Edward S.   149, 152-5, 158, 160-1, 163, 194-5, 197-8, 241, 245-9, 253, 278, 281-2, 284, 307, 346-7, 356
Godide kaNdlela   134
Godwin-Austen, Lt. Frederick   227
Goes Ahead   274
Golden, Pat   248
Goldin, Theodore   170
Goodwin, James   279, 286
Gordon, Gen. Charles G.   124
Gossett, Maj. Matthew   138, 176
Grant, Lt. F.D.   18
Grant, Orvil   68-70
Grant, Ulysses S.   1, 7, 16-17, 20-1, 30, 35-8, 52, 69, 71-5, 97, 105, 303, 351-2
Greeley, Horace   2
Grouard, Frank   57-8, 117, 320
Hairy Moccasin   274

Half-Yellow-Face   160, 274
Hamer, James   185, 215, 218, 230, 236, 237
Hamilton-Browne, Commandant George   174-6, 288
Hancock, Gen. Winfield S.   5, 204
Hare, Bishop W.H.   18
Hare, Lt. Luther S.   160, 190, 198, 246, 283, 356
Harness, Lt. Col. Arthur   174-6, 244, 310, 367, 373
Harney, Col. W. S.   5
Harrison, Gen. William H.   351
Hartford, Capt. Henry   140, 171, 290-1
Hassard, Col. Fairfax   310, 367, 373
Hawkins, Villiers   178
Hayden, Pvt.   297
Henderson, Lt. Alfred   225-7, 259-60
Henry, Capt.   118
Herendeen, George B.   156, 158, 160-2, 201, 205, 244, 252, 275
Hicks Beach, Sir Michael   28-32, 41-2, 44-5, 63, 81, 309, 312
Higginson, Lt. Walter   182
Hitch, Frederick   260-2, 265-6, 268, 296
Hodgson, Lt. Benjamin H.   10
Holcroft, Lt.   140
Hook, Henry   261, 263-6, 296
Horner, Jacob   10
Howard, Arthur   265
Hughes, Col. Robert   73, 299
Hughes, Sgt. Robert   283
Iron Hawk   212
Jackson, Andrew   351
Jackson, Will   254
Jenny, Prof. Walter P.   18

Johnson, Andrew   4-5
Jones, Robert   265
Jones, William   265
Josephine (steamboat)   18, 76
KaMvundlana   228
Kanipe, Sgt. Daniel A.   195, 200, 203, 205
Kein, Ralph   151
Kellogg, Mark   79, 105, 120, 165, 286, 361
Keogh, Capt. Myles   208-10
Kidder, Lt.   5
Kumbeka   238
Lame Deer   329-30
Lame White Man   209
Langalibalele   12, 84
Lanyon, Col.   44
Lee, Lt. Jesse M.   349
Lee., Gen. Robert E.   1
Lell, Corp.   250-1
Little Face   273
Little Hawk   118
Little Wolf   325-6
London, Quartermaster W.   226-7
Long Feather   323
Longhurst, Vet. Seaward   314
Lonsdale, Col. Rupert   135, 138-40, 172, 181, 216, 230, 287-90, 368
Lord, Dr. George E.   76, 282
Lorentz, George   190
Louis Napoleon, Prince   338
Luard, Col. Charles   315-6
Lytton, Lord   29
Madden, Michael   279

Maguire, Lt. E.   278
Mainwaring, Lt. Henry   175, 296
Mansel, Insp. George   129, 297, 308
Marsh, Capt. Grant   106, 286
Marsh, Prof. Othniel C.   36
Marshall, Gen. Sir Frederick   293
Martin, John   196-7, 201, 203, 206, 245
Matshana   126, 135, 144, 172
Mavumengwana   137
Maxfield, Sgt. Robert   265
Mbilini kaMswati   43
McDougall, Capt. Thomas M.   165, 195, 198, 200, 203, 354, 356
McIntosh, Lt. Donald   152, 192, 277, 356
McKenzie, Gen. Ranald S.   325-6
McLaughlin, James   20
Meeker, Ralph   68, 70
Mehlokazulu   225, 237
Melville, Lt. Teignmouth   234, 236, 375, 380
Meyer, J.R.   189, 191
Miles, Col. Nelson A.   56-7, 321, 322-5, 328-30, 343
Mills, Capt. Anson   58-9, 118, 119, 320
Milne, Lt. Berkeley, R.N.   174-5
Mitford, Bertram   347
Mnyamana   123
Molife, Jabez   215, 224
Moore, Capt.   58-60
Moore, Major   76
Moriarty, Capt. David   331
Mostyn, Capt. William   221-2, 375
Moylan, Capt. Myles   199, 211, 283-4
Munger, Rev. Dr. T.T.   299

Muziwento   230, 238
Myrick, Andrew   20
Newdigate, Gen. Edward   337
Norris Newman, Charles   120, 176, 330
North, Frank   325
North, Luther   325
Nourse, Capt. Cracroft   181, 372
Noyes, Capt.   58-9
Ntshingwayo kaMahole   133, 137, 144, 216-7
Nzuzi   132
Otis, Col. E.S.   322, 323, 329
Parr, Capt. Henry Hallam   173
Parsons, Lt. C.S.B.   176
Paulding, Dr. Holmes O.   103, 106, 276, 279
Pearson, Col. Charles   92, 124, 134, 337
Penn Symons, Capt. William   136, 172, 292
Phillips, Portuguese   4
Phillips, Sub-Insp.   130
Pigford, Edward   248
Pine, Lt. Governor   84, 277
Poland, Capt.   51
Ponsonby, Gen. Sir Henry   311
Poole, Capt. Ruscombe   132
Pope, Lt. Charles   223, 227-8
Porter, Dr. Henry R.   193, 198, 247, 279, 356
Pretty Shield   3
Prior, Melton   293-4
Pulleine, Lt. Col. Henry   143-4, 173, 177-83, 202, 215, 218-9, 220-1, 228-9, 232, 307-8, 310, 316, 369-72, 374
Pullen, Quartermaster James   229
Rain-in-the-Face   319
Raw. Lt. Charles   181, 184-5, 214, 229-30, 235

Reagan, Ronald   352
Red Bear   155
Red Cloud   4, 6, 8, 36
Red Star   148, 155, 162-3
Reed, Autie   75
Reno, Maj. Marcus A.   74-6, 107-13, 115, 117, 148, 153, 156, 159, 165-71, 183-4, 189-99, 201-8, 213-5, 226-7, 235, 243-55, 266, 268-9, 276-7, 279, 283, 285, 291, 301-7, 311, 325, 346, 349, 351, 353-62, 365
Reynolds, Charley   74, 79, 98, 100-2, 104, 162, 259, 277, 361
Reynolds, Dr. James   263
Reynolds, Gen. Joseph J.   55, 58-60, 78
Roberts, Lt. Joseph   184, 222
Roe, Corp. William   340
Roe, Lt. Charles   275-6
Rosser, Gen. Thomas   305
Royall, Maj.   118
Rullin, Roman   189
Russell, Lt. Col. Cecil   174-5, 289, 295, 333
Russell, Maj. Francis   183, 217
Ryan, Fst. Sgt. John   282
Salisbury, Lord   45
Scheiss, Cpl. Christian   267
Schreuder, Bishop   124
Scott, Lt. F.J.D.   178, 237, 294
Seip, Robert C.   70
Shaka   22
Shepherd, Dr.   291
Shepstone, Capt. George   215, 218-9, 221, 230, 231-2, 313, 370
Shepstone, Capt. Theophilus (Offy)   313-6

Shepstone, John W.   23, 28, 62
Shepstone, Sir Theophilus   24-8, 32, 43-4, 62-3
Sheridan, Gen. Philip   9, 15, 18-21, 36-7, 39, 50-2, 71-74, 76, 113, 287, 301-2, 347
Sherman, Gen. William T.   3-4, 6-7, 9, 21, 35, 51, 71-3, 81, 305
Sibley, Lt. F.W.   319
Sihayo   42, 121-3, 136, 225, 238
Sitting Bull   8-9, 17, 19, 39, 47, 50-2, 57-8, 74, 77, 116, 155-6, 169, 207, 319, 322-5, 329, 341, 344-5, 348-9, 353
Slade, Lt. Frederick   334, 340
Slavey, Cpl.   56
Smith, E.P.   36-7, 40, 49
Smith, J.Q.   51
Smith, Lt. Algernon E.   211
Smith, Maj. Stuart   222, 373
Smith, Rev. George   256, 259, 262
Smith-Dorrien, Lt. Horace   142, 225, 235-7, 239, 372, 380
Spalding, Maj. Henry   256-8, 267, 332
Stabbed   157, 164
Stafford, Capt. Walter   181, 221-2
Stanley, Col. Frederick   308, 312
Stanley, Gen. David S.   9-11, 98, 100-1, 109, 151
Stephenson, Capt. William   260
Strahorn, Robert   56
Sturgis, Col. Samuel   277, 302
Sturgis, Lt. James   277, 282, 360
Symons, Capt. William P.   136, 172, 292
Taylor, Muggins   275-7, 286
Taylor, William   170-1, 191-3, 213, 243, 247, 279, 281
Terry, Gen. Alfred H.   15, 50-4, 70-1, 73-80, 91, 97-107, 110-

7, 119-20, 125, 147, 154, 157-60, 183, 202-3, 206-7, 212, 248, 255, 271-287, 291, 299-304, 307-8, 360
Thesiger, Gen. Sir Frederick (see Chelmsford, Lord)
Thompson, Peter   110, 306
Torrens, Gen. Henry   306
Trollope, Anthony   24
Turley, James   187
Tyler, John   351
Upcher, Maj. Russell   267
Varnum, Lt. Charles A.   78, 156, 162-3, 192-3, 201, 244, 304, 356,
Vause, Lt. W.   221
Vic (Horse)   165
Victoria, Queen   90, 256, 311-2, 329, 340, 348
Von Luettwitz, Lt.   320
Vroom, Lt.   118
Walker, Judson E.   344
Wallace, Lt. George   152, 167, 192, 284, 306, 356, 365
Walsh, Maj. James M.   329, 345
Washington, George   1, 351
Washita battle   38, 85, 102, 151, 204-5, 248, 278, 351
Wassall, Samuel   236
Waters, John   264
Watkins, Erwin C.   39-40, 42, 49-50
Weir, Capt. Thomas B.   100, 195, 243-5, 281, 356
Westwood, Private   236
White Antelope   319
White Bull   207-10, 212-4, 323, 346-7,
White Swan   274
Whitelaw, Pvt.   178
White-Man-Runs-Him   169, 274
Whittaker, Frederick   306

Williams, John   263-5
Williams, Dr. John   279
Williams, Joseph   264
Windolph, Private   250
Witt, Otto   135, 255, 259-60,
Wolseley, Sir Garnet   332, 338, 349
Wood, Col. Evelyn   90, 92, 333-4, 337
Yates, Lt. George W.   211, 277, 260
Yellow Nose   326-7
Younghusband, Capt. Reginald   232, 239, 376